FIGHTER COMBAT
IN THE JET AGE

David C. Isby

HarperCollins*Publishers*

HarperCollins*Publishers*
77-85 Fulham Palace Road
Hammersmith
London W6 8JB

First Published in Great Britain by
HarperCollins*Publishers* 1997

1   3   5   7   9   8   6   4   2

Copyright © David C. Isby

The author asserts the moral right to
be identified as the author of this work

ISBN 0 00 470822 9

Editor: Ian Drury
Design: Rod Teasdale
Line artwork: Peter Harper
Production Manager: Bridget Scanlon

Contents

1 The Me 262 and the Origins of Jet Fighter operations   8

2 Contrails over the Yalu: Fighter Operations in Korea 1950-53   24

3 Early Cold War Fighter Operations   44

4 Vietnam: From 'Thud Ridge' to 'Topgun'   70

5 Arab-Israeli Conflicts 1956-82   94

6 The Rebirth of Fighter Operations: The Last Decades of the Cold War   114

7 Sea Harriers and Skyhawks: Fighter Operations in the Falklands War   138

8 The Gulf War and Post-Cold War Fighter Operations   156

Fighter Directory   172

Index   188

The Me 262 and the origins of Jet Fighter operations

The attacking enemy fighter that overshot the two P-47 Thunderbolts was like nothing the two American pilots had ever seen.

'It's got wings like a C-47.'

'Ever see a C-47 traveling at 500 miles per hour?'

'It's got a tail like a P-51.'

'Ever see a P-51 with a paint job like that?'

The subject of this Socratic radio dialogue between Captain 'Val' Beaudralt and his wingman, Lieutenant 'Pete' Peters, of the 356th Fighter Group was a Messerschmitt Me 262, the first jet fighter to enter air-to-air combat. This particular Me 262 demonstrated that however revolutionary its technology, if its pilot did not take advantage of its capabilities, its life expectancy was about the same as any outnumbered German aircraft in late 1944. The two P-47s chased it and maneuvered with the Me 262 until it ran out of fuel – its turbojet engines were thirsty at high power settings. The pilot, *Oberfeldwebel* 'Ronny' Lauder bailed out. A bomber pilot by training; he possessed plenty of aggressive courage but little air combat maneuvering skill. Lauder repeated this type of attack several weeks later against two US Army Air Force (USAAF) P-51 Mustangs and again failed to shoot his targets down.

The Messerschmitt Me 262 was the first jet fighter to enter air-to-air combat. Its first appearances over Germany in late 1944 caused understandable concern to Allied air commanders. This one was captured on film by an Allied fighter's gun camera.

With an 18 cylinder engine rated at 2300 hp for take-off, the P-47 Thunderbolt represented the ultimate in wartime piston-engine technology.

However, this time Lauder himself was shot down and killed.

In 1944-45, other Me 262 jagdflieger would fare better in air combat. They would demonstrate that the new technology of the jet engine would make obsolete all previous combat aircraft. Many of the tactical and operational lessons gained in both how the Germans developed and used the Me 262, and how the Allies defeated it, have remained valid to this day. 'Ronny' Lauder showed how not to do it, using the new technology in small numbers with the same tactics as its piston-engined predecessors. The operational goals of this particular Me 262 mission were also uncertain. Destroying one or two P-47s was not going to make life appreciably easier for the hard-pressed German Wehrmacht, who destroyed far more marauding USAAF fighters every day with low-technology anti-aircraft fire. Rather, the operational success in the first use of jet fighters in combat went to the Luftwaffe's USAAF

and Royal Air Force (RAF) opponents, who lacked comparable aircraft, but were able to use their tried and tested operational tactics and planning to effectively negate the Me 262's performance advantage.

Despite intense bombing and enormous disruption to its industry, Germany had jets in frontline service before the Allies.

A Messerschmitt Me 262A-1a. The four nose-mounted 30 mm cannon were capable of bringing down a four-engined bomber with a short burst.

Heinkel He 162 – the first light jet fighter

The Luftwaffe quickly realized the need for more than one type of jet fighter, with a light, single-seat single engine machine intended to make up numbers by being cheaper and easier to produce than the Me 262. A 'mixed force' of jet fighters has been a feature of many air arms since then – the RAF's Meteor and Vampire squadrons of the immediate post-war period and the USAF's use of F-15s and F-16s (plus the US Navy's employment of F-14s and F/A-18s) in the 1990s are other examples of this force structure. That 'quantity has a quality all of its own' was emphasized by the high loss rate experienced by Me 262s engaging technologically inferior, but numerically superior, adversaries in March-April 1945.

The Heinkel He 162 was conceived, designed, built and flown within 90 days – a remarkable feat under any circumstances, but even more so in the closing months of 1944, using immature jet engine technology. Named the Volksjager (Peoples' fighter), the He 162 was constructed mainly of plywood. Its pilots would be hastily trained Hitler Jugend, with much of their flight time in gliders. It was a desperate plan for a desperate time, and was opposed by both Adolf Galland, due to its diversion of resources from vitally needed Me 262s, and by leading aircraft designers.

Despite this, the program forged ahead. The basic requirement was issued on 8 September 1944, drawings were completed by 29 October, and the building of prototypes and mass-production aircraft started immediately. The first prototype flew on 6 December and crashed four days later, but increasing numbers of prototypes were built and committed to an intense development program. Production aircraft started coming off the lines on 24 January, and JG 1 commenced its conversion onto the He 162 soon after.

The He 162 was never committed to combat as part of Luftwaffe defensive operations, although Allied pilots reported a few skirmishes with developmental or training aircraft in the last days of the war – French ace Flt Lt Pierre Clostermann ran into two whilst leading his Tempest flight over Schleswig-Holstein, which resulted in a number of air-to-air kill claims by both sides. The combat effectiveness of the Volksjager remains questionable. The He 162 was a 'hot ship' from a simple flying point of view, for it possessed the deadly combination of a high landing speed and narrow track undercarriage, which would have no doubt exacted a heavy toll on the glider-trained volunteer pilots.

By the end of the war about 170 He 162s had been delivered to the Luftwaffe, 100 more were awaiting flight testing, and some 800 were in the advanced stages of construction. While Galland was right – the He 162 had contributed nothing to the Luftwaffe's last battles – it nevertheless remains the best example of a true 'panic jet fighter'. Today, some ten or twenty years may elapse between a fighter being conceived and it finally entering operational service.

Desperate measures for desperate times: the jet-propelled 'Peoples' Fighter' was to be flown by volunteers from the Hitler Youth to overcome the shortage of pilots.

Above: A handful of Heinkel He 162s flew during the last weeks of the war, but the type was not fully operational before the collapse of Nazi Germany.

Left: A Heinkel He 162A-2 of JG1 stands among other captured German aircraft ready for testing by the Royal Aircraft Establishment at Farnborough in October 1945.

Below: This He 162A2 was to crash on its fourth evaluation flight by the RAE Aerodynamics Flight, on 9 November 1945.

The problems of emerging technologies

A Messerschmitt Me 262A-1a of II./JG7, the world's first operational jet fighter wing.

Germany had jet fighters in air combat before the United States or Great Britain despite the political confusion of the Third Reich, and the multitude of research and development programs – some brilliant, others simply draining scarce resources – competing with its evolution. The incessant Allied air bombardment, and the increasing tempo of battlefield defeat, provided the motivation of desperation. The Germans turned to the immature technology represented by the Junkers Jumo 004 turbojet in an attempt to counter the ever-increasing number of combat aircraft ranged against them. The Me 262, and other jet- and rocket-propelled fighters, offered some hope of redressing the advantage bestowed upon the Allies through their numerical superiority.

While the Messerschmitt fighter's turbojet engines made it a revolutionary engineering advancement in the story of flight, it was unable to claim a similar

advance in the history of air combat operations. The jet engine would not revolutionize air combat in 1944-45. It would take a generation to do this, and required technologies unavailable in 1944 – reliable turbojets, designs for transonic (and eventually supersonic) flight and adequate weapons. Tactics and operations that took advantage of both the jet's capabilities and limitations were in their infancy. None of the air arms that used jet fighters in 1944-45 were able to take more than the first steps.

By 1944, it was obvious to the Luftwaffe, RAF and USAAF – the Royal Navy's Fleet Air Arm, and their equivalent in the US Navy, were more hesitant – that the future belonged to the jet. Piston engine technology, pushed to its limits, exacted increasing burdens in return for marginally higher performance. However, bigger and more efficient powerplants of this type had appreciably increased fighter performance during the course of the Second World War. For example, the original Spitfire design of the mid-1930s was initially formulated around a 600 hp engine. However, the frontline Spitfire that fought the Battle of Britain in the summer of 1940 was powered by an 1,100 hp Rolls-Royce Merlin II engine, and by the time the Me 262 came into action in the autumn of

1944, late-model Spitfire Mk XIVs boasted a 2,400 hp Griffon 'up front'. The United States was already producing turbo-compound powerplants, and a 3,000 hp engine was under test. But the development of the piston engine had by now all but reached its engineering limits – propeller-driven powerplants of this type could not be made any bigger.

The USAAF and RAF were able to devise an effective operational counter to German jets with their piston-engined fighters because of numerical superiority, their generally higher level of tactical and operational competence, and because the jet pilot's advantage over his best propeller-driven opponents was that slender that he had to use all of his performance envelope if he was to survive, let alone prevail, against numerically-superior opponents.

The ultimate Mustang: a North American P-51H as delivered in late 1945.

The skill of individual jagdflieger, however great, could not assure victory against well-trained opponents employing effective operational tactics refined over years of combat. The Me 262 could pose a threat to individual machines, and even formations of multi-engined aircraft, but the combination of their lack of numbers and the overwhelming Allied response never allowed them to threaten the ability of massed ranks of USAAF and RAF bombers to wage total war from the skies over Europe.

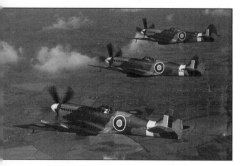

Spitfire F 21s and F 22s had Griffon engines four times as powerful as those in the 1930s prototype.

Rocket Fighter

The first rocket-propelled fighter, the Messerschmitt Me 163 was, in effect, a re-usable manned missile. Its descendants were not fighters, but the surface-to-air missiles (SAMs) that would assume increasing significance in aerial combat over the next 50 years. Since 1945, the SAM has replaced heavy flak as an integral part of modern defensive operations ranged against any airborne threat.

The Me 163 carried enough highly caustic and toxic T-

Above: The rocket-powered Me 163 undoubtedly killed more of its own pilots than Allied aircrew. This one was sabotaged by the slave laborers on the production line; it would have exploded on take-off.

Left: With just 12 minutes of powered flight, the Me 163 could make one or two firing passes against the US bombers. Then, low on fuel and ammunition, the pilot had to escape Allied fighters and glide down to land.

Stoff and Z-Stoff rocket fuel for 12 minutes of powered flight. When enemy aircraft were detected, the Me 163s would first come to alert and then launch when the bomber stream was within striking range. Take-off had to be made directly into the wind on a two-wheel dolly, which fell away as the Me 163 became airborne.

Once safely aloft, the aircraft's rocket engine gave it a rate of climb far in excess of any contemporary fighter, either Allied or Axis – it could reach its operational altitude of 32,000 ft (higher if required) in less than six minutes. The Me 163 was then positioned for a slashing attack on a bomber formation, attacking from the rear at 560-590 mph. However, with that rate of closure on its much slower target, the brief time the Me 163 was in range of a bomber before it overshot was usually not long enough for the pilot to inflict lethal damage on the latter with the Komet's two slow-firing 30 mm cannon.

Whilst in theory an Me 163 could pull up into a zoom climb for a second attack, in practice the pilot was usually faced with having to glide back to his field while avoiding the attention of escort fighters alerted by the initial attack.

The jet employed a single retractable skid under the fuselage for recovery, although this was often unreliable at the high landing speeds encountered with the Me

163. Despite the pilot being provided with a reinforced torsion-suspension seat to help absorb some of the shock experienced with the impact of landing, severe spinal injuries were a frequent occurrence for Komet jagdflieger. Worse still, if the aircraft landed too hard, or was gripped by a crosswind, it would then flip over, which usually resulted in the detonation of any residual rocket fuel remaining in the tanks. Major Wolfgang Späte, commander of JG 400 and a five-kill Me 163 ace, remembers, 'After crash landings, which would have resulted in no more than broken bones for the pilot, we had to bury pilots who had literally been dissolved through T-Stoff, or reduced to a gelatin-like mass, or blown to smithereens through an explosion'.

Adding to the risks faced by Me 163 pilots was the knowledge that their aircraft were built by slave laborers, who would risk summary execution to sabotage aircraft on the production line. For example, the unflown Me 163 in the National Air and Space Museum in Washington D.C. was found to have scrap steel wedged behind the pilot's seat to slice open the fuel tank upon accelerating when it was examined after the end of the war in Europe. Scratched in the fuel tank was the under-stated French-language graffito, 'My heart isn't in my work'.

The origins of the Messerschmitt Me 262

The Me 262's design started in autumn 1938, Messerschmitt engineers aiming to take advantage of promised advances in turbojet technology. Prototype contracts for the Me 262 and the rival Heinkel He 280 were issued in March 1940. While a prototype Me 262 flew in April 1941, suitable turbojets were not available until July of the following year – jet technology had failed to keep pace with airframe development.

Some of the Luftwaffe's leadership – especially First World War ace Generaloberst Ernst Udet – originally insisted that there was no need for jet propulsion, but soon the Me 262 found high-level supporters, most notably the General der Jagdflieger, Generalleutant Adolf Galland, who had scored nearly 100 kills in the west in 1940/41.

Galland first flew the Me 262 in April 1943, exclaiming soon after his short flight, 'It felt as if the angels were pushing'. From that moment on he knew that the jet was the future of fighter design. While the Luftwaffe would never again have numerical superiority, with the Me 262 it could again have qualitative superiority. Galland was convinced that to change

the course of the air campaign, the technology of the Me 262 needed to be married with not only effective weapons and tactics, but also a new operational concept. Like the German generals of a previous generation, who were focused on preparing for a decisive battle, Galland envisioned Me 262s being massed to defeat the USAAF's strategic bombers, which had already started their campaign against the Reich. Even long after the war, Galland stated, 'that with only 300 Me

Substantially faster than Allied piston-engined fighters, the Me 262's advantage was more theoretical than practical. High closing speeds made accurate shooting difficult, and its unreliable Jumo 004 turbojets only had a operational life of ten hours.

The Me 262 was delayed by the opposition of General Udet whose dogmatic pronouncements on aircraft design hindered many other projects. Adolf Galland saw the Me 262 as the only way to regain air superiority: to fight quantity with quality.

262 fighters we could on any day have shot down a minimum of 200 bombers. If this had been continued for a week or so the day bombing would have had to be stopped'. He realized that without a concept of operations, and sufficient numbers with which to carry it out, the capability of individual Me 262s and their pilots would matter little.

Benefiting from Galland's strong support, the Me 262 was released for production in June 1943, but the Luftwaffe leadership, reflecting the concerns of Hitler himself, would not go along with Galland's demand that at least a quarter of future fighter production be Me 262s. This time, Hitler and the high command's assessment of the suitability of the technology for mass production proved to be more accurate than the fighting man's, despite Galland's operational and technological expertise.

The Führer's well-known insistence in late 1943 that the Me 262 be introduced into service as a bomber delayed its introduction much less than serious engine problems – its Junkers Jumo R004 turbojets had a service life of just ten hours (later increased to fifteen), and never lost their tendency to explode and burn due to the engine's metal alloy being progressively weakened by the high temperatures experienced in flight. It was simply not feasible to have put the Me 262 into action any faster than was done, regardless of the impact of Hitler and others. The problem was basically one of technology, rather than politics or resource allocation. It also underlined the weakness of relying on technological solutions to solve operational problems.

Like the Luftwaffe's Bf 109, the Supermarine Spitfire was in service from the beginning to the end of World War II. With its Griffon engine, four 20 mm cannon and bubble canopy, this F 22 is a radically different aircraft from the Spitfires of 1940.

The Me 262 in combat

Hitler's insistence that the Me 262 be re-designed as a fighter-bomber is often advanced as the reason for its delay in entering service. However, the real culprit was the Jumo turbojet, which was prone to flame out and had a chronically short operational life. The handful of Me 262A-2 bombers attacked targets in Britain and the Low Countries in 1944-5, but could only inflict token damage.

The Jumo 004 turbojet was 'frozen' for production in June 1944, and soon after a combination of developmental aircraft and an increasing number of production machines were committed, in ones and twos, to combat. Me 262s from the first operational units – including those from former bomber gruppe such as that flown by the unfortunate 'Ronny' Lauder – clashed with Allied fighters. Starting in August 1944, Me 262s shot down several of the high-flying Allied reconnaissance aircraft (especially RAF PR Mosquitos and USAAF F-5 Lightnings) that had proven largely invulnerable in the past to the Luftwaffe's piston-engined fighters.

The first few Me 262s were used for relatively ineffective high-altitude fighter-bomber attacks, starting in late July and continuing throughout 1944. Whilst fulfilling this role they first encountered Allied fighters – they could be intercepted when carrying bombs – and engaged in some of the initial

combats with USAAF and RAF aircraft. While the Me 262s were unable to hit pin-point targets with their bombs, the fact that they were often able to evade standing patrols of piston-engined fighters showed how jet aircraft had made the former virtually obsolete overnight. While their bombs did little damage, it was obvious that the technology available to the Allies in 1944-45 could not consistently defeat a jet bomber threat. Developing this capability would be a priority in the post-war years.

As the number of Me 262s increased in 1944, they finally started to be used for what Galland realized must be their main operational role – intercepting Allied bombers. This was the mission of Kommando Nowotny, put together under the command of seasoned Luftwaffe ace, Major Walter Nowotny. The unit received its first jets in September, and on 7 October made its operational debut when it attacked a

The Me 262B-2 Sturmvogel was the first jet night-fighter and a potentially serious menace to the RAF's Mosquito intruders.

USAAF B-24 Liberator formation over western Germany. That interception, where three Me 262s were shot down by escorts for the loss of three bombers, set a pattern that was to be repeated many times over during the next few months. The fighter escorts usually caught one or two Me 262s and discouraged repeated attacks from others, but the number of bombers lost to the jets started to climb, even though Kommando Nowotny itself had been pulled out of action soon after the loss of its commander during a sortie on 8 November. Its handful of surviving

Walter Nowotny – the first jet fighter leader

Major Walter Nowotny, the Austrian-born ace who scored 258 kills prior to his death, organized the first Me 262 unit to see combat – Kommando Nowotny – in September 1944. His task was formidable, for he had to both command a unit equipped with untried (and often dangerous to fly) aircraft, whilst simultaneously starting to find answers to the technical, tactical and operational problems of jet combat. Like the great First World War ace Max Immelmann, who was responsible for evolving basic fighter combat techniques in 1915, Nowotny was writing on a clean slate, with few examples and less institutional wisdom to aid him. The Major and his pilots had no shortage of piston-engined combat experience to draw from, but that really wasn't the problem. The issue was understanding what had changed with the advent of the new technology, and what – including some of Immelmann's basics – would remain the same.

The limited range of the Me 262 meant that they would have to measure their combat endurance in minutes. There would be no time to join up into large wing formations, as favoured by their opponents flying P-47s or Tempests, even if there had been sufficient Me 262s available. Kommando Nowotny, despite the quality of its aircraft and pilots, failed to achieve success. From its maximum strength of 30 Me 262s in early October, it was eventually reduced to just three jets within the space of four weeks.

Killed in action on 8 November 1944 soon after scoring his final two victories, Nowotny's death brought home to the Luftwaffe's leadership that the Me 262's introduction to combat had been premature. Kommando Nowotny was withdrawn from operations, and several of its surviving pilots posted to the newly-formed III./JG 7. It would only be at the end of the Me 262's career, when another first-class fighter leader in the shape of Adolf Galland started to build upon Nowotny's work, that effective jet fighter tactics were finally evolved.

aircraft and personnel joined new Me 262s and freshly-trained pilots within the recently formed Jagdgeschwader (fighter wing) 7, the first jet fighter wing. The latter would not become operational until February, 1945.

Like most solutions employed to counter new threats in the air combat environment, the Allied reply to the Me 262 menace was based on three levels of response – technical, tactical and operational. Due to the fact that there was no time available to develop new aircraft, weapons or sensors, the technical response was limited to improvisation, and the implementation of rapid turn-around elements – some of which were surprisingly effective. For example, airborne Me 262s could be located by a tracking device mounted to a suitably-modified USAAF fighter, and this in turn could trigger IFF (Identification Friend or Foe) transponders fitted to aircraft over 100 miles away. Tactical responses were limited by the need to remain effective against the piston-engined fighters that still constituted the bulk of the Luftwaffe's strength.

The American fighters opposing the remnants of the once all-conquering Luftwaffe found themselves in a situation operationally similar to that

Meteors versus Flying Bombs

In stark contrast to the Luftwaffe's desperate reliance on jet technology, the RAF's only wartime jet fighter element was a solitary unit equipped with Gloster's Meteor I. No 616 'South Yorkshire' Sqn debuted the aircraft in aerial combat when it was tasked with countering V1 rocket attacks on targets in the south-east of England in the mid-summer of 1944.

The only jet to see action with the Allied air forces was the British Gloster Meteor, which remained in RAF service through the 1950s.

Although the Meteor's Rolls-Royce W.2B Welland turbojet engines were not fully developed at the time of the aircraft's introduction to combat, they fortunately lacked the Jumo 004's propensity for self-destruction in flight. Underpowered and lacking maneuverability (especially at high altitude), the Meteor I was still faster than any of its piston-engined contemporaries, especially at low to medium ceilings.

Originally intended to be used for high-altitude interception, the Meteor was rushed into action on 27 July 1944 from RAF Manston, in Kent, following V1 attacks on London. In this role, its speed was more important than its tactical limitations, although it was not until August that, having resolved teething troubles with the jet's lethal quartet of 20 mm Hispano Mk 5 cannon, the Meteor started to take a toll of V1s, eventually destroying 13.

After the rocket threat had subsided, No 616 Sqn's aircraft became the first 'aggressor' jet fighters, being used as stand-ins for Me 262s in large-scale exercises with fighter elements of the Eighth Air Force in October 1944, their aim being to develop effective anti-jet tactics. In early 1945, equipped with the faster and more maneuverable Meteor III, No 616 Sqn moved firstly to Belgium and then the Netherlands. Its mission was high-altitude interception, but scrambles against increasingly rare German threats like the jet-powered Arado Ar 234 Blitz bomber and photo-recce aircraft were never successful. In the last few weeks of the war, Meteors were finally used for ground attack work, thus failing to score any manned air-to-air kills in the Second World War.

Despite this lack of success in its chosen field, the Meteor nevertheless proved to be an effective first-generation fighter. Improved versions remained in RAF Fighter Command service well into the 1950s, and many more were sold to air forces across the globe. Its wartime performance, while lacking the drama or success of the Me 262, showed it to be a good design, and the RAF made much use of it as a 'bridging' type between the piston-engined fighter of the Second World War and the turbojet interceptor of the Cold War.

Right: No 615 Sqn flying Meteor F 8s in the post-war finish that harked back to the glory days of the 1930s. Seven years after its introduction, the Meteor was to be drastically out-matched over Korea.

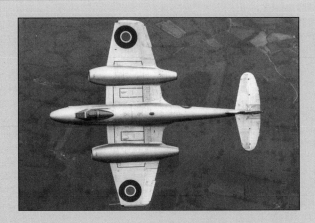

This Gloster Meteor F 4 is similar to the type that established a new world air speed record of 606 mph over Herne Bay, Kent in November 1945.

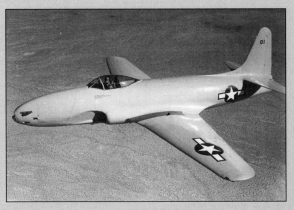

Designed around a de Havilland H-1B jet unit supplied by Britain, the prototype Lockheed XP-80 Shooting Star was built and flown in only 143 days.

encountered by their successors over Korea, North Vietnam and Iraq. While ground air defenses were inflicting the most casualties, it remained that offensive fighter operations were needed to prevent even a numerically inferior fighter force such as the Me 262s in 1944-45 (or MiG-21s in 1967-68) from preventing Allied aircraft from taking full advantage of their air superiority. This was one of the reasons why the USAF has continued to emphasis air-to-air combat even though enemy fighters have accounted for a small percentage of the total aircraft it has lost in action over the past 50 years.

The Allied operational response to the Me 262 was not limited simply to catching the latter when they took the initiative and went into action. Rather, they had learned how to 'use scouts offensively', to hearken back to Major-General Hugh 'Boom' Trenchard's directions to the Royal Flying Corps in France in 1916. Against Me 262s, the counter-air operations ranged from high and low altitude bombing of known jet airfields (the effect of these strikes was limited by a combination of

flak and the use of dispersal fields), to 'capping' them – keeping standing patrols of fighters just out of range of an airfield's heavy flak defenses, waiting for Me 262s to return to base low on fuel and unable to use their superior speed to avoid combat.

'Capping' was the most effective operational response to the Me 262s, as the Allies' numerical superiority, and the greater endurance of their piston-engined fighters, allowed them to keep sizeable combat air patrols (CAPs) in the air. Half of the 160 Me 262s claimed by USAAF fighters were destroyed near their airfields. In the words of Oberstleutnant Heinz Bär, the most successful Me 262 ace with 16 kills, 'It was a petrifying experience to be low on fuel, preparing to land, and find that Allied fighters had followed you home'.

To defend the Me 262s when they were at their most vulnerable – when taking off and landing – the Germans deployed not only massed flak guns but also units of piston-engined Fw 190 and Bf 109 fighters at their bases. Bitter large-scale battles at low altitude resulted, but the Germans were often

Right: Adolf Galland accepted that the Me 262s were likely to be outnumbered, but the actual delivery rate proved sadly disappointing. Committed in ones and twos, the jets faced such overwhelming odds that they failed to inflict significant losses.

Below: One of the most effective answers to the Messerschmitt Me 262: a P-47 carrying bombs. By attacking the jets on their airfields, the Allies further reduced the jets' already poor sortie rate.

able to protect the Me 262s. The jet fighter could not operate independently of other elements like radar for early warning and fighter direction, and 'friendly' flak and fighters for protection. Over the next 50 years the elements would change, but the need for jet fighter operations, offensive or defensive, to be part of an integrated operational approach to an air campaign remained.

While fighter-bomber operations continued – 20 Me 262s took part in the 1 January 1945 Bodenplatte attack on Allied fighter airfields which Galland opposed on the grounds of it weakening the build-up of an anti-bomber force – more Me 262s were made available to attack Allied bombers and their escorts, starting in February. The jagdflieger of JG 7, bolstered by a cadre of Kommando Nowotny veterans, were starting to intercept multi-engined formations more effectively that the ex-bomber pilots who had flown the bulk of the operational Me 262s in previous months.

But it was only as Germany was finally starting to collapse at the end of March 1945 that the improvements in pilot and groundcrew training, and the

Ejection seats

The ejection seat was one of the technologies made necessary by the introduction of jet propulsion. The airflow associated with low-drag/high-speed design meant that bailing out in the traditional manner was likely to lead to the pilot being either trapped in the cockpit by 'g' forces if the aeroplane was in a spin, or being hurled against the aircraft if not.

As with the introduction of the parachute to fighting scouts in 1918, the Germans were the pioneers in the use of the ejection seat – the Allies would not make their fitment in aircraft universal until their post-war designs were in service.

The first ejection seat to be used operationally was on a Heinkel He 280, the premier German jet fighter design (flying both as a glider and under its own power in March-April 1941), and the loser to the Me 262 in the competition for the first production jet fighter. Its ejection seat used compressed air, rather than the explosive charge that has since become standard. On 13 January 1942, during an unpowered test flight, test pilot Flugkapitan Otto Schenk found that his He 280 had become uncontrollable at altitude due to the icing up of his flying surfaces. He subsequently did what thousands of other pilots have since done – ejected. The first ejection in an emergency situation (the seat had been deliberately fired during previous developmental test flights) was successful.

However, production Me 262s did not have an ejection seat, and if bailing out at speeds in excess of 250 knots, the pilot would often be thrown against the high tail of the jet. The development of reliable ejection seats was another of the technologies absent in 1944-45 that would go on to become a pre-requisite for effective jet fighter operations in the post-war years.

provision of the improved Jumo 004B engine with a service life of 25 hours, allowed the Me 262 force to more consistently engage in the uneven battles against the Allied bombers that continued to strike the Fatherland literally around the clock. By this stage Galland himself was commanding a new elite Me 262 unit, known as JV 44, which participated in the last battles at the end of March.

The high-water mark of the Me 262s' fight against the bombers came on 31 March when JG 7 was able to generate 38 sorties, destroying 14 heavy bombers and 2 fighters for the loss of 4 of their own number – the 14 bombers represented less than one per cent of the attacking force, however. High-speed attacks by the Me 262s penetrated screens of escort fighters,

and their improved armament – they now carried R4M air-to-air rockets – made their head-on attacks against bombers highly lethal. In these weeks, night operations by 10./NJG 11's handful of converted Me 262 nightfighters (which included radar-equipped two-seat versions as well as single-seaters) started to claim a rising toll of their RAF Mosquito counterparts, which had previously prayed on piston-engined Luftwaffe nightfighters with virtual impunity.

The increased tempo of Me 262 operations led to renewed 'capping' and massive counter-air strikes – 1,000 heavy bombers struck jet airfields on 21 March, but, as was also to be seen repeatedly over the next 50 years, these operations did not prevent the enemy fighters from continuing their operations. Galland's JV

44 joined the fight in the first week of April, but the odds against their success were high. During the course of 47 Me 262 sorties flown on 4 April, eight Me 262s were shot down and five damaged. In reply, the Germans claimed seven bombers and two fighters destroyed. Six days later some 55 sorties were undertaken, resulting in 27 Me 262s being lost in return for claims of just 9 bombers. Despite their heavy losses – evidence of the effectiveness of the Allied operational response – the Me 262 units remained in action until their bases were overrun in April, with JV 44 flying some of its last missions on 26th of that month.

The Messerschmitt jet was the most significant fighter of its type to see action in the Second World War, and post-war tests went on to demostrate

A typical Me 262 battle, March 1945

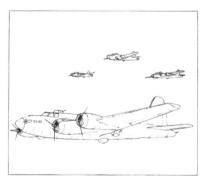

1. B-17s take off from bases in England, joining long range fighters en route for Germany.

2. Tactical fighters based in Europe take off to fly combat air patrols above known Me 262 bases.

3. Once at altitude, the B-17s are detected by German radar and the fighter defenses are alerted.

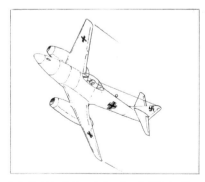

4. German piston-engined fighters scramble first while the limited endurance jets wait until the last moment.

5, As Allied CAPs engage the Bf 109s or Fw 190s, the Me 262s take off from autobahn strips.

6. Vectored by flight controllers, the Me 262s position themselves above and ahead of the bombers.

its superiority over its Allied contemporaries in the shape of the RAF's Meteor I and the USAAF's P-80A Shooting Star. A total of 1,294 Me 262 were built, although only half to three-quarters of this number were actually delivered to frontline units.

The effectiveness of the German design was not proven by its kill figures. The Luftwaffe claimed that Me 262 pilots downed about 780 Allied aircraft, 179 of them falling to the first 22 jet aces in history. The top scorer, Oberstleutnant Heinz Bär, claimed 16 victories, whilst Galland calculated that JV 44 had a 5-to-1 kill ratio in its favor. However, the US Eighth Air Force claimed that only 52 bombers and 10 fighters were lost to Me 262s, and despite adding losses of aircraft that were not witnessed, as well as the losses of the Ninth Air Force, French Air Force, RAF, RCAF and the Soviets to this total, it is still unlikely that the two figures can be reconciled. One contemporary estimate is that about 150 Allied aircraft were shot down for the loss of about 100 Me 262s in air-to-air combat. In addition to the 160 jets claimed by USAAF fighters, a further 30 Me 262s were purportedly downed by the RAF and RCAF, plus smaller numbers lost to AAA, bomber gunners and Soviet aircraft and ground fire. The bitterness of the Luftwaffe's desperate final battles is further emphasized by the destruction of a number of Me 262s in mid-air collisions with Allied aircraft.

Adolf Galland's last battles and the R4M

Generalleutnant Adolf Galland, dismissed from his post as General der Jagdflieger by Reischmarschall Herman Göring in January 1945, formed Jagdverband (fighter group) 44. Many of its pilots were aces and veteran fighter leaders whose commands had been all but wiped out in combat, or grounded for lack of fuel. Organized in February 1945, JV 44 arrived at its operational base on 31 March, and in April Galland's last battles saw him flying an Me 262, armed with R4M air-to-air rockets, against heavily escorted formations of USAAF and French B-26s.

The Me 262 only started to realize its potential lethality against heavy bombers when the R4M was introduced. Because of the Me 262's closing speed when using the favored method of head-on attack to maximize the vulnerability of Allied bombers, the four 30 mm cannon sited in the jet's nose were unable to hit the target with a lethal burst. Despite the power of the Me 262's armament, the Germans discovered that the jet fighter would be limited by relying on guns alone. In the words of Me 262 ace Oberst Johannes 'Macki' Steinhoff, 'the bullet velocity was so poor that in a turn you could see the bullets fly'.

The R4M rocket was developed to give German fighters the ability to down bombers in fast slash-and-run head-on attacks without having to resort to carrying the externally-mounted cannon or rocket launchers that made the Fw 190s and Bf 109Gs so armed almost totally unmaneuverable. Indeed, the latter required fighter escort to protect them from USAAF bomber escorts. The advent of the R4M re-introduced the unguided rocket to air combat and it would remain the anti-bomber weapon of choice until the air-to-air missile matured in the late 1950s. Steinhoff found that, 'when you placed the target in the reticule (of the Revi gunsight) for the gun and released the rockets, the kill was guaranteed'. Each Me 262 carried 24 rockets, normally fired as a single salvo at a distance of about 600 meters – extreme range for the bombers' guns. Jagdverband 44 used the R4M rocket in its last battles against the B-26s in April 1945, even though on his final mission before being shot up by a Mustang, Galland himself forgot to arm the rockets. While the Generalleutnant's ultimate confirmed kill – a USAAF B-26C of the 17th Bomb Group – was to be downed with cannon, he had helped demonstrate the potential of the rocket.

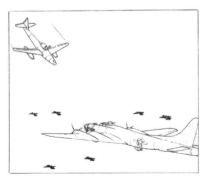

7. The Me 262s dive through the bomber formation, firing 30 mm cannon or R4M air-to-air rockets.

8. A second attack was often prevented by P-51 escorts and the Me 262s forced to break off.

10. The most dangerous moment for the Me 262: its straight and relatively slow approach to land.

Contrails over the Yalu: fighter operations in Korea, 1950-53

In the first air combat operations universally dominated by jet fighters, it quickly became apparent that although the aeroplanes had changed significantly from those involved in the Second World War, much of the tactics and technology required for effective fighter operations remained the same. Korea was a 'limited' war that placed restrictions not only on the type of forces involved, but also the operations which could be conducted by them and, ultimately, perceptions by the participants of the validity of the operational lessons learnt during the three years of conflict. A prime example of this was the fact soon after the end of the war, the United States Air Force (USAF – the Air Force had become independent of the Army in 1947) began buying fighters and preparing for operations that were very different from those that had proven so successful over Korea.

A production model Lockheed P-80B Shooting Star production model. Just too late for World War II, the P-80 was outclassed by the time of the Korean war.

USAF air missions: 1950

The conflict commenced with the invasion of South Korea by the Communist North on 25 June 1950. Even as the latter's army scored impressive victories on the ground principally through the element of surprise, its small air force (mainly comprising ex-Soviet aircraft of Second World War-vintage) was soon outclassed by the fighters committed to action by the USAF – piston-engine F-51Ds and F-82s, plus turbojet F-80Cs, the latter being much improved versions of the first-generation P-80s of 1945.

With air superiority virtually secured by the USAF fighter force, bomber elements from US Navy carriers joined with B-26 Invaders (a different bomber entirely from those Adolf Galland had

encountered over Germany in 1945) and B-29s in striking at North Korean airbases. The lack of fighter opposition over the battlefield also left United Nations (Australian and South African F-51s) fighters and Royal Navy Fleet Air Arm (FAA) carrier aircraft (piston-engined Sea Furys and Firefly Vs) to concentrate on air-ground operations.

These 'mud-moving' sorties soon proved to be the most important element of the air war in Korea, as UN fighter-bombers were used to counter the numerical advantage held by the Communist ground forces. Aircraft also became essential tools in reconnaissance and interdiction work. Such was the importance assumed by bombing and attack aircraft that air

USAF fighters like this F-80C soon disposed of any threat from the North Korean air force, enabling US and Allied bombers to engage enemy ground forces throughout the South.

combat operations in-theatre were sharply defined by air to ground taskings. Simply put, the Communist goal was to prevent the attacking aircraft from hitting targets, both in the frontline and to the rear, whilst the UN fighters' goal was to ensure that the bombers got through to neutralize enemy forces.

Soviet intervention: the MiG-15

The first serious attempt to interfere with UN air-ground operations came in November 1950 when UN forces, having counter-attacked after repulsing the initial Communist invasion, were approaching the Yalu River, which signified North Korea's border with China. In the first surprise of the month (the second would be a massive Chinese counter-attack that would send UN ground forces reeling), Soviet MiG-15 fighters rose from bases inside China to challenge B-29s on interdiction missions. On the eighth of that month, the first all-jet dogfight saw Lt Russell Brown, who was escorting B-29s in an F-80C, score the premier MiG kill of the war.

Despite this early success, it quickly became apparent that the MiG-15 posed a serious challenge to UN air superiority. The presence of these fighters served notice that the war in Korea may be limited, but it would be fought with the latest weaponry. By late 1950 it was suspected that the MiGs were ex-Soviet Air Force machines flown by seasoned pilots from its country of manufacture, but this could

be confirmed for some time.

The MiG-15 totally outclassed the F-80C, F-84 and Meteor straight-wing jet fighters in Korea. Even the US Navy, which had stayed committed to straight-winged aircraft because of their superior landing characteristics on the smaller carriers then in use, found that its F9F and F2H jet fighters did not measure up to the MiG. Finally, the latter's superiority over piston-engined fighters such as the F-51 and F4U – mainstays of the UN close-air support effort – was even more pronounced.

The MiG-15 relied heavily on the

As UN forces drove the North Koreans back, MiG-15 fighters, supplied and manned by the Soviet Union, rose to attack the USAF bomber formations. This MiG-15 was captured towards the end of the war when the pilot defected to the South.

Like all the straight-winged US jets, the F-80C was unable to stay with a MiG-15 in a turn.

experience gained by Soviet aircraft manufacturers during the Second World War, whose products had got progressively better as they gained access to western types through lend-lease agreements. Traditionally highly maneuverable at low to medium altitudes, as well as being easy to produce, Soviet fighters now also began to benefit from an increased level of technological sophistication through exposure to advanced British and American designs.

This resulted in the rapid development of the MiG-15 in the immediate postwar years, Soviet designers also benefiting greatly from captured German wartime research and the acquisition of advanced British

The MiG-15's RD-45F turbojet was developed from the Rolls-Royce Nene engine, given to the Russians by the Labour government in Britain soon after the end of World War II

Left: The US Navy preferred straight-wing aircraft like the Grumman F9F Panther because they were safer to operate from aircraft carriers, but this duly meant the fighter was completely outclassed by the MiG-15.

Royal Australian Air Force Meteor F 8s, with a T 7 two-seat trainer in the background of No 77 (Fighter) Sqn are seen over the Korean coast.

jet engines – the MiG-15's Rolls-Royce Nene-inspired RD-45F turbojet engine was arguably a better powerplant than the British original.

Unlike its piston-engines predecessors, the MiG-15 was truly a Cold War design. The former had been built to defend troops in the field against German attack aircraft, whilst the raison d'être of the MiG-15 was to defend cities and industrial centers against high-altitude US strategic bombers like the B-29. Reflecting this operational requirement, the Mikoyan jet had an excellent rate of climb, and was armed with one 37 mm and two 23 mm

cannon – slow firing, but capable of doing lethal damage to heavy bombers, even if they placed the MiG-15 pilot at a disadvantage if the latter encountered a maneuvering target.

The MiG-15s initially engaged by UN fighters in November 1950 were part of the 64th Fighter Aviation Corps of the Soviet Air Force – its three fighter aviation divisions had moved into airfields around Mukden, Anshan and Antung, in Manchuria, just days before making their combat debut. Throughout the war these airbases would remain barred to US bombers due to UN restrictions on overflying China. Despite this ban, however, numerous F-86 'hot pursuits' went as deep into forbidden territory as the landing pattern at Antung.

Although the Soviet pilots were inexperienced in jet combat, and were operating from bases even more austere than those back in the 'motherland', this did not prevent them from quickly establishing air superiority through both superior numbers and performance over 'MiG Alley' – the airspace in the north-western corner of North Korea, adjacent to the key Yalu crossings bounded by the towns of Sinuiju, Chosan and Chongju, and the Yalu and Chongchon Rivers.

The First Jet-versus-Jet Victories

The first all-jet dogfight in history occurred over North Korea on 8 November 1950. In the days leading up to this historic encounter, UN ground forces in-theatre had recoiled in the face of a massive Chinese counter-attack, launched on 25 October. The MiG-15 added to the shock of the Chinese intervention, and following two bloodless attacks on F-51D fighter-bombers, the Soviet fighters challenged a flight of F-80Cs undertaking defense suppression strikes against North Korean AAA in support of a B-29 attack on Sinuiju, near the Yalu – an area that soon became known as 'MiG Alley'.

USAF 1st Lieutenant Russell Brown of the 16th Fighter Interceptor Squadron (FIS)/51st Fighter Interceptor Wing (FIW) was flying one of the F-80Cs at 20,000 ft when he saw eight MiG-15s some 10,000 ft above him. The Soviet fighters were from Colonel A V Alelyukhin's 28th Interceptor Air Division (*Istrebeitel Aviatsionnaya Polk*), based at an airfield just across the Yalu at Antung, in Manchuria. As soon as they had been given the word to scramble, the Soviet pilots immediately utilized the MiG's superior rate of climb to reach 30,000 ft. Once at their pre-briefed patrol height, they simply waited for their targets to come into view, before initiating a diving attack on the bombers. Through employing this 'slashing' tactic, the Soviet pilots allowed their airspeed to carry them back over the Yalu in order to safely regain an altitude advantage in airspace closed to US fighters. They would then form up to commence another attacking pass.

During the first interception, one MiG pilot made the mistake of getting too close to 1st Lieutenant Brown's F-80C, and thus lost the mutual covering support of the rest of his flight. At lower altitudes, the MiG's performance advantage against the F-80C was canceled out, and Brown quickly closed on the diving Soviet fighter and shot it down with a well-aimed five-second burst, despite the fact that all but one of his .50 cal machine guns had jammed soon after he opened fire. The rest of the Soviet pilots returned safely to base, with only a solitary claim for an F-51 – subsequently not borne out by US loss records – by Lt Shchegolev (the Soviet's first MiG kill of the war) to show as compensation for the downed MiG-15.

The next day the Soviets finally drew blood when MiGs shot up an unescorted 91st Reconnaissance Squadron RB-29 sent north on a photo mission. Badly damaged, it made it back to base but crashed while trying to land, killing five crewmen. RB-29 gunner Staff

Armed with large caliber, but slow-firing cannon, the MiG-15 was primarily designed to attack four-engined bombers like the USAF's B-29s.

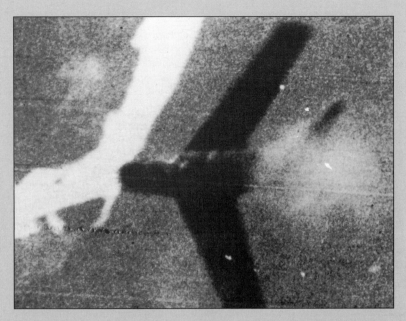

Gun camera film from a USAF F-86 catches the last moments of a MiG struck by a hail of .50 cal bullets.

Sergeant Harry J Lavene claimed a MiG kill in return, but this is not borne out in Soviet sources. On 10 November Maj Khar'kovskiy (a squadron commander in the 28th Interceptor Air Division) and his wingman shot down a B-29 of the 307th Bomb Group over Uijiu, and thus registered the first confirmed Soviet kill of the war. From then on only jet reconnaissance aircraft would be allowed to operate near the Yalu unescorted. The 28th also claimed to have destroyed an F-80 and a P-47 – there were none of the latter in-theatre, the Soviet pilots clearly mis-identifying their target, which was probably a US Navy AD-4 Skyraider (there were a number of them operating near Sinuiju on this day).

The Allies also scored their second and third MiG kills on the 10th when two jets fell to US Navy fighter pilots escorting the Skyraiders over Sinuiju. The first was claimed by Lieutenant Commander William Thomas Amen of VF-111, who notched up the Navy's premier jet-versus-jet kill in the process. Attempting to down one of the 'low and slow' AD-4s, the MiG-15 literally 'dropped into the lap' of the F9F-2 Panther pilot, who quickly despatched it. The Panther, like the F-80C, was no match for the MiG thanks to its straight wing and underpowered engine, but because of the Soviet pilot's (Guards Captain M F Grachev, a veteran of the Second World War, and a squadron commander in the 139th Guards Interceptor Air Regiment) error in losing momentum at low-level, Amen had no difficulty in destroying the jet fighter. Grachev's wingman claimed an F9F (mis-identified as a F-80C) in return, but again their was no evidence of a loss in US Navy listings. The second MiG was shared by two Panther pilots from USS *Valley Forge*.

The first bomber interception battle was fought on 15 November when Major Khar'kovskiy led eight MiGs against a formation of 21 (the Soviets claimed to have counted 40) B-29s, escorted by F-80Cs. Two B-29s were damaged (the Soviets claimed three kills) and the bombing of Sinuiju disrupted.

These early kills by both sides established themes that would be seen throughout the remainder of the Korean war. While MiG-15s could defeat straight-wing jets at high altitude, low down, Soviet pilots lacked both the performance and the tactics to consistently defeat US and allied aircraft. These limitations would remain in place for the duration of the conflict, and were major reasons why the Soviets were never able to clear UN fighter-bombers from North Korean skies. However, the vulnerability of B-29s – or any other piston-engined bombers for that matter – to jet fighter attacks had been clearly demonstrated. Despite this, American military strategists refused to commit USAF jet bombers into action over Korea, and this decision resulted in a number of bloody battles being fought between B-29s, escorting fighters and MiG-15s during the war.

Finally, the importance of training and tactics, and the US superiority in both these areas, was also graphically demonstrated. In the Soviet units sent into action, only senior pilots, such as the squadron commanders had any real combat experience, and when the air divisions first sent to Korea were rotated back to the USSR, none of pilots who had encountered USAF jets were left behind to teach recent arrivals from the Soviet Union. Therefore, any combat knowledge accrued by the units in-theatre had to be learnt the hard way – in action against veteran Sabre pilots out over the Yalu.

The F-86 Response

Below: The F-86F was the ultimate Korean war version of the North American Sabre. Despite statistics being confused by AAA losses and accidents, the F-86s still achieved a kill ratio of about 7:1 against the MiGs over Korea.

Far below: The earlier F-86A lacked power-boosted controls but was nevertheless superior to the MiG-15 below 25,000ft.

On 17 December 1950 the first MiG-15 was downed by a USAF F-86A of the 4th Fighter Interceptor Wing, which had been rushed to the theater after the arrival of the Soviet jets. The two fighters were, on paper at least, closely matched. The MiG-15 was lighter than the F-86, and duly had a superior climb rate, a higher ceiling, better initial acceleration and greater turning ability above 35,000 ft – both types had comparable rates of turn between 25,000 and 35,000 ft, but even the basic A-model Sabre, which lacked power-boosted flight controls, was superior beneath 25,000 ft. The F-86 had higher 'red line' speeds and a better rate of roll, but its armament of six .50 caliber machine-guns lacked lethality, although they provided a higher rate of fire than the MiG's cannon armament.

Despite these drawbacks, the F-86 maintained a combat edge over the MiG-15 in Korea right from the word go. Sabre pilots quickly learnt to exploit the MiG's lack of power-boosted controls, which meant that the later E- and F-models could 'pull G' more rapidly. The MiG pilot was at a further disadvantage when embroiled in violent maneuvering, for he did not have a G-suit like his opposite number in an F-86, which allowed the latter to better sustain 'high-G' turns without 'blacking' or 'redding' out through blood flow problems to the brain. The MiG-15's transonic control capability was also more restrictive than the F-86, and this became further pronounced when the later models of Sabre arrived in-theatre with their 'all-flying' tail. Transonic control problems arose when the MiG approached speeds of Mach 1.0 – the transonic barrier that was to prove so significant for the jet fighters of the 1940s and early 1950s – and it saw the pilot struggle to make the flying surfaces (ailerons, stabilizers and rudder) respond to his control inputs.

Due the wide variety of problems experienced by Allied and Communist pilots alike, neither possessed a decisive advantage over the other in terms of outright performance. What would determine the outcome of fighter operations over Korea would be the skill of the man ensconced in the

cockpit, which had instilled in him through a rigorous training regime. Here, the USAF pilot had a clear advantage over his Soviet rival.

In Korea, as throughout the history of fighter combat, about five per cent of the fighter pilots generally accounted for 40 per cent of the air-to-air kills scored. Similarly, pilots on their first few combat missions accounted for a disproportionate percentage of those shot down. The UN squadrons (and especially the USAF units) had a broader pool of trained pilots to draw from.

Soviet pilots were often at a disadvantage, in part, because their air force was more concerned with having as many of their aviators exposed to jet combat as possible, rather then restricting operations to a chosen elite. The 64th's three original air divisions of fighters were replaced, in rotation, by a further nine during the course of the war, as well as four independent regiments – new units dedicated specifically to air defense and radar were also added as the war ground on. As a result of this near-constant change, Soviet pilots could experience a tour of duty that lasted just 40 sorties. Although unit rotation ensured tactical integrity, it also prevented hard-won tactical lessons being passed on to the new men at the frontline.

As mentioned earlier, the MiGs were operating out of austere facilities at the end of a very long supply line, and the Soviets also had to further devote their resources to training the Chinese and North Korean air forces. Often, only two air regiments, with 30 combat-ready aircrew each, comprised the entire MiG-15 force charged with protecting the burgeoning Communist armies spilling into the south in the first half of 1951. The opening of a new airfield at Myaougou in June of that year drastically increased the frontline

The First Jet Aces

For the USAF, the Korean War saw a greater emphasis placed on publicizing the deeds of the 'fighter ace' than had been the case in the Second World War. Rather than just showing the fighter pilot as a component part of the UN war effort in Korea, the media tended to the idolize the new breed of jet aces in a way not seen since the press coverage of First World War aces. This was principally due to the similarities that existed between the two conflicts in the bitter fighting on the ground – bitter, bloody, stalemate, that resulted in long casualty lists for little geographical gain. The American media, therefore had to publicize the clean, heroic, side of the conflict in Korea – the almost medieval duels that were taking place in the skies over the Yalu between US and Soviet jet fighter pilots. The unmitigated success of the F-86 pilots also helped boost the image of the fledgling USAF, which had only been formed as an independent service in 1947.

The first jet ace of the Korean War was Captain James Jabara, a veteran of the Second World War (with 1.5 kills in Mustangs over Europe) who had been amongst the first F-86A pilots in the 4th FIW. The combat experience and pilot skill embodied within this unit were critical factors that allowed the American pilots to prevail in the initial air battles over North Korea. Jabara scored his first confirmed MiG kill on 3 April 1951, and swiftly added to his score over the next few weeks. By 20 May he had claimed his fifth and six victories, and although pulled out of action the very next day (USAF generals considered it too great a risk to lose their first jet ace in combat), Jabara eventually managed to return to Korea for a second tour as a major in early 1953 and remained in action up to the end of the conflict. With a final tally of 15 jet victories, he finished second only to 16-kill ace Captain Joseph McConnell of the 51st FIW in the USAF jet ace listings for the Korean War. In third place was fellow 4th FIW pilot Captain Manuel Fernandez with 14.5 victories.

Despite having been portrayed for decades as mere cannon fodder for American F-86 pilots, recent Russian writing has shown that the claims of some Soviet pilots were higher than their USAF counterparts. For example, the leading Soviet ace of the conflict was Colonel Yevgeni Pepelyaev, commander of the 196th Interceptor Air Division, who claimed 23 kills. He was closely followed by N V Suyagin with 22, whilst the third-ranking ace, L K Shchukin, finished with 15. The Soviets also produced a solitary jet nightfighter ace in the form of Major Karelin, who claimed six B-29s. However, the total of Soviet claims exceeds the number of Allied aircraft lost during the war.

strength of the MiG-15 force to five regiments, but skilled Soviet technicians – especially in Chinese and North Korean units – remained a scarce commodity throughout the war.

Another advantage enjoyed by the USAF was the employment of better tactics, Sabre units proving more adept at matching successful tactics to their

aircraft's performance envelope than the Soviets. In broader terms, this allowed USAF generals to make better use of their fighters in relation to the overall theater strategy. At squadron level, the Americans also had superior fighter leaders within their F-86 wings.

Many were veterans of the Second World War, whose experience in the conflict was still fresh enough in their minds to mean that their operational requirements were taken seriously by the high command both in Washington and Tokyo. Those who followed them in Vietnam in 1965-68 would not be so fortunate. Seasoned fighter aces such as Colonel Harrison Thyng and James K Johnson (both commanders of the 4th FIW) not only led F-86 formations, they helped improve tactics, integrate jet operations within the overall UN air offensive and tried to extract more resources for their units from the high command.

The Soviet fighter leaders included men such as Ivan Kozhedub, a MiG-15 division commander who was their leading Second World War ace (62 victories, including an Me-262). They too had an appreciation of the applicability of the lessons of the Second World War, A I Podkryshkin (another wartime ace) writing at the time, 'Results do not become obsolete – they only need to be rethought and

turned into a method which applies to the actual conditions present'. But they were limited in their effectiveness by the stringent control enforced by senior Soviet commanders back in Moscow.

Their allies in the Chinese and North Koreans lacked both leaders and trained aircrew, and therefore experienced the inevitable problems encountered by any Third World air arm trying to quickly transition to jet

fighters in a time of conflict.

All these factors combined to make Korea a limited war in respect to the use of air power. Neither the USAF, the USN or the Soviet Air Force – all of whom were trying to build up their jet fighter strength in case the Cold War turned hot – would commit the majority of their forces to the conflict. Another world power in the form of Britain was even more restrictive in its commitment to the war in respect to air power, choosing to deploy elements of the all-piston-engined FAA from Royal Navy carriers off the Korean coast. The RAF refused to send any jets at all (through fear of them being outclassed by the MiG-15 perhaps!?), although, like the Canadians, they sent dozens of fighter pilots to fly with USAF units.

As proof of this watchful eye kept focused on the Cold War, one has to look no further than the brief deployment of Strategic Air Command's (SAC) 27th Fighter Escort Wing, equipped with F-84D/Es, to Korea in November 1950. This specialized unit was only permitted to stay for a six-month tour, before being returned to America in case it was needed to protect SAC B-29s despatched on a nuclear strike against the Soviet Union.

The limited numbers of aircraft sent to Korea by both sides meant that low-level tactical considerations held a

Above: F-86Fs reached Korea in the Fall of 1952. With power-boosted controls they could sustain high 'G' turns better than the MiGs.

Left: A great deal of money and effort was expended to obtain flyable MiG-15s for testing. This example is seen under evaluation on Okinawa during 1953.

With Sabres confined to bases in Japan during the Chinese ground offensive, it fell to F-84 Thunderjet fighter-bombers to escort B-29s over North Korea.

greater sway in the eventual outcome of this conflict than in an all-out war like that which had ended just five years before.

Further compounding the adverse effect the limited number of F-86s had on the UN war effort was the problem encountered with their basing. This had serious repercussions on USAF fighter operations throughout the conflict, but was felt most acutely in 1951, when the

poor condition of American bases in Korea (particularly in the harsh winter months) forced most F-86 units to fly from Japan. The move further afield not only reduced the amount of time Sabre pilots could spend over 'MiG Alley', but also the sheer volume of sorties that could be put into that key airspace because of the time taken up in cruising to and from the operational area. Furthermore, additional maintenance

requirements created by these long transit flights placed an added strain on an already overstretched supply chain.

The key to successful fighter operations often wrests on the sheer volume of sorties that a given force is capable of flying against an enemy. If this number is halved, the ability to defeat the enemy is reduced accordingly, regardless of whether the reduction due to massive operational

losses (actual attrition), or the effects of mud-clogged airfields (virtual attrition). This logic is borne out by the fact that throughout the Korean War, the MiG-15 force averaged about half the sorties per fighter in theater than did the F-86 wings. This duly had the result of effectively negating much of the advantage the Communists should have been able to derive from their position of numerical strength.

1951 – The Bomber Escort Battles

As just previously mentioned, in the early stages of the F-86's involvement in the Korean War, units operating the jet flew from bases in Japan until the summer 1951. This was primarily because airfields in South Korea were usually inoperable, or threatened by the Chinese Army. The end result of this was that the Sabre force now lacked sufficient range to escort B-29s attacking targets in North Korea.

If they reduced airspeed in order to conserve fuel, and thus keep station off the bomber formations for much of the mission, the F-86 pilots would then become as vulnerable to the MiGs as their charges, lacking the acceleration to either respond to an attack or to implement a surprise diving interception. Further compounding this performance problem was the fact that more often than not, the Sabre's drop tanks would hang up despite the pilot's best efforts at 'punching' them off. This

F-86s were unable to escort B-29 bomber formations deep into North Korea in 1951 as their drop tanks proved to be unreliable.

Republic F-84 Thunderjets were a poor substitute for F-86s in the escort role, and rising losses to MiGs meant that daylight B-29 raids had to be abandoned.

further reduced its maneuverability, thus making it even more vulnerable to surprise attacks. A combination of these operational restrictions meant that the F-86 force in Korea was never able to implement effective B-29 escort tactics, and in the spring of 1951, escort of the bombers on daylight missions against interdiction and infrastructure targets over North Korea fell to inferior F-84 Thunderjets, RAAF Meteors and US Navy F9F Panthers.

Aside from attacking key industrial targets, USAF bombers and USN attack aircraft were also used in the counter-air mission to bomb airfields in North Korea. Despite the fact that these sites were often empty (the North Korean Air Force had decamped en masse to the safety of Chinese airfields early on in the conflict as these were out of bounds for the Allies), the USAF thought that periodic strikes would help

prevent the Communists from bringing MiG-15s forward into North Korea.

The Soviets began to challenge these raids in increasing numbers as the weeks passed by, and this eventually led to the air battle of 12 April 1951, when 39 B-29s (a maximum effort raid, although small-scale when compared with the bombing missions of 1945) were attacked by mass MiG formations. After suffering heavy losses, the B-29s were pulled out of daylight operations in 'MiG Alley', and resorted instead to night attacks.

With the Chinese ground offensive halted in the spring of 1951, the airfields in South Korea were quickly improved to allow F-86s to return to the mainland from Japan. This upgrading of Allied bases was completed just in the nick of time, for the number of MiGs thrown into action drastically increased through the spring and

The jet battles intensified in 1951, with both US and Russian pilots achieving 'ace' status. However, most F-86s remained deployed in the USA or Europe, ranged against the Soviet threat.

summer of 1951. The F-86 wings responded accordingly, and usually emerged victorious – on 20 May, Captain James Jabara of the 4th FIW became the first jet-v-jet ace in history, although the Soviets also claimed that their first jet ace, Senior Lieutenant Fedor Shabanov, achieved this status in the same air battle.

Despite the increased tempo of the air war the 4th FIW remained the only F-86 wing in theater, Washington steadfastly refusing to pull any more units away from continental air defense, or from Europe. As a result of this, the Soviet pilots were able to push their patrols out of 'MiG Alley' for the first time and range throughout western North Korea.

Despite months of B-29 night attacks against North Korean airfields, the UN still believed that they could be use by forward-deployed MiGs (which they never were), so daylight raids where reinstated once again. After more heavy losses to MiGs in October, the B-29s reverted once more to just night operations

In these battles the MiG pilots not only had the benefit of fighting near to their bases (the escort fighters were at the limit of their operational radii), but also the advantage of good Ground-Controlled Intercept (GCI) radar coverage. They also used the superior high altitude performance and rate of climb of their Mikoyan fighters to gain the altitude advantage before making diving attacks.

The USAF's response to these attacks was limited, as MiG bases in Manchuria could not be capped due to the ban on flying in Chinese airspace. With many of the targets close to the Yalu, sweeps could not be interposed between the MiG bases and the bombers without violating the ban. Fighter sweeps were also restricted by the F-86's range, whilst the limited number of Sabres available in-theater further reduced operational options. The MiG-15's defeat of the daylight bombing campaign on two separate occasions was a major success for the Soviet fighter force.

Lucky to be home: although the MiGs occupied the headlines, enemy AAA fire inflicted mounting losses on USAF squadrons.

Right: RAAF Meteors in their revetments. With four 20 mm cannon, the Meteors had enough firepower, but lacked the performance to tackle the MiGs on equal terms.

The Bandit Trains

Despite the fact that the MiGs were proving effective against the B-29s, they were still coming out second-best to the F-86s in increasingly larger aerial engagements. Like the Superfortresses, the fighter-bombers carrying out the interdiction campaign over North Korea were also encountering increasing resistance from both MiGs and Communist anti-aircraft guns, although neither were not part of an integrated air defense system. Such was the growing effectiveness of these weapons that by the fall of 1951, the air interdiction campaign waged by Allied airpower in an effort to counter the Chinese Army's numerical superiority was in serious jeopardy of being overwhelmed.

The Soviets had decided to take the offensive to the fighter-bombers by using massed MiG-15 formations dubbed 'bandit trains' by their Allied opponents. These were made possible by the increased use of external fuel tanks, and the introduction of the improved MiG-15bis fighter powered by the uprated Klimov VK-1 engine. The MiGs came south in strength to hold off F-86s while dedicated flights 'dropped off' to attack the fighter-bombers, the multiple 'trains' trying to employ pincer and envelopment tactics against UN aircraft.

At their height the 'bandit trains' posed a serious threat to Allied fighter-bombers, especially those carrying out interdiction missions deep in northern Korea. Yet the MiGs lost much of their high-altitude performance advantage when they descended to medium altitudes to try and engage their targets. Often, instead of carrying out successful dive-and-climb attacks like those used against B-29s, the MiG pilots found themselves engaged in dogfights with less capable aircraft whose pilots, at low speeds and altitudes, found that the straight wings on their often piston-

engined mounts gave them an acceptable turning performance when up against the Soviet threat.

The USAF responded by re-quipping an F-80 wing with improved F-86Es, thus creating a second F-86 wing in-theater. But even then, this still only meant that there were a maximum of 150 F-86s available for operations, ranged against at least 350 MiG-15s in the bases across the Yalu – granted, a fair proportion of these were flown by the less skilled pilots of the North Korean and Chinese Air Forces. The MiGs maintained this numerical superiority throughout most of the

MiGs destroyed. By the end of the year the offensive was beginning to fail as the USAF had draughted in F-86s to counter the MiG threat. The 'bandit trains' subsequently reduced in size and frequency just in time to prevent the USAF fighter force from total collapse, as by year's end, the tempo of operations against the Communists, combined with the appalling conditions at the South Korean air bases, had left just 55 per cent of F-86s in-theater serviceable. Allied to this, many combat-experienced F-86 pilots had also returned home having become tour-expired.

conflict, and of the 275 MiG-15 versus F-86 battles identified by the USAF in a study conducted after the war, the former had numerical superiority in 197 of them.

Despite this, the F-86 pilots maintained the advantage. For example, on 13 December 1951 two 'bandit trains' with a combined total of some 150 MiG-15s failed to destroy a single Sabre, while the USAF claimed 14

The pilot of this MiG-15 won the reward offered by the US government for the first defector to arrive with his airplane intact. It was flown directly to the USA aboard a C-124 Globemaster.

Night Operations

The shift in B-29 operations to nocturnal attacks also resulted in a dramatic increase in the night operations of the MiG-15 force as the Communists attempted to counter this new threat. The jet fighters lacked the technology to perform accurate night interceptions, even though a specialist nightfighter air regiment had arrived in-theater as early as March 1951. Realising that the MiG-15 alone did not provide the answer to the nocturnal raiders, Communist forces also enlarged their AAA arsenal and received more radar equipment from the Soviet Union.

To counter MiG nightfighters (a very limited number at first), USMC F7F Tigercats and then USAF F-94 Starfires and Corps' F3D Skynights were deployed to Korea and, with improved IFF equipment, were able to destroy a number of Communist jets. However, these operations also revealed a number of limitations in the equipment available to do the job. IFF technology at the time was rather unreliable, meaning that crews were unable to take full tactical advantage of the improved radar and fire control systems built into their fighters at night and in bad weather. Also, because the nightfighter's armament was limited to 20 mm cannon, targets had to be visually identified before opening fire – this rather negated the advantage of surprise that the radar and IFF systems offered nightfighters.

Communist offensive night operations were largely limited to 'Bedcheck Charlies', the US name for harassment raids by Chinese and North Korean Po-2 biplanes and Yak-18 trainers, dropping light fragmentation bombs. Operating at low altitude and airspeed, these machines proved difficult targets for US nightfighters. The most successful response came through using piston-engined US Navy and Marine Corps F4U-5N Corsairs, operating with gear and flaps down in order to reduce the great overtaking speeds encountered when attacking the Communist machines. The top proponent of this style of attack was Lieutenant Guy Bordelon, who became the only Navy ace of the war whilst flying Corsair nightfighters.

As a final twist to the nocturnal war, Soviet MiG pilots have since claimed to have shot down US jet nightfighters by using Po-2s as live bait!

The First Night Jet Fighter Battles

Having forced the USAF to finally shift its B-29 bombing raids from day to night time in June 1952, MiG-15 pilots soon adapted to the change in tactic and began carrying out successful nocturnal interceptions. The Soviets had deployed specialist nightfighter units – initially the 351st Independent Air Regiment – to Manchuria, but these had arrived in-theatre with piston-engined La-11s, which had little effect against the high-flying B-29s. A hasty change of plan saw a number of seasoned MiG-15 dayfighter pilots already in Manchuria swiftly converted onto the nightfighter role. Despite their GCI capability being limited at night, and having to cope with North Korean and Chinese ground air defenses that fired first and asked questions later, the MiG pilots were able to score a number of B-29 kills in 1952.

Their success forced the Americans to commit nightfighters to Korea to support the bombers, although there was much reluctance amongst senior officers in the Pentagon in approving jet fighters with the most modern radars and fire control equipment to accompany the bombers over enemy territory – they feared the technological comprise that could arise should they be shot down over enemy territory far outweighed the loss of a few B-29s. However, piston-engined F7F Tigercats of the USMC soon proved inadequate in the bomber escort role, forcing the latter to substitute F3Ds Skyknight jets in their place. Soon, the USAF's premier jet nightfighter in the shape of the F-94 Starfire was also sent north, having been restricted for a number of months to defensive patrols over South Korean bases.

IFF problems initially placed both the B-29s and their jet escorts at risk to incidents of 'friendly fire', but these were soon overcome, allowing USAF F-94s and USMC F3Ds to operate effectively over North Korea against the MiGs. The Skyknights initially flew barrier patrols some 20 to 50 miles north of the bomber stream, and scored the first jet-versus-jet night kill on 2 November 1952. When F-94s were committed, they took over the barrier patrols, releasing the F3Ds to fly close escort.

Starfire crews reported deterring many potential MiG attacks, the Lockheed interceptor eventually being credited with four kills (three MiGs and a Po-2 biplane) – total claims for the F3Ds stood at six by war's end. Aside from a number of B-29s, Soviet MiG pilots claimed three F-94s, two F-84s and a solitary F3D at night.

Sorties in Korea proved that jet fighter operations could be successfully carried out at night, but only with aircraft equipped with a suitable search radar. Even with GCI, MiGs were often left 'groping in the dark' for B-29s, and had the Americans been willing to send their best nightfighters north earlier, Soviet losses would have been far greater. The latter, quickly realizing that the strategic bomber threat to their homeland would probably come at night, invested in more all-weather fighters and greatly extended their radar and GCI coverage.

Over the ensuing decades even radar-equipped non-specialist fighters, and their aircrew, found nocturnal operations difficult to master, and it was only in the 1980s that US fighter forces truly became capable of round-the-clock operations in both air-to-ground and air-to-air (highly lethal BVR missiles were one of the key requirements) modes. By proving their proficiency in this, the most demanding of combat environments, American aircrews have outstripped many of their allies, and most of their adversaries, in their ability to wage war 24 hours a day.

Left: Lockheed F-94 Starfire two-seat nightfighters were deployed to Korea after the B-29s were forced to attack at night. The F-94s were to seek out MiG-15s operating at night, but most North Korean night missions were flown by Po-2 biplanes!

Right: US Marine Corps' Douglas F3D Skynights were also dispatched to Korea to dominate the night skies. Llke the F-94s, they found their high closing speeds a serious problem when attacking enemy piston-engined aircraft.

1952 – Situational Awareness

By 1952, both sides had made efforts to improve operational situational awareness. Air force studies have shown over the years that the majority of fighters shot down in air combat have not seen the aircraft that got them, the victor, in effect, having won through superior situational awareness. At a tactical level, superior situational awareness relies on sensors on the fighters themselves, whilst at an operational level, it means using sensors on separate platforms. Despite these key differences, at both levels, effective communication between allied fighters is a vital part of situational awareness.

By 1952, the Soviet radar coverage along the Yalu had been supplemented by an enhanced GCI capability which allowed the MiGs to both climb to altitude and be directed against F-86s with a height advantage. It also meant that Communist squadrons could mass in superior numbers in response to a threat prior to engaging, and then maintain the initiative by choosing when and where to fight.

In response, the USAF forward-deployed warning radars onto the Cho Do islands off the north-west coast of South Korea. Although this provided warning and control for fighters operating in 'MiG Alley', their situational awareness in Korea was still compromised by the fact that they did not have the benefit of passive sensors. USAF passive electronic intelligence data such as radio intercepts were normally too highly-classified to be passed onto fighter pilots in the frontline, period – let alone in real time.

Fighter Operations Against 'Bedcheck Charlie'

'Bedcheck Charlie' was perhaps the most unusual opponent encountered by US forces in Korea, and one that proved to be the most difficult for jet fighters to neutralize. The generic name given to piston-engined aircraft – mainly biplane Po-2s and monoplane Yak-11s and -18s – flown by the North Korean Air Force on nightly harassment bombing raids over UN positions, the 'Bedcheck Charlies' used their low altitude and speed as their primary defensive weapons, being able to 'terrain mask' in flight and usually ingress under UN radar coverage.

Different US nightfighters were flown against 'Bedcheck Charlies', with the F7F Tigercat – designed for classical Second World War GCI night interceptions – initially scoring several victories over the intruders. However, the North Koreans soon learned that the big Grumman could not follow the highly-manoeuvrable Po-2 at low-level, and their attack profiles were modified accordingly. The F-7F's effectiveness was drastically reduced.

In a gross case of overkill, the USAF then committed its high-technology F-94 to patrolling the skies over South Korean airbases in search of antiquated Po-2s that rarely achieved speeds in excess of 130 mph, but as the former's landing speed was in excess of the Polikarpov's top speed, interceptions of any kind could hardly have been expected. Indeed, due to the immense overtaking speeds between the two combatants, a number of near-misses occurred during the course of interceptions, and it is believed that at least one F-94 was lost when it actually flew through a Po-2.

After the war a Soviet MiG-15 pilot also claimed to have used the Po-2 as 'live bait' for attracting US fighters. He recounted how he followed a biplane until it was shot down in flames, then destroyed a F-94 whose

Independence Day – MiG Alley 1952

1. F-86s in 'finger four' formation approach the Yalu at high altitude, covering F-84s which will bomb the North Korean installations at Sakchu.

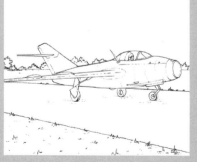

2. About 50 MiGs from the Soviet 97th and 190th Fighter Divisions are scrambled as GCI radar plots the Americans' course.

crew were busy watching their kill crash to the ground – USAF records do not bear out this claim.

In the end, the most effective fighters against 'Bedcheck Charlie' proved to be 1944-vintage piston-engined USN and USMC F4U-5Ns. Flying with gear and flaps down, their pilots would first use their radar to detect the slow-flying targets, and then move in at near-stalling speed behind the unsuspecting enemy and swiftly shooting it down, before being forced to overshoot. One of the most effective at employing these tactics was Lieutenant Guy P 'Lucky Pierre' Bordelon, who became the US Navy's sole ace of the war in mid-1953.

US attempts to counter 'Bedcheck Charlie' were neither an aberration or a dead-end in fighter operations. They pointed out a problem that has remained constant through to this day, with the slow, low-flying, threat of the Po-2 in Korea having now

been replaced by the helicopter.

While helicopters in the desert are vulnerable to aircraft (the Egyptians suffered severe losses on a number of occasions in 1973), in European terrain it can make use of the varied topography to hide. In the case of an attack helicopter, its crew can fire a cannon or pods of rockets at an attacking fighter – indeed, some machines like the AH-1W SuperCobra and the Ka-50 'Hokum' can even fire AAMs.

In order to help fighters cope with the advent of 'dogfighting' helicopters, a number of longer-range AAMs like AMRAAM have been fitted with seeker heads that can pick up a slow, low flying, target against a geothermal background. However, despite the successes of these 'more sensitive' missiles in controlled tests, helicopters still remain difficult targets. Just as the Americans used piston-engined aircraft to counter other piston-

engined machines in the Korean war, helicopters may yet prove to be the best counter against other helicopters.

Ironically, many decades after the cessation of the Korean War, USAF and South Korean fighters still confront a biplane threat in-theatre today. The North Koreans have several hundred Antonov An-2 biplane transports which would no doubt be used for the massive insertion of special operations forces in the opening stages of any new war with the South. Flying down valleys at night at tree-top height, these biplanes would likely prove to be a tricky target for most fighter pilots sent to confront them. Indeed, even if these biplanes were to be engaged by F-15C Eagles firing AMRAAM missiles in a look-down/shoot-down mode, the weapon used to kill the An-2 would no doubt be worth more in monetary terms than the target itself!

3, Flying in columns of squadrons, each about two miles apart, the MiG-15s are guided into action by their ground controllers.

4. Some of the MiGs 'bounce' the F-86s and in the melee, at least one American pilot saw the obviously slavic face of his opponent.

5. With the F-86s engaged, other MiGs attacked the F-84s, but at low altitude the MiG no longer enjoyed a real advantage and no kills were scored.

1952 Fighter Operations

In 1952, as the stalemate on the ground continued, the Communist approach to offensive fighter operations shifted. It was thought that green units – Chinese or Soviet – were being introduced to combat, and only venturing south when they had attained some experience over 'MiG Alley'. The USAF, reinforced by new F-86E/Fs, and benefiting from the radars on the Cho-Do islands, still managed to keep the advantage in air combat despite lacking full situational awareness.

With the introduction of the F-86F that year, the Sabre's suitability for air-ground operations was fully realised thanks to its superior engine thrust. It had also had the leading edge slats of the earlier models replaced with a 'solid' wing, thus improving the jet's maneuverability at high speeds for a trade off in faster landing approaches and less agility at the lower end of the performance scale. The F-86E also boasted a radar-ranging gunsight in place of the 1945-style gyroscopic equipment fitted to the F-86A. The improved system on the F-model proved difficult to maintain under operational conditions, however.

With its new strength and capability, the USAF was able to take the offensive against the Communist fighter force in the summer of 1952. Their main tactic was to escort daylight

bombing attacks on targets in 'MiG Alley', knowing that this would draw the MiGs up to engage the B-29s. This strategy soon resulted in some of the most intensive air battles of the war.

By June 1952 there were an estimated 1000 MiG-15s in-theater, the Soviets being joined by the first two Chinese air divisions, which had become operational in December, 1951. These had been reinforced by three more units of divisional size in March and another two just eight weeks later. The North Koreans had one air division operational by the start of 1952, with two more forming later that year. The employment of these various divisions in action along the frontline allowed the Communists to not only meet the F-86s head to head over the Yalu, but to go on and re-

Above: Evaluation of captured MiGs helped the USAF perfect its tactics. It was just as well: by the summer of 1952, there were over 1000 MiG-15s in action.

launch their own offensive operations.

The fall 1952 Communist fighter offensive was not a repeat of the 'bandit trains' of the previous years, however, as the formations were now smaller and the MiG pilots far more aggressive. This, combined with the effect of the improved F-86E/Fs at all altitudes, and increasing USAF numbers, meant that the outcome of the 1952 battles still remained in the F-86's favor. Numerical superiority did not give the Communists air superiority, but the USAF, remembering how brittle their single F-86A wing had been by the end of 1951, realized that quantity as well as quality was required in fighter operations.

1953 Fighter Operations

By 1953 the tide was turning firmly in the USAF's favor. There were now four (five by June) wings of F-86s operational in-theater, and the South Korean bases had been upgraded to allow them to remain operational in all weather conditions.

In Manchuria the 64th Fighter Aviation Corps remained in action,

although the increase in the number of new units rotating into the frontline had resulted in many of the more experienced regiments being withdrawn. Changing Communist strategy also led to many of the final air battles of the war being contested by the less experienced Chinese and North Koreans squadrons – indeed,

many of these units were still trying to incorporate the increased flow of Soviet aircraft within their ever-growing ranks, whilst at the same time being tasked with conducting operations over the frontline.

The most significant arrival in terms of hardware in the final year of the war was a force of over 100 Il-28 jet bombers that flew into a variety of Chinese airfields from the Soviet Union. Although never used operationally, these machines were viewed by the UN as having the capability to deploy nuclear weapons, and thus drastically escalate the scale of the conflict. The USAF, as well as looking to improve the air defense of their bases in Japan as a result of the Il-28s' arrival, also started planning for nuclear-armed counter-air missions against the Ilyushin bomber

bases. An immediate response implemented by the Americans was the training of F-84 units in the deployment of nuclear bombs – the Thunderjets had to be hastily modified in order to be able to carry such weaponry.

The tempo of operations remained high until the armistice was signed on 27 July, F-86 pilots gaining some of their most significant victories in the seven months of war in 1953. For

example, there were 56 MiG kills claimed in May, with Captain Joseph McConnell, the highest ranking USAF jet ace in Korea, scoring his 16th, and final, victory that month. In June some 77 enemy fighters were claimed destroyed without loss, and in July F-86s added another 32 claims to the total in just four weeks.

A Grumman F9F Panther of the USMC's VMF-311 operating as a fighter-bomber from a Korean airstrip.

The Impact

For a number of years after the war, the USAF claimed that their F-86 Sabres had achieved a 14-1 kill ratio (792 MiGs versus 78 F-86s, plus a further 26 Sabres lost to unknown causes), which they later revised downwards to 7-1 after the findings of their Sabre Measures Charlie report. The Soviets, for their part, reported similar ratios, but in their favor – 1,097 (651 of them F-86s) UN aircraft shot down by Soviet fighters for 335 losses (they claim their Chinese and North Korean allies scored 271 kills, including 181 F-86s, for 231 losses). The Soviets also complained that many UN aircraft listed as lost to AAA (especially F-86s) actually fell to MiGs.

Both the UN and Communist fighter operations were defensive in nature, the former attempting to use its aerial

might to neutralize the enemy's infrastructure and supply lines, whilst the latter employed its MiGs to attack that effort. Despite this, the fighter still remained an offensive weapon, even when used as part of a defensive operation.

The US victory in the air superiority stakes over Korea had limited applicability to the overall course of the conflict, however. Granted, the F-86's successes meant that bombers and fighter-bombers could strike infrastructure and interdiction targets throughout North Korea virtually at will, and that close air support, reconnaissance and air re-supply missions were also important to the overall UN effort.

However, despite its relative lack of vulnerability to MiGs, Allied airpower

simply could not turn the tide in Korea due to several key reasons. The weather conditions were bad; there were simply not enough aircraft; and air-to-ground weapons employed by UN units were just not accurate enough to allow the command of the air to translate itself into meaning the defeat of an enemy ground offensive, or the breaking of a stalemate. Finally, and perhaps most significantly, strategic bombing and sustained counter-air operations against the airbases in Manchuria were ruled out for political reasons.

Successful fighter operations may lead to air superiority and the free use of airpower yet, in limited wars worldwide, the advantage provided by this control has often proved to be limited by other factors.

Early Cold War Fighter Operations

To the fighter forces embroiled in the Cold War, this long running 'conflict' was every bit as fierce as any of the 'shooting' wars which raged in the Third World throughout its 40-year duration. The casualties were also just as real on both sides – during this period member nations of NATO and the Warsaw Pact lost over two per cent of their aircraft to accidents each year on average, with a number of air forces exceeding this figure. One Soviet fighter unit that converted from MiG-17s to MiG-21s at the time of the Cuban Missile Crisis in 1962, reportedly lost a jet a day during the Caribbean stand off.

The Cold War also occasionally deteriorated into open conflict when western reconnaissance aircraft (or those simply in the wrong place at the wrong time) were shot down by Communist fighters. Elsewhere, even those pilots who never fired a shot (or a missile) in anger in over 20 years of frontline flying still stood alerts, participated in exercises and generally trained for the day when the klaxons would sound in earnest.

In the first two decades of the Cold War, the fighter forces of the major

A Soviet MiG-21 accelerates rapidly skyward thanks to the added boost provided by strap-on SPRD-99 solid fuel rocket boosters. Developed for use in the field in Eastern Europe, the MiG-21/rocket combination was heavily used in North Vietnam during the USAF's Linebacker II operations of December 1972.

powers all had to adapt to the rapidly changing technology becoming available, and the new missions this allowed them to perform. Two innovations that were first used operationally in 1945 – the jet engine and the atomic bomb – changed the world, fighter operations included. The early Cold War years were shaped by fighter forces struggling to come to grips with these major changes. Other innovations introduced in the early Cold War years would reach fruition later, including technology such as the air-to-air missile and techniques like air-to-air refueling.

However, despite the profound changes introduced by the jet and nuclear age, there was still some continuity between the old piston-engined fighter pilots of the wartime years and the new Cold War air forces. Perhaps the most important link was in fighter leadership, as throughout this period, those who were responsible for planning and leading frontline operations had all learned their business in the cockpit during the Second World War or Korea. This experience led these men to keep alive the concept of fighter operations even in services such as the USAF which, during the SAC-dominated era of 'massive retaliation' from the mid-1950s to early 1960s, saw offensive fighter operations as basically taking 'nasty neutrons' on a quick one-way trip to Omsk.

One of the great force multipliers quickly adopted in the 1950s by the USAF was air-to-air refueling, the first tankers employed by the Americans being ex-SAC Boeing B-29s and B-50s. Seen here 'topping off' the tanks of a thirsty F-101A, this particular example is a KB-50J.

Fighter Operations and Changing Technology

The most obvious elements to undergo rapid change during the Cold War were the fighters themselves. In the immediate postwar years, the last, and most powerful, of the piston-engined fighters served alongside increasing numbers of first generation jet fighters. These were straight-wing aircraft such as the USAF's F-80 and F-84, the USN's FH-1 and FJ-1 and the RAF's Vampire and Meteor. The Soviets also followed suit with such comparable designs such as the Yak-15 and MiG-9.

The second generation of jet fighters was already on the drawing boards as the Cold War began to warm up – most notably the F-86 and MiG-15 that dominated the course of fighter operations in Korea. These incorporated the results of German wartime development and improved transonic aerodynamic design.

The advent of third generation jet fighters soon after the Korean War had ended signalled the arrival of the first frontline types capable of achieving supersonic speeds in level flight. Although developed whilst the conflict in Asia raged, these fighters were nevertheless designed too soon to take advantage of lessons and requirements that arose from the war – the F-100 and MiG-19 were the first of this new generation.

The Armstrong Whitworth Meteor NF 11 was a dedicated two-seat radar-equipped nightfighter variant of Gloster's more austere single-seat day fighter, and along with the improved NF 14, remained in frontline service with the RAF until 1961.

Despite being found wanting in the air-to-air role during the Korean conflict, Republic's F-84 Thunderjet remained a key fighter-bomber within the USAF well into the late 1950s, firstly with frontline units and then with the reserve and Air National Guard. These decoratively-marked F-84E-30s were assigned to the 9th FBS/49th FBG in Korea.

The first three generations of Cold War jet fighters all shared a number of characteristics. The standard fighter was still a fair weather/blue sky aeroplane, with larger. less nimble, two-seat machines handling night and all-weather duties, just as their invariably twin piston-engined forerunners had done In the Second World War. All these aircraft relied on cannon as their primary armament, although unguided rockets – the descendants of the Me-262's R4M – had became increasingly widespread by the mid-1950s, especially with all-weather fighters.

After the F-100s and the MiG-19s, the neat distinctions that had so delineated the initial generations of jet fighters started breaking down. Interceptors emerged in the mid-1950s that were capable of Mach 2 and relied on air-to-air missiles (AAMs) for their offensive weaponry – the F-104 and MiG-21 (both long-lived designs) fell into this

grouping. Both combined the lessons of fighter operations over Korea with the requirements of Cold War interceptor tactics, but by the mid-1950s, fighters were becoming even more specialized, intended either to deliver nuclear weapons or shoot down bombers trying to carry out the same mission.

Above: Meteor NF 11s of No 29 Sqn at the Queen's Review of the RAF at Odiham on 15 July 1953.

Just as the F-84 remained in the frontline despite its performance shortfalls when compared with the MiG-15, so too did the Shooting Star. Seen in the late 1940s these assorted F-80As and RF-80As, hail from a number of different units including the 4th FG, who would soon be re-equipping with F-86As.

The radar-equipped F-86K was a specially-designed export version of the USAF's D-model 'Sabre Dog', the APS-6 search and track equipment and Hughes fire-control system making this variant more of an all-weather fighter than the 'radarless' Sabres that were then in use principally with America's NATO allies. This natural-metal aircraft was assigned No 700 Sqn of the Royal Netherlands Air Force.

The Yak-25 was the Soviet equivalent of the F-94 or the Meteor NF 11/14, although unlike these two types, this fighter was an all-new design rather than a conversion of a day fighter. Some 480 Yak-25s were constructed over a five-year period starting in 1953, and the jet was principally employed guarding the northern borders of the Soviet Union. This particular aircraft is a Yak-120, a number of which were built prior to the definitive Yak-25 in order to test systems for inclusion in the service fighter – it carried out avionics development work.

The MiG-19 was the first Soviet fighter capable of sustained supersonic level flight and it entered frontline service as a straight day fighter in 1955. This shot shows the PM limited-weather version of the MiG-19, which boasted an Izumrud-2 radar and a quartet of beam-riding K-5M missiles in place of the standard trio of NR-23 23 mm cannon.

The MiG-19's equivalent in the USAF was the Lockheed F-104A Starfighter, which first flew in 1954. A futuristic aircraft which looked unlike any other design, the F-104 was tailored specifically for the air superiority bomber interceptor role.

The Rise of the Air Defense Mission

The rotund Saab J 29 was the first European swept-wing fighter to enter service. Over 600 were built in Sweden, and it served from 1951 until 1976. Although a neutral nation during the Cold War, the Swedes modelled their unit structure and tactical operations on their western neighbors.

Some of the first Yak-25s to reach the frontline perform a flyby at the Tushino airshow in the summer of 1955. Squadrons were not declared operational with the all-weather interceptor until later that year.

The first three generations of Cold War fighters on both sides of the Iron Curtain had, as a primary mission, not the destruction of enemy fighters in order to secure air superiority over a theater of operations, but rather air defense against enemy bombers. Hiroshima and Nagasaki showed the potential costs of letting even a single bomber get through.

The nuclear threat was delivered firstly by piston-engined types of ex-Second World War vintage, but these were soon replaced in the 1950s by jet- or turboprop-powered designs. The Soviets, who lacked a true strategic bomber in 1945, soon responded with a reverse-engineered 'B-29' of its own, designated the Tu-4 – it was essentially a copy of an aircraft that had landed at Vladivostok in 1944, and Tupolev went on to build some 1200 examples. As soon as Stalin had the bomb, the Tu-4 posed a threat to Europe, Japan and, on one-way missions, the US. More disturbing yet was the appearance of the Soviets first successful jet bomber in the shape of the Il-28, which entered service in the early 1950s.

The sheer destructive strength of the atomic bomb had eradicated the need for massed formations of bombers. Armed with a nuclear weapon, a single aircraft could cause as much damage as a fleet of conventionally armed bombers. Flying independently to its target, it would rely on high altitude, or the cover of weather or darkness (precision bombing was not a

requirement), to escape interception.

Defensive fighter operations relied on ground-based radar to detect the incoming target, just as they had done since the summer of 1940 and the Battle of Britain. The single-seat day interceptors had no radar, whilst the two-seat all-weather interceptors had primitive equipment that provided limited range and coverage when in operation. Essentially, ground-based radar would provide the early warning of incoming targets, and fighter controllers would then vector interceptors against the attackers. The controller's job was to get the fighter within range of its own on-board sensors, which could be either the jet's own radar, or more probably the pilot's 'Mark I eyeball'.

The atomic bombers that were the projected targets of these tactics were now flying higher and faster than those of the Second World War. Because these targets were harder to detect visually, or were expected to operate at night, the controllers would often have to use ground radar data to position fighters against each target in

turn, as had been done with night-fighters during the Second World War. This was made possible at the time because in most cases, the short-ranged jet fighters of the period were not expected to double as bomber escorts. This meant that controllers did not have to be concerned with placing their interceptors at a tactical advantage against jet fighters sent along as escorts for the atomic bombers.

Improving this ground-controlled interception (GCI) capability from its basic tactical employment in the Second World War was the goal of all the major powers in the first decades of the Cold War. The integrated air defense system also spread (along with the jet fighter) into the Third World in the late 1950s, thus ensuring that it too would be a factor in future fighter operations in regional conflicts as well.

The Soviet Union had recognized the advantages of integrated air defense to defend its strategic heartland even before Britain built the first such system in the years immediately preceding the Second World War. However, they had neither the technology, resources

Bearing a strong family resemblance to other Yak twin-engined fighters, the Yak-28 entered service as a replacement for the subsonic Yak-25 in the late 1950s. This aircraft is actually a Yak-28P, which was a dedicated all-weather interceptor capable of supersonic speeds. It made its service debut with IA-PVO units during the winter of 1961-62.

Left: An impressive looking aircraft from any angle, the Gloster Javelin was built as a replacement for the Meteor nightfighter in the all-weather interception role. Photographed near their home base of Odiham in March 1956, these F(AW) 1s belong to No 46 Sqn, which was the first unit to declare itself operational to NATO with the jet in that same year.

Below: The delta-shaped wing adopted by Gloster when designing the Javelin was very much cutting edge technology back in the 1940s and 50s, and several prototype aircraft were lost due to handling problems induced by the radical flying surface prior to it entering squadron service. This particular aircraft (WD804) was the first prototype and it was lost in a crash landing at Boscombe Down on 29 June

Right: The other key fighter to enter RAF service in the early Cold War years was the English Electric Lightning, which boasted an unrivalled ability to climb to operational altitudes thanks to its powerful Rolls-Royce Avon engines and sleek aerodynamic styling. These F 1s were the first to enter Air Force service, and are seen at Coltishall in mid-1960 bearing the distinctive tiger head badge and striped roundel 'fighter bars' of No 74 Sqn.

nor the threat (the Luftwaffe's strategic bombing attacks in the east were limited in their scope) to facilitate the creation of their own system. However, by the end of the Second World War, Soviet priorities had changed.

The B-29, and its ten-engined successor, the B-36, provided motivation enough for Soviet air defense development. The vast nation's vulnerability to Allied strategic air forces (their power was evident by the ruins throughout Soviet-occupied Germany), combined with their access to improved technology – especially radar, developed domestically, captured through the Germans, or extracted from Lend-Lease – was a great motivator. Finally, Stalin's personal intervention made the deployment of an integrated air defense system a priority. A new service, the National Air Defense (PVO Strany), which brought together fighters, surface-to-air missiles, radars, and their associated communications and command, was formed in 1948 to oversee its successful introduction into the frontline.

The Soviet air defense system would continue to expand throughout the Cold War. From its original requirement to defend Moscow and the oil center of Baku against strategic bombers, it expanded to cover the whole country. Soviet jet fighter operations were developed to fit in with this system. Soviet fighter operations remained dominated by the air defense mission and GCI tactics throughout most of the Cold War.

Unlike its former allies, the RAF already had its air defense system in place from the Second World War, and had made identifying the strengths of German search radar an immediate postwar priority. Soon, Meteors and Vampires were exercising effectively alongside Spitfires and Tempests, and the British system was incrementally improved on its wartime base throughout the 1950s. But even as higher-performance, but still subsonic, Hunters and all-weather Javelins took over from the straight-wing jets in the late 1950s, it soon became apparent during the years of exercises against USAF and RAF bombers that Fighter

Command could not defend the whole of the UK against a co-ordinated nuclear strike from the air.

In Britain, as with other NATO nations, military strategy changed orientation from the defense of home airspace to massive nuclear retaliation, if deemed necessary, against an aggressor. As a result of this fundamental revision of strategy, Fighter Command's tasking duly shifted from the protection of the country as a whole, to the defense of key bomber bases. This change in role was still adhered to even when the rise of the ballistic missile in the late 1950s started to make air defense against manned attacking aircraft a secondary consideration.

The advent of the nuclear missile, and the fact that it was virtually impossible to intercept in a manned fighter, led the British government to declare in 1957 that they had decided to get out of the interceptor business, and would only field one last design. This turned out to be the Lightning, which would remain in frontline service until 1988 – long after those who had written off its validity in a modern combat

The Air Defense of North America in 1962

During the Cuban Missile Crisis of 1962 the USAF came closer to finding out whether its fighter defenses could protect North America from attack than at any other time during the Cold War. Ironically, by 1962 air defense fighter operations had been scaled down from the peak force strength reached in 1958. However, the 1,000 interceptors made available to NORAD when it went onto alert provided a substantial all-weather defensive capability. Considerable diplomatic leverage was required to bring the USAF's RCAF partners 'north of the border' up to alert status as well.

The fighters defending North America relied on the chain of early warning radar lines (three in total) across Alaska and Canada known as DEW (Distant Early Warning), Mid-Canada and Pinetree Lines. On the flanks were other radars including those fixed to concrete 'Texas Towers' that had been mounted on the continental shelf off the north-east United States and in the freezing waters off the Aleutians and Greenland. Air- and ship-mounted radars filled gaps in the coverage.

This extensive radar chain had to assure a high probability of interception for the attacking NORAD fighters – certainly far higher than that achieved during the Second World War, when a large percentage of interceptor sorties never actually made contact with the enemy. The different radar lines therefore served not only as force multipliers, but also increased the percentage of sorties that would contact the enemy, and thus reduced the possibility of a nuclear-armed bomber 'leaking' through the multiple layers of detection radar.

All the radars faced north – the direction that (before 1962) all believed the Soviet attack would come from. So, when the USSR deployed Il-28 bombers to Cuba, they immediately the 'soft underbelly' of the USA. This shock move required the rapid redeployment of both USAF and US Navy fighters southward in order to defend against the possibility of nuclear

The F-89 Scorpion was a key player in the NORAD defense strategy throughout the 1950s, examples equipping units based across the continental USA. No fewer than 1,050 aircraft were built by Northrop, with the final F-89H variant being the most effective of them all. This photo shows an H-model commencing its take-off run in the late 1950s. The fixed wingtip tanks on this version housed three Hughes AIM-4 Falcon AAMs and 21 2.75 in unguided folding-fin aircraft rockets (FFARs).

attack. US Army HAWK and Nike-Hercules SAMs were also ranged against this new 'all azimuths' atomic bomber threat.

In 1962 the Pentagon estimated that the Soviets could attack North America with over 200 bombers, but it is now known that the total strategic bomber strength of the USSR at that time was just 58 M-4 'Bisons' and 76 Tu-95 'Bear-As' – even these could not physically reach all US targets. Their ranks could be bolstered by an infusion of Tu-16 'Badger' medium bombers tasked to fly one-way missions, but these were already heavily committed to theater operations.

It is thought that Soviet nuclear planning for a strike on the United States in 1962 would have stressed counterforce targeting. Fears of the 'missile gap' had earlier led SAC to both disperse its US bomber force and keep a percentage of its B-52s on continuous airborne alert. It is likely that these types of targets, along with a number of command and control centers and possibly some urban/industrial targets, would have been the Soviet priorities in a counterforce strike.

Faced with engaging a force of barely 130 strategic bombers at most, NORAD fighters would probably have acquitted themselves very well in the fight to protect North America from nuclear devastation. Further helping their cause was the fact that we now know the Soviet bomber force not only lacked up-to-date ECM equipment, but also relied on tactically-poor battle plans. What would have reduced the effectiveness of the NORAD defenses was the electro-magnetic pulse (EMP) of the nuclear explosions unleashed by both the attacking forces (nuclear-armed Genie air-air rockets and BOMARC and Nike-Hercules SAMs) and the 'dead-men's fuzes' that detonated weapons still carried within downed Soviet bombers. Little was known about the effects of EMP in 1962, so both terrestrial and aircraft radars and communications links boasted only limited degrees of hardening against nuclear blasts.

The Boeing CIM-10A Bomarc was a surface-launched pilotless missile that was guided from the ground until near its aerial target, when an in-built seeker would complete the interception. The A-model had a range of over 260 miles, and entered service in 1960 – improved B-models were issued to NORAD sites across North America the following year. The Bomarc was finally phased out of USAF service in 1972.

The F-86D 'Sabre Dog' formed the backbone of Air Defense Command during the early 1950s, its nose-mounted APS-6 radar giving it limited all-weather capability. Over 2,500 D-models were produced by North American Aviation.

The Lightning F 6 was a far more capable interceptor than the earlier versions of the English Electric fighter of less than a decade before, boasting a greater range, improved weapons and better handling. This particular aircraft was originally built as an F 3A, but was later converted to F 6 specification. Seen at Akrotiri, in Cyprus, this jet wears the diving eagle emblem of No 23 Sqn on its slab fin.

environment had retired from politics.

Unlike the RAF, the USAF was a newcomer to the air defense mission. During the Second World War there had been a basic air defense system in operation in the United States, but its primary mission in the absence of a credible threat after the 'dark days' of 1941-42 was to train fighter units prior to being posted overseas. This swiftly changed with the development of the Soviet nuclear and long-range bomber threat in the early Cold War years. Operational priorities for the USAF

fighter force rapidly shifted their focus onto the air defense of the United States. This change in emphasis was marked by the formation of Air Defense Command (ADC) in 1951. It was to control an integrated air defense system like that in place in Britain, and as well as possessing dedicated fighter interceptors, ADC also deployed firstly AAA and then Nike SAMs throughout the US in the 1950s (the latter would remain until the early 1970s.

However, unlike the RAF, the USAF did not have a honed wartime system to inherit. Rather, it had to create an air defense network from scratch, and this included the construction in the 1950s of early warning radar lines across Alaska, Canada and Greenland. These were intended to give a warning of Soviet bombers coming across the North Pole.

New interceptors were designed and rushed into service in the early 1950s to respond to any such alerts. The XP-89, an experimental ground attack and escort heavy fighter, became the F-89, whilst the T-33 (the trainer version of the F-80) was dramatically enlarged into the F-94 – both types overcame severe teething troubles to become mainstays of air defense in the 1950s. RCAF CF-100s joined them in the all-weather air defense mission, whilst the original F-86A was soon joined by radar-equipped F-86Ds in the single-seat interceptor class to fulfil the low altitude end of ADC's 'high-low mix'. As the 1950s progressed, supersonic F-

101s, F-102s and F-104s assumed the interception mission, being joined in 1959 by the ultimate dedicated ADC interceptor, the F-106.

Labelled the 'automatic' all-weather fighter-bomber by its manufacturer Republic due to its then state-of-the-art navigation, radar and fire control suites, the mighty F-105 Thunderchief was designed to be equally adept at carrying either nuclear weapons or AAMs. This F-105D was photographed serving with TAC in October 1960.

Left: Taxying out at the start of yet another alert patrol from the typically ice-covered Elmendorf Air Force Base (AFB), in Alaska, in January 1958, this F-102A Delta Dagger was assigned to ADC's 317th FIS. Arguably the first effective all-weather interceptor to enter USAF service, the F-102 commenced frontline operations in June 1955.

Fighter Operations and 'The Bomb'

Left: F-104Cs of 479th TFW. Although built for bomber interceptor with ADC, the Starfighter saw more widespread service in the USAF with TAC-assigned units. The jet closest to the camera also has a bolt-on refueling receptacle fitted - a must for TAC units operating the Starfighter due to the jet's notoriously short range.

Right: The Yak-27 was seen as a supersonic replacement for the subsonic Yak-25, but it failed to progress beyond the prototype stage because of handling problems at high angles of attack.

Below: The fourth pre-production F-101B Voodoo is seen carrying a pair of nuclear-tipped Douglas AIR-2A Genie missiles on its underfuselage weapons rack.

Fighter operations in the first two decades of the Cold War – when not being dominated by the need to defeat attacking nuclear-armed bombers – were dominated by the requirement to deliver bombs, either by escorting friendly bombers or carrying out tactical nuclear delivery missions.

Fighter escort of bombers remained a significant mission for the USAF (and, secondarily, the USN) through much of the 1950s. SAC had fighter escort wings in its order of battle from its inception in 1946 through to 1957. These were the operational descendants of the P-51 groups of the Eighth and Fifteenth Air Forces of the Second World War. Because SAC warplans envisioned its bombers operating out of forward bases, it would be possible to have forward-deployed long-range fighters available to accompany them on their penetrating missions, at least one-way.

The classical escort mission of the Second World War was never truly adaptable to strategic bombing in the jet age, as F-86 pilots had found out in Korea. SAC did not invest in the large number of fighter wings that would have been required to effectively implement these tactics principally because they were convinced that the bombers could get through to the targets by themselves.

Point Defense against Soviet atomic bombers

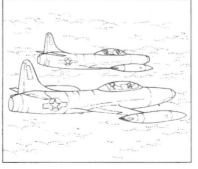

1. Before geting in range of the point defense interceptors, the bombers would be attacked by long range fighters like the F-94 or Canadian CF-100s.

2. F-86D 'Saber Dogs' were on alert across the northern USA. It took 4 minutes to get airborne because of the need to spin-up onboard systems.

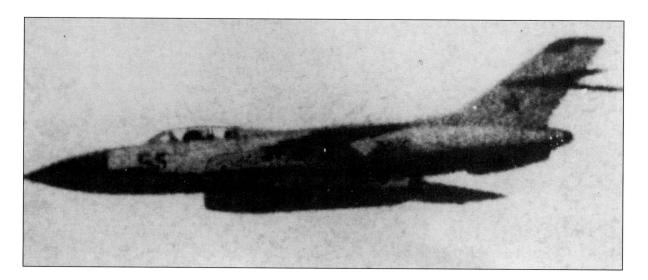

The nuclear delivery mission became an increasingly important element of fighter operations in the 1950s, firstly in the USAF (with F-84D/Es becoming nuclear capable by 1952), and later among its NATO allies. The latter either received nuclear-capable US-built fighter bombers (or, in the case of the RAF, used indigenous designs such as the Canberra), and trained on the delivery of nuclear weapons held under a 'dual key' arrangement with the US government.

Increased production of fissile material in the America, and the advent of smaller atomic bombs that could be carried under a fighter, meant that the remit of nuclear attack from the skies

now straddled bomber and fighter communities alike. The latter worked on delivery improving tactics, with programs such as the USMC-developed over-the-shoulder climb-bombing Low Altitude Bombing System (LABS), allowing a low-flying fighter-bombers to remain out of the nuclear blast caused by the dropping of its ordnance. Technology such as the buddy-tanking equipment adopted by the USN, which allowed one fighter-bomber to refuel another, also meant that a single-seat fighter could traverse great distances (usually only associated with a much larger bomber-type machine) in order to hit its target.

This new mission came close to

replacing the idea of offensive fighter operations that had evolved since 1915. Proponents of the nuclear delivery mission believed that its effective implementation rendered air-to-air fighter operations obsolete. In theory, two fighters armed with nuclear weapons could destroy an entire airfield full of enemy aircraft on the ground far more effectively than a squadron could shoot them down in air-to-air combat. This equation fitted well with the strategy of massive retaliation that emerged after the Korean war, and endured in the USA, Britain and the Soviet Union until long after NATO's adoption of 'flexible response' defense strategy from 1967.

3. It took 11 minutes to reach the enemy altitude of 45,000 ft. The SAGE system monitored the bombers and gave intercept courses to the fighters.

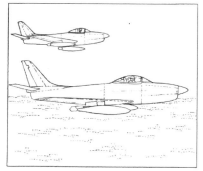

4. Vectored to within the 30-mile range of their own APG-36/37 radars, the F-86Ds' onboard computer plotted the course to the target.

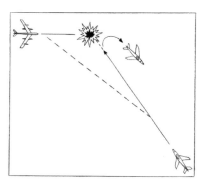

5. When SAGE's radar showed the fighter converge with the bomber, the pilot was ordered to fire. It took less than a second to fire all 24 rockets.

Fighter Operations in the Age of Nuclear Primacy

In the late 1950s and early 60s, fighter operations in the air arms on both sides of the Cold War (but most notably the USAF and USN) were dominated by nuclear weapons delivery – either preventing their delivery by the enemy, or attacking said foe with similar weapons of mass destruction. Aircraft, tactics and operations reflected this contingency throughout the period.

Planning for a war that would be massive, nuclear and brief obviously had to done in advance of the conflict. There would be one plan for a brief nuclear spasm, which would obviate the need for fighters to secure air superiority over enemy territory. Thus, there were no follow-ons to USAF fighters such as the F-86 and the F-100 (North American Aviation, the manufacturer of these machines, plus the P-51 of the Second World War, was one of the commericial casualties), and when the fourth generation of

fighters did emerge in the US, they were capable of Mach 2 to allow them to be employed primarily as bomber destroyers (such as the F-106), or nuclear bombers themselves (such as the F-105).

For the Soviets, there was little change in operations under Stalin, but under Khruschev, the Soviet Frontal Aviation suffered from their own version of nuclear primacy. Even then, the rise of theater (and tactical ballistic) missiles was viewed by many in the Kremlin as sounding the death knell on conventional aircraft even in the nuclear delivery role. Thus, theater offensive air operations that had been developed during four long years of war on the Eastern Front were de-emphasized until the 1970s.

Air defense fighter operations in the mid to late 1950s featured both longer-ranged area defenders (multi-seat and multi-engine) and short-range point

defenders (single seat and single engine). Both were faced with a serious problem in that rapidly evolving airframe and engine technology meant that the next generation of bombers – anticipated in the early 1960s – would be flying higher and faster than these machines could climb to altitude and carry out their GCI interceptions. The key capability that soon became most desirable in any new fighter was a superior, and sustained, rate of climb. The future of the interceptor lay in it becoming, in the buzz-words of the period, a 'manned missile'.

These point defense interceptors such as the British SR.177, with its revolutionary dual-engine propulsion system that comprised a ramjet for high-speed climbing, and a whole host of US programs – most notably the XF-108 – were intended to get a fighter up to a bomber's operational altitude as fast as possible. The direct

descendants of the Me 163 of 1945, these highly specialized machines were not built to enter into combat with other fighters along the way. Not surprisingly, these 'manned missiles' were all replaced by actual missiles in the form of SAMs before they could become operational.

Even during this missile-crazy period when air-to-air combat was de-emphasized in favor of air defense and nuclear delivery, it was never totally eclipsed. Units within the RAF, RCAF, USN and even the USAF in Europe (despite that service's near-total domination by the 'bomber barons') continued to keep the tactics alive, while operational continuity, and experience, remained in the hands of senior fighter pilots — even if staff colleges now considered their knowledge and experience of historical interest only.

Above: The USAF's partners in NORAD were of course the Royal Canadian Air Force, and the one indigenous type that they operated in the 1950s was the rather antiquated Avro Canada CF-100. Equipped with a Hughes APG-40 radar, and associated fire control system, its principal weapon was the 2.75 in unguided FFAR, housed in wingtip pods. These CF-100 Mk 4s of No 428 Sqn lack the rocket armament, although the ventral gun pack housing eight 0.5 in Browning machine-guns is in place between the engine intakes.

Left: This F-106 of the Missouri-based 71st FIS came to rest in a snow-covered field after its pilot had been forced to eject due to technical malfunctions. It was soon repaired and returned to service.

Left: Like the Yak-27 before it, the more successful Yak-28 relied on a pair of podded Tumansky turbojet engines to acheive speeds of Mach 1.5+, essential if the fighter was to have any chance of catching the B-58 Hustlers of Strategic Air Command.

Right: TAC units also performed their fair share of interception missions in the Cold War, and none more so than those forward deployed in Europe with NATO. This F-100F was part of the British-based 20th TFW in 1961 — three other bases in western Europe hosted Super Sabre-equipped wings at the time of the Berlin Wall crisis..

Communications, Datalinks and Fighter Operations

Left: The Su-7 'heavy fighter' was the VVS-FA equivalent of the F-105. Capable of carrying a heavy war load at supersonic speeds at low level, this fighter-bomber posed a serious threat to NATO.

Right: The world's first guided AAM was the Hughes F-98, which had originally started life as an 'unmanned fighter'. Developed into the GAR-1 Falcon, it relied on semi-active radar homing. By the time this shot was taken in the early 1960s, its designation had changed to AIM-4. Here an F-102A fires two AIM-4Ds.

Below: Like all other Soviet interceptors of the period, the Su-9 boasted little in sophisticated radar equipment, its pilot instead relying almost exclusively on GCI instructions from the ground.

Effective communication during peacetime is often taken for granted, yet it is perhaps the most singularly important factor in the execution of successful fighter operations during a time of conflict. In the future, when it is likely that fighter missions will become more dependent on vital long-range weapons and 'off-board' sensors that will allow a pilot to defeat stealthy adversaries (or just survive against them), communications will assume even greater importance. Today, a fighter without effective communications is even more of a burden to its own side than one without effective weaponry.

The 1950s and 60s introduced the use of datalinks, rather than voice transmitters, for passing radar data to interceptors as part of GCI tactics. The datalink meant that data on threats and orders of which direction to steer could also be passed directly to the aircraft and its systems, rather than have to be provided to a fighter controller, who would then impart it verbally to the pilot on station. The datalink reduced both time delay and the opportunity for errors to be imparted in audible transmissions between a controller and a pilot. It also meant that GCI personnel were no longer limited to just one intercept at a time – previously a key limitation when the latter were airborne in AEW aircraft. Now, a single controller could monitor multiple interceptions through datalink transmissions with numerous patrolling fighters.

An alternative approach to GCI that was introduced in the 1950s was broadcast control, which had been developed by the Royal Navy as a counter to saturation attacks. Rather than give fighters specific directions, speeds and courses to steer as in a classic GCI engagement, a ship would simply broadcast over a radio channel the threat's position, speed and heading in relation to its own position. FAA fighter pilots, orienting themselves onto the directing ship by determining range

and bearing from the ship TACAN (tactical air navigation) beacon and DME (Direction Measuring Equipment), could then work out the intercept course for themselves.

The fighter forces most enthused about datalink were those whose mission it was to carry out all-weather interceptions against bombers or cruise missiles – USAF Air Defense Command, the US Navy's F-14 squadrons and the Soviet IA-PVO Strany. The most tactically flexible of these systems was the US Navy's Air and Naval Tactical Data Systems (ATDS NTDS), which emerged in the 1960s. Its Link 4 TADIL-A and later Link 11 datalink connected AEW aircraft with both interceptors and fighter controllers back aboard the aircraft carrier.

Other fighter forces placed less value in the datalink. Its reliability was often questioned, so much of the data had to be confirmed by voice. The Israelis were concerned that it would keep the pilot's eyes inside the cockpit, which could be lethal when enemy fighters were near. They preferred the blanket coverage of broadcast control tactics. The limitations of defending Israel against high altitude jet bomber attack using classic GCI techniques had soon been realized once Israel faced a jet bomber threat. This was a major reason why the Israeli fighter

force championed offensive counter air operations.

The USAF's Tactical Air Command thought that datalink had the potential to override the judgment of a fighter pilot embroiled in the heat of battle, and therefore chose not to adopt it. Indeed, it was only in the 1980s, when the increasing lethality of modern weapons put a premium on situational awareness, and new technology emerged offering an unprecedented degree of sensor-fusion in the cockpit, that TAC (and its ACC successor) re-considered the datalink.

Ever since the Allied 'Y Service' voice radio intercepts provided intelligence against marauding Me-262s over Europe, unsecured radio transmissions have posed the problem of providing audible communications without supplying the enemy with intelligence. In the early decades of the Cold War, scientists overcame this problem by introducing UHF communications, which not only meant more channels on which to broadcast, but also more security for these transmissions due to the frequency of the signal. The revival of air-to-air fighter operations in the second half of the Cold War was also facilitated by reliable UHF communications.

In the 1970s the US improved secure voice radios for its fighters through programs such as the 'Have Quick' system. However, communications interoperability, like IFF remained an issue, especially within NATO. This problem led to the latter issuing a requirement for a secure, interoperable, datalink, which could also be made compatible with whatever system the US joint services eventually adopted.

The end result of this technologically challenging request is Link 16, which will eventually be used as part of the current American fighter datalink JTIDS (the Joint Tactical Information Distribution System) that is scheduled to replace current US airborne data communication systems.

Link 16 is programmed to display all facets of synthetic situational awareness directly in the cockpit through the employment of seamless all-source data fusion. This can bring to one screen in a fighter's cockpit, or head-up display, inputs from a number of different radars, ESM devices, infrared and other sensors, either ground-based or fitted to other aircraft.

The US Navy, having operated datalink systems for many years, are putting JTIDS on all their ocean-going combat aircraft, including E-2Cs, F-14s and F/A-18s. The USAF, meanwhile, recently declared their first JTIDS-equipped F-15Cs operational – both USAF and NATO F-16s are scheduled to receive a cheaper version of the Link 16 in due course. The JTIDS Wide Area Surveillance Net is monitored by all suitably-equipped air assets, permitting high lethality engagements to occur based purely on datalink information – for example, JTIDS is capable of passing targeting information for BVR AAMs directly from an AWACS to a fighter's fire control system in real time. Based on this information, an F-15C pilot can then designate a specific track file to be a target without having to lock-on to it. Note that modern fighters do not have to commit all their radar coverage to prosecuting one aircraft – unlike 1960's fighter which sacrificed all situational awareness in the process.

Yet in training exercises with JTIDS, pilots still want UHF voice communications. They are concerned about over-reliance on Link 16, and are afraid that the potential for seamless data fusion may burden pilots with too much non-germane information. Pilots also want to be able to hear the tone of voice reports, to hear if the transmitter is panicked or reassured - itself a useful guide to decision-making. The isolation experienced by fighter pilots in their individual cockpits is also better assuaged by regular communication with a human voice.

Improved Weaponry – Cannon

The Hawker Hunter was an important fighter within NATO in the 1950s and early 1960. This camouflaged F 4 is serving as a target tug for No 323 Sqn of the Royal Netherlands Air Force. The large bulge on the underside of the forward fuselage on this jet served as the ammunition link collector box for the Hunter's four 30 mm Aden cannon.

The rapidly improving performance shown through the development of the first three generations of jet fighter was never properly exploited in the operational sense because of the limitations placed on the aircraft concerned by their respective armament. In the early 1950s the 20 mm cannon was still the world standard for fighter armament – just as it had been in 1945. Even with higher rates of fire and the advent of radar-ranging gunsights (as used so effectively in the last 18 months of war in Korea by F-86s armed with even less-lethal .50 calibre machine-guns), 'aerial combat' still meant engaging a target at short range. The cannon's relatively low muzzle velocities, and the short time available to engage in head-on attacks against bombers, were not as pronounced in Korea as they had been

for the Me-262, but nevertheless they still limited the fighter's capabilities.

One answer was to improve the gun by making it fire either a bigger round (such as the slow-firing Russian 37 mm cannon seen in Korea) or at a faster rate (the US Vulcan six-barrel electric-driven 20 mm Gatling gun emerged in the mid-1950s, and has been the western world's standard weapon for fighters virtually ever since). The two solutions could be combined, most notably in the Hawker Hunter, which had four 30 mm ADEN cannon using a Mauser revolving chamber – its employment effectively reduced heavy bombers to aluminium powder. But it was increasingly apparent that relying on the gun alone in combat would not be an effective operational response to a fast-moving, all-weather, threat. The fighter needed to extend its lethal reach.

Improved Weaponry – Rockets

The prototype YF-89D Scorpion (49-2463) unleashes a full salvo of FFARs during flight testing in 1952. When fired like this, the 104 rockets from the wingtip pods would reputedly blanket an area the size of a football field. A further 682 D-model Scorpions followed on from this aircraft.

All 104 rounds had to be loaded by hand and then the fuzed charge in the head of the rocket carefully screwed onto the body of the weapon. So fast turnaround times between sorties were difficult for the F-89, particularly in bad weather.

The immediate weapons upgrade applied to fighters in the 1950s was the same as it had been for the Me-262 – lots of unguided rockets. These were intended to be used mainly against non-maneuvering bomber targets, for their main drawbacks were that they lacked accuracy and suffered from high ballistic dispersion. This was compensated for by providing large numbers of rockets, which were housed in pods at the wing-tips or hung under the wings, fuselage or in retractable internal mounts.

The mid-1950s saw the arrival of the first gunless fighters such as the single-seat F-86D and two-seat F-89. These relied on heavy missile armament to fulfil their mission of all-weather air defense, GCI vectoring these fighters close to an enemy aircraft so that they could unleash a lethal cone of rocket or missile fire in a single salvo. The fighter pilot did not have to make visual identification – he just fired and broke away. Interceptions in all weather conditions using GCI equipment such as the SAGE (Semi-Automatic Ground Environment) air defense system over North America (which had become operational in the mid-1950s) became central to US air defense operations. With this precise GCI, beam attacks – the bane of the gun-armed fighter due to the high deflection angles involved – became the tactical goal of all-weather interceptors.

However, the low accuracy and limited lethality of individual rockets still limited the weapon's effectiveness. For the air defense mission, the USAF came up with a weapon that greatly enhanced lethality, and made shortfalls in accuracy irrelevant. Through the proliferation and miniaturization of nuclear weapons, an atomic warhead could now be fitted into an air-to-air missile.

The Ding Dong – an air-to-air unguided nuclear-armed rocket – was developed and put into service as the AIR-2A Genie, and it remained operational until the 1970s. The Genie had one great advantage over other aerial weapons of the time – the overwhelming strength of its warhead

meant that a single round had a high probability of downing a bomber even without achieving a direct hit on its intended target.

Nuclear-tipped SAMs also became popular at the time for it was realised that a conventional kill of a nuclear-armed bomber near a target could mean its bomb, if fitted with a 'dead man's fuze', would detonate as the bomber spun in. With a nuclear-tipped SAM, however, the fireball caused by the weapon impacting with the target would easily consume the incoming bomb as well. Nuclear SAM warheads were used by the US Army's Nike-Hercules batteries, as well as by the USAF's BOMARC system and larger Soviet SAMs.

The Air-To-Air Missile, and its Impact on Fighter Operations

The Genie may have been effective for all-weather point defense against nuclear bombers, but against maneuvering fighter targets (which were also likely to be hard to 'swat' except by large numbers of Genies) the unguided rocket failed to provide the answer, just as it had done with the Me 262.

The Germans had worked on the idea of air-to-air guided missiles during the Second World War. Immediately after the war, the US Navy, still bearing the scars of the bitter fighting off Okinawa, wanted a weapon that could keep future jet-propelled kamikazes away from its carriers. It started a number of AAM programs mainly aimed at tackling beyond visual range (BVR) targets. To perform this task the weapon had to be radar-guided, the first examples being beam-riding (following a narrow beam locked onto the target by the firing aircraft's radar). Later in the 1950s, as technology progressed, semi-active homing was introduced, the firing aircraft's radar 'painting' the target to give it a high-energy radar return which the missile's basic seeker head would then fly towards. Neither were 'fire and forget' guidance methods, however, the firing aircraft having to remain nose on to the target until the missile had hit home.

After progressing quite rapidly in the early 1950s, AAM development was stymied in the US when the focus shifted to the development of nuclear weapons. USAF strategists believed the only fighter operations that would be required in the age of nuclear primacy were those flown in conjunction with the defense of nuclear bombers – and so it remained from the mid-1950s through to the early 60s. At the time it was believed that an effective AAM could be achieved through improving the accuracy of the air-to-air rocket. This the USAF did in the form of the Hughes Falcon, which was designed to be fully integrated with the on-board weapons system fitted into ADC all-weather interceptors. By the late 1950s, the Falcon was replacing rockets in the air defense role.

The USN, however, came up with a design that was to make the AAM more than just an improved bomber-destroyer rocket – their weapon would eventually change the shape of fighter operations and tactics the world over. It was the Sidewinder. Intended to destroy incoming Soviet bombers, it was basically a guided version of the standard five-inch air-to-ground rocket. It was a passive homing missile, which meant it used infra-red emissions to home in on the heat of an engine's exhaust – this technology allowed the Sidewinder to be a true 'fire and forget' weapon, being able to follow a maneuvering target independently of its host aircraft's radar emissions.; although it was well into the 1960s before upgrades allowed it to follow a fighter successfully. Later versions of the Sidewinder – retaining only the name and the basic airframe layout – will remain operational well into the next century.

The Sidewinder was adopted by virtually all the world's air arms, including the Soviet Air Force. The latter relied on espionage, and an captured example supplied by their erstwhile Chinese allies, to provide them with up-to-date Sidewinder technology in the late 1950s. Just as with the Tu-4 a decade previously, the Soviets decided that reverse engineering would allow them to keep apace with the superior US product. The Sidewinder duly entered Soviet service as the K-13, and was known

A No 19 Sqn pilot and his groundcrewmen rush to get their Lightning F 2A airborne as quickly as possible during a Zulu alert for Battle Flight at Gutersloh, in Germany. Nestled beneath the refueling probe is a live Firestreak missile.

within NATO ranks as the AA-2 Atoll.

The USAF came to the Sidewinder more reluctantly than the Soviets. When, in the early 1960s, the USAF had to once again consider fighter operations other than delivering or destroying nuclear weapons, they found they lacked a suitable AAM for these missions. The Sidewinder entered USAF service on the F-110A (soon to be redesignated F-4C) Phantom II, a Navy fighter that they had hastily procured to allow them to perform more conventional fighter operations.

While the Sidewinder was entering service, the Navy had finally made a practical BVR radar-guided missile following a decade of research – it was dubbed the Sparrow III. Operational in the late 1950s, the weapon at last gave

the Navy a carrier defense weapon for the jet age. The Sparrow was initially carried under older fighters such as the F3H and F3D, but the all-new F-4B Phantom II had been designed from the outset to tote the BVR weapon .

Fighter operations were not immediately revolutionized by the first AAMs, however. Throughout the 1950s and 60s, their performance would remain limited – it would soon become apparent just how limited over Vietnam and the Middle East. Indeed, it was almost 20 years after their initial introduction to the frontline that both AAM technology, and the operational thinking that would guide their use, evolved to the point where the implications of the guided missile in fighter combat would be fully realized.

The first medium range AAM to enter service with the US Navy was the AAM-N-2 (later AIM-7) Sparrow I, which entered fleet service with the suitably-modified McDonnell F3H-2M Demon in the late 1950s. This example boasts a full complement of AAMs, and is seen on a test sortie over coastal California in 1957.

Surface-to-Air Missiles and Fighter Operations

The emergence of the SAM altered the shape of fighter operations. The first examples such as the US Nike-Ajax and Soviet SA-1 were intended for point defense against mid-1950s-technology bombers, flying at high altitude. Later in the decade more capable weapons emerged such as the US Nike-Hercules and the Soviet SA-2. These SAMs had the potential to solve the problems associated with point defense by interceptors against high-flying bombers. The use of SAMs rather than interceptors meant that even bombers capable of a supersonic dash (such as the US B-58 and Soviet Tu-22) could be hit and shot down.

The SAM was first viewed as a replacement for the fast-climbing point defense interceptor. The enthusiasm for the new weapons was such that some – most notably Britain's infamous defense minister in 1957, Mr Duncan Sandys – thought that the SAM would soon replace the fighter for all missions. This conviction, elevated to dogma, brought British fighter development to a grinding halt.

However, by the early 1960s the bomber was being supplanted by the ballistic missile as the primary nuclear delivery system. Those bombers that stayed in the strategic penetration business did so by shifting to low-level tactics, which placed them well beneath the SAM's operational ceiling, and presented interceptors with a new challenge. The requirement for a 'look-down, shoot-down' AAM was soon apparent, but would not be met until the 1970s.

The SAM had been quickly integrated into the air defense systems in place of AAA, which had for many decades been used in a similar way. The USAF employed the ramjet-powered, long-range, nuclear-armed BOMARC from the late 1950s to the early 1970s. It was integrated with the use of manned interceptors, operating via the SAGE system to get within range of its on-board terminal homing radar – it had a troubled development, however. The RAF's Bloodhound SAMs were deployed from the early 1960s to provide protection for the air force's nuclear bomber bases, and enable the alert force to scramble in order to make their contribution to massive retaliation.

The USN liked SAMs because they allowed surface warships to defend both themselves and a carrier battle group effectively for the first time in the jet age. The Soviets liked SAMs because they seemed the obvious way to counteract allied airpower which always had the technological, if not the numerical, edge. They were pleased at having scored the first live SAM kill when an SA-2 downed the U-2 spyplane of Francis Gary Powers over the Soviet Union on Mayday 1960. The SAM also appealed to the Soviet view of war in that it employed applied science, with minimal human inputs. SAMs were easier to plan for than fighters, plus it meant having to train and employ fewer fighter pilots, who were an expensive commodity in the jet age.

By the 1960s, SAMs were not limited to homeland defense against nuclear bombers, having taken over tactical missions as well. Permanent Nike-Hercules and SA-2 sites sprouted on opposite sides of the Inner German Border, whilst mobile low-altitude-capable US HAWK and Soviet SA-3 batteries took their place on the battlefield. The large, static, systems were designed to defeat not only bombers, but fighters as well, and they would remain important throughout the Cold War, defending troops, forward installations and airfields. In the late 1960s the Soviet SA-6 became the first operationally self-propelled SAM, able to cover advancing armored

columns. Even the infantryman received a SAM capability with the arrival of the shoulder-launched Soviet SA-7 and US Redeye in the 1960s.

The rise of the SAM transformed fighter operations, though its full impact would not be apparent until the 1970s. It all but took over the point air defense mission from purpose-built interceptors, whilst the rise of tactical SAMs meant that the fighter's environment over the battlefield would also become more deadly. Perhaps most significantly, the IFF issue became even more important. Fighters, especially those not under strict GCI control, would have operate fully with allied SAM sites, otherwise they would fall victim to 'friendly fire'..

As well as making the skies over the battlefield more dangerous for fighters, the SAM also gave more freedom to mission planners. With SAMs providing

Above: By the late 1950s the Javelin had matured into an effective all-weather interceptor that combined US radar (APQ-43) with powerful engines (Sapphire ASSa 7Rs) and a new AAM (Firestreak).

The distinctively 'waisted' lines of the F-102A conformed to the 'area rule' design philosophy exposed by leading NACA dynamicist, Richard Whitcomb. It was dubbed the 'Coke bottle' fuselage by pilots and groundcrews.

defensive coverage, fighters could be massed at decisive sectors, or could be freed purely to undertake offensive operations, rather just bomber escort. This was particularly important as in the 1960s fighters were becoming more sophisticated and more costly, and few air arms could afford to replace the cheaper single-engine/single-mission fighters of the 1950s on a one-for-one basis. New types would have to justify their price tags by being multi-role weapons of war.

Vietnam – From 'Thud Ridge' to 'Topgun'

Fighter combat in Vietnam started in 1965 when the first bomb-laden F-105s fell victim to gun-firing MiG-17s, and finished some eight years later when the last MiG-17 went down to a missile fired by a Navy F-4B. Much had changed between the first and last kills. America had entered the conflict with fighter forces configured primarily for nuclear conflict – such as the silver F-105s lost in 1965 – and motivated by the willingness to 'bear any burden' in opposition to Communism in Vietnam. The fighter forces of 1973 – such as the F-4Bs – were better trained and equipped for conventional war-fighting. But they served a country whose will and purpose had been severely weakened by the hard lessons learnt in Vietnam.

Fighter operations do not take place in a vacuum. They are shaped by both broader (strategic) and more focused (tactical and technical) requirements and constraints. Effective fighter operations are much harder to achieve if they are not consistently tasked, at a higher level, with the overall campaign strategy. They will often prove impossible to perform if they cannot make use of effective tactics, training and technology (including aircraft and weapons).

Between March 1965 and October 1968 (the period of Operation Rolling Thunder), US fighter operations against North Vietnam often proved near-impossible to perform effectively because neither overall US strategy, nor the fighter forces which were required to implement it, were designed to make the goal of these operations achievable. However, the limitations of the North Vietnamese Air Force (NVAF) and the quality of American fighters, aircrew and fighter leaders were enough to allow USAF operations to succeed, even if their overall strategic goals went unfulfilled.

Motivated by the setbacks to US fighter operations in 1965-68, both the USAF and the USN implemented extensive changes to their fighter tactics during the four-year bombing

Above: Considered by many to be the most suitable fighter for Vietnam, Chance Vought's F-8 Crusader blended a lithe design with a gutsy engine. An effective armament of four 20 mm cannon and four AIM-9 Sidewinders completed the package.

Right: The natural metal finish of the Thunderchief was quickly daubed over with three tone tactical camouflage once the jets arrived in South-east Asia. With its centerline multiple ejector rack groaning under the weight of six cluster bomb units, an anonymous F-105D is throttles up and taxied out from the squadron ramp at Korat AFB.

Left: The F-105D was TAC's primary weapon of war in the first years of the Vietnam war. As the conflict escalated, jets were purloined from units operating on the other side of the globe, like these F-105Ds of the Bitburg, Germany, based 23rd TFS/361st TFW

moratorium that ended when US aircraft again attacked targets in North Vietnam in 1972. As a result of this overhaul, fighter operations were much more successful during Operations Linebacker I (April-October) and Linebacker II (December). Other contributing factors to the success of these offensives included less interference on fighter operations by US strategic requirements, greatly improved tactics for aerial combat and improved fighter aircraft.

The North Vietnamese fighter operations were, by comparison, largely defensive, and operated as part of an integrated air defense system. They had little difficulty in making their operations consistent with the overall strategy of the NVAF, and access to Soviet support provided them with the tactics and technology that so often proved frustrating to their US opponents in 1965-68. By 1972 the strategy remained the same, but the North Vietnamese were at a greater advantage in both tactics and technology.

The Soviet Advisory Effort

When the first US bombs fell on North Vietnam in 1965, the latter country's air arm was comprized of just a few dozen MiG-15 and -17s, plus a handful of Il-28 bombers. Yet, by 1967-68, the NVAF often found itself challenging the US for air superiority over Vietnam. Much of the credit for this remarkable achievement belongs to the North Vietnamese pilots and groundcrews, who exhibited great courage and adaptability in the face of a numerically (and technologically) superior enemy. However, as praiseworthy as the NVAF's efforts were, it was the Soviet Union that provided the hardware, the understanding of the operational aspects of running an air defense system, and the advisers who both trained the North Vietnamese pilots and sometimes participated in combat themselves.

For example, the first NVAF SA-2 sites were set up by Soviet Air Force technicians, who went on to command them in action for several years to follow, shooting down a number of US aircraft during this time. Other advisers were to be found throughout the North Vietnamese air defense system. That the NVAF returned so effectively to fighter operations after their setbacks in mid-1967 at the hands of Colonel Robin Olds and his 8th TFW was due in no small part to an advisory team led by ex-Soviet Air Force General M I Fesenko.

The capability that the USSR provided the NVAF with is known to the USAF as 'force reconstitution'. The North

Vietnamese air defense system was hit repeatedly during the three years of the Rolling Thunder campaign, yet the immediate provision of expertise and hardware from the Soviet Union allowed it to reconstitute itself equally repeatedly. In 1972, a combination of Linebacker II's greater operational tempo and the blocking of re-supply routes from outside North Vietnam at last denied the NVAF this 'force reconstitution' capability.

Chinese advisors were also instrumental in NVAF fighter operations, for they too trained many pilots and technicians. North Vietnam's neighbors also supplied equipment to the NVAF in the shape of Chinese-built MiG-17Fs, known as J-5s. A handful of J-6s (licence-built MiG-19s) were also encountered in action in 1972. Soviet advisors finally relinquished their fighting role – which had apparently included some air combat – in 1968 following the cessation of the Rolling Thunder campaign by the Americans, but they continued to train both North Vietnamese SAM crews and pilots. Returning to base with a low fuel state, one such instructor was in the back-seat of a MiG-21US two-seat trainer on 11 September 1972 when he was bounced by four F-4Js. The Soviet pilot managed to out-maneuver the first two attacks made by the Phantom IIs, but was forced to eject through a lack of fuel just before Major Lee T Lasseter and Captain John D Cummings of VMFA-333 shot him down with a AIM-9G –

Above: Essentially an enlarged MiG-15, the MiG-17 had a 'sickle' wing, with variable chord-sweepback to improve compressibility at high speed. The F-model used by the NVAF also featured the VK-1F engine, an afterburning version of the turbojet that was so effectively employed in the MiG-15bis.

Left: The diminutive MiG-17F proved to more than a match for the more advanced USAF and US Navy types in a close quarters dogfight.

Right: Unlike in Korea, Soviet advisors stopped short of flying in combat against the Americans, although they trained NVAF pilots both in North Vietnam and the Soviet Union. However, they did have a 'hands on' role in operating GCI and SAM sites.

both the Soviet instructor and his North Vietnamese student survived the ejection. Their victors were not so lucky, however, for later in the same sortie their Phantom II was hit by a SAM which killed Major Lasseter and saw Captain Cummings made a PoW.

The importance of the advisory effort expended by the Soviets in North Vietnam was paralleled by US attempts to expand the South Vietnamese Air Force. Then, the Americans also stressed the significance of advisors in both training Third World air arms, and then helping them maintain proficiency on their high-technology equipment. Even with committed external support from a 'superpower', only a handful of countries have been able to make the successful transition to integrated jet fighter operations. This is perhaps because these fledgling air arms have not been left to evolve their own approach to both operating and integrating fighters into an overall operational force. Some, notably the Egyptian and Afghan air forces improved markedly after the departure of their Soviet advisors.

1965-68 – Strategic Influence on Fighter Operations

The might of US naval airpower in Vietnam was perhaps best encapsulated in one combat type – the F-4 Phantom II. This F-4B of VF-92 'Silver Kings' was assigned to USS Ranger (CV-61) during the carrier's first war cruise of 1964/65

Fighter operations often reflect an overall national strategy. The USAAF and RAF mission against the Me 262s was to allow the continuation of the offensive against Germany by strategic bombing, whilst in Korea airpower was used to allow the successful conduct of a limited war against numerically superior forces. As with Korea, the USAF/USN again limited the air campaign against North Vietnam in 1965-68 because, conversely, its strategic goals were now much broader. The US government wanted a 'graduated response' to secure South Vietnam from Communist forces (without provoking Chinese intervention), rather than to defeat North Vietnam outright.

As a result of this policy, there was less scope for effective fighter operations. All air operations were subject to tight political limitations that included bombing sanctuaries, both in North Vietnam and in bordering countries, and a constant pattern of offensives and that always gave the North Vietnamese the opportunity to regroup and make good their losses.

This political control was manifested in the refusal – until 1967 – of the US government to either allow fighters over North Vietnam, except as close escorts to bombers; to authorize offensive operations against the NVAF, or their ground air defenses; or to close the ports and railroads down which weapons flowed into North Vietnam from the Soviet Union and China. The NVAF was part of an integrated air defense system, and to be effective, US fighter operations needed to defeat the system, not just shoot down aeroplanes. These restrictions effectively made airfields, radars, SAM sites, communication links and headquarters buildings out of bounds for American combat aircraft.

Air Combat With China

During the execution of Rolling Thunder, there were a number of clashes between US and Chinese aircraft over the South China Sea. The Chinese played a key role in NVAF fighter operations, and in addition to providing training and aircraft, they allowed the North Vietnamese to intercept US aircraft directly from their own bases during the intense air battles of mid-1967. American intelligence had, by that stage, ascertained that Chinese early warning radars (including those on the island of Hainan) were 'netted in' to North Vietnamese air defense system. China set up massive AAA defenses in North Vietnam from 1965-68. Pre-empting this overt assistance to its beleaguered neighbor, the Chinese had drawn blood on 9 April 1965 by claiming the first US Navy air-to-air loss of the war. An F-4B from VF-96 (crewed by Lieutenant(jg) Terence M Murphy and Ensign Ronald J Fagan) was lost in combat with four J-5s (Chinese-built MiG-17s) of the 8th Naval Air Division. Murphy and Fagan claimed one J-5 (hit with an AIM-7) as the first US kill of the wa, but this is not confirmed by Chinese sources. Flying from USS Ranger on a high-altitude BarCap near Hainan Island at the time of the engagement, both crew were lost. Reports emanating from China soon after the action stated that the Phantom II was hit by a misdirected AIM-9 fired from another VF-96 jet. Chairman Mao then ordered the best Chinese air units to the Vietnamese border,

Chinese fighters also destroyed two USAF F-104Cs in separate incidents later that year when the Lockheed jets, operating out of Da Nang, clashed with J-5s over the South China Sea. The Communists claimed kills on 20 September (reportedly confirmed by the USAF at the time) and 5 October 1965, although postwar Air Force records admitted no air-air losses for the F-104C – the three reportedly lost to AAA in 1965 may include these two 'Chinese' kills. The Americans did manage to strike back on 12 May 1966: an F-4C crew from the 390th TFS shot down a Chinese J-5, supposedly over North Vietnam. The Chinese claimed that it was on a training flight over Yunnan province and they filed a diplomatic protest. Chinese fighters operated over North Vietnam on several occasions during 1966 but saw no combat However, they did intercept some US aircraft on ferrying missions from the Philippines to Vietnam. A US Navy KA-3B tanker (on 12 April 1966) and a USAF F-4C (on 26 June 1967) were reportedly shot down in this way.

The Chinese claimed to have downed an additional three US aircraft (and damaged two others) during this period, with the last confirmed kill of the war according to US records being an A-1H Skyraider of VA-25 that was shot down on 14 February 1968 – its pilot, Lieutenant(jg) J P Dunn, was posted as MIA. Total Chinese claims were 12 shot down and four damaged as a result of 2,138 sorties.

Improved relations between the US and China helped prevent any clashes when air strikes resumed in 1972. These skirmishes provide another example of the type of 'quasi-war' often fought against fighters of neighboring powers during regional conflicts (US and Soviet aircraft also traded shots during the Korean War).

Clearly visible in this shot of a Soviet MiG-17F is the jet's formidable armament, comprising one N-37D 37 mm cannon and two NR-23 23 mm weapons.

1965-68 – Tactics, Training and Technology

Left: One of the first ASMs to be fired in anger was the AGM-12 Bullpup. Built to fulfil a US Navy requirement, the USAF adopted the weapon in the early 1960s. One of its chief proponents was the F-100, and many thousands were fired from underwing rails on Super Sabres between 1965 and 1970.

Right: One of the most specialized, and dangerous, combat roles that evolved during the Vietnam conflict was that of electronic defense suppression. Perhaps the most effective 'Wild Weasel' of the war was the F-105G, which earned an enviable reputation for 'SAM busting'.

Below: The F-102 saw limited service in Vietnam: under the 'Water Glass' and Candy Machine' codenames – detachments of jets were based at Da Nang and Tan Son Nhut AFBs.

The USAF still had limited interest in fighter operations in 1965, despite its increased commitment to being able to fight a non-nuclear conflict, which had been guiding defense policy since 1961. A lack of appropriate air-to-air training was one reason that the first air battles of 1965-66 included some embarrassing setbacks for both the USAF and USN. Those units such as the USN's F-8 squadrons, which had never abandoned the ideal of classic fighter missions, were among the most successful in the early engagements with the NVAF.

Like their pilots (nearly half of whom were over 36), the aircraft of 1965-68 could trace their lineage back to the 1950s. Despite an escalation of the conflict in 1965, the Department of Defense blocked the expansion of both aircraft production and pilot training. When the order to was finally given to increase both elements in 1967 to make good US losses, the effect was not seen until 1972. As a result, the more experienced fighter pilots of the opening campaigns of 1965-66 had been rotated home by 1967-68, and the services were forced to send combat novices into the frontline, further contributing to operational losses.

F-105 'Thuds' (the noise they made

when they hit the ground!), intended to deliver nuclear bombs at low-level and high speed, inherited the heavy bomber mission of the Second World War – the delivery of unguided conventional bombs from medium altitude. Politically limited to clear weather day bombing, Thunderchief losses mounted so rapidly that the high ground to the west of the Red River Valley became known as 'Thud Ridge'.

The F-4 Phantom II – intended to defend the fleet against Soviet nuclear-armed bombers with Sparrow AAMs – became the workhorse of both the USAF and USN in the air combat role because its large, twin-engined, two-

seat, mulit-roledesign allowed it to perform both as a fighter and a bomber. The USAF had adopted the F-4 in the early 1960s, having no new fighters of its own capable of conventional air-to-air combat that were ready for production .

Other improvisations were less successful, however. A squadron of F-102 interceptors, equipped with the usual 1950s armament of unguided rockets and possessing infrared sensors to detect bombers with radar jammers was sent to South Vietnam and ordered to fly around the mountains in the of southern half of the country looking for Viet Cong camp fires with

their infrared. Once they had acquired a target, they were to fire on it with their rockets. The initial humor associated with these ludicrous missions soon disappeared when a number of the less than maneuverable F-102s were lost in low-level crashes caused by the sheer misuse of technology.

Weapons also had to be improvised. The nuclear primacy of the 1950s meant that a conventional bomb shortage hindered operations in 1965-66, and the only precision-guided munition (PGM) available to US fighters was the rather inadequate Bullpup air-to-surface missile. Anti-Aircraft Missiles designed for use against bombers, rather than highly agile fighters like the MiG-17, turned out to be relatively inaccurate – about ten per cent of those fired hit their target. Because so many rounds were being expended in an effort to secure a single kill, an acute shortage in the stockpile of air-to-air missiles soon occurred.

A particular disappointment in this period were the results achieved in combat by the F-4's main weapon, the semi-active radar homing Sparrow. Then relying on vacuum-tube technology within its seeker head, the missile was very unreliable, especially as a round could be left exposed to the elements beneath an aircraft for weeks at a time. More significantly, the rules of engagement (RoE) imposed on US fighter operations negated the Sparrow's BVR capability, as all targets had to be visually identified before a missile could be fired. The MiGs, without BVR AAMs and often (in the case of the MiG-17s) any AAMs at all, liked nothing better than fighting within visual range.

The low accuracy of the AAM brought about a re-evaluation of the much-maligned cannon. Long considered secondary (or, in the case of the gunless F-4, superfluous) to the missile or, before that, the rocket, the success of cannon armament in the MiG-17 saw air-to-air gunnery – long a neglected art in the USAF – being re-emphasized . Indeed, the air force was so desperate to incorporate guns into the F-4 that it ordered external cannon pods for its F-4s, whilst design work started on a new version, known as the F-4E, which boasted an integrally-mounted 20 mm gun.

Other modifications to the aircraft themselves came as a result of these early dogfights with MiGs, with later F-4Es having wing leading edge slats that enabled them to turn with a MiG in a dogfight – not a maneuver the F-4 was originally designed to perform. However, during the combat of 1965-68 the USAF and USN found that its aircrew were more at sea in the unfamiliar world of dogfighting than their aircraft. With the mythical 10-1 kill ratios achieved in Korea not being replicated, senior officers in the American armed forces began to take a long, hard, look at the adequacy of tactics and training following the bombing halt of 1968.

Dissimilar Air Combat

Most of the air combat over North Vietnam in the 1965-68 period saw subsonic, cannon-armed, MiG-17s tackling supersonic (when unloaded), AAM-capable, fighters such as the F-105, F-4 and F-8. With the help of their Soviet and Chinese advisors, the NVAF was able to evolve combat techniques that not only took advantage of the MiG-17's strengths, but also exploited the limitations of their US opponents.

The MiG-17 was a small aircraft with a smokeless engine, which made it difficult to acquire visually. NVAF pilots would often operate at low altitude, popping up in a climb when behind US strike aircraft, and thus minimizing the chance of them being spotted either by their opponents or by radar – the latter was often confused by surface clutter as it tried to acquire a MiG-17 using terrain masking to great effect.

US fighters, on the other hand, were physically much bigger than the MiG-17, which made them that much easier to see at distance. In addition, early F-4s tended to leave long smoke trails when flying at full military power – Phantom II pilots would often light their afterburners in combat zones, burning much more fuel, in an effort to lose the smoke trails.

The MiG-17 relied on cannon, while the Phantom II was devoid of a gun until the pod-armed USAF F-4D came into service in 1967 – even then, the underslung 20 mm Vulcan cannon often proved difficult to aim accurately in the heat of battle. As a result of their gun-only armament, MiG-17 pilots would normally try quick, hit-and-turn, attacks that were aimed at getting US strike aircraft to jettison their bombs. If cornered by F-4s, the MiG-17s would form up into a 'Lufbery Circle' – a maneuver that had its origins in the First World War. Essentially, it

consisted of a flight of aircraft following each other's tails in an ever tightening circle. By adopting such a tactic, the defending fighters protected each other's tails from enemy aircraft that tried to attack from astern. Indeed, any pilot that managed to penetrate the 'Lufbery Circle' and latch onto a target would soon find the next circling fighter stuck to his 'six o'clock'.

While US Navy F-8s often 'waded in' and broke up this favored defensive maneuver by matching the MiG-17s' high-g turns, the latter successfully used the 'Lufbery Circle' against the less agile F-4 on numerous occasions. At low altitude, and maneuvering in the horizontal plane at slow speeds, there was no way the gunless Phantom II could fight the MiG-17 on its own terms. On one occasion, however, two F-4 flights broke a 'Lufbery Circle' wide open by firing Sparrow AAMs towards the MiGs from some distance away – they were forced to evade these missiles, and in so doing lost the mutual support of each other. Although the initial rounds had missed the

Top: Crews who achieved five or more kills in the Vietnam War were a rarity, with the US Navy producing just a solitary pilot and RIO combination with the prerequisite score of five kills. Lts Randy Cunningham and Willie Driscoll were flying an F-4J with this unit – VF-96 'Fighting Falcons' – when they achieved this unique accolade in May 1972.

Left: A small number of RP-5 Izumrud radar-equipped MiG-17PFUs were supplied to the NVAF in the mid-1960s, and these were able to operate with AA-1 Alkali AAMs. One was credited with shooting down an EB-66C EW aircraft in 1968.

NVAF fighters, the scattering of the MiG-17s resulted in at least two jets being chased down and destroyed by other F-4s equipped with Sidewinders.

The lessons of 1965-68 contributed heavily to the emphasis placed by the Americans on dissimilar air combat training (DACT) later in the decade – this has remained a major facet of peacetime fighter operations to this day. The need for DACT was a key finding of the US Navy's Ault report of 1968, which looked into why the US Navy's kill ratio was just 3.7-to-1 at the end of 'Rolling Thunder'. Its findings led directly to the US Navy's implementation of improved fighter training techniques like the creation of the Fighter Weapons School, better known as 'Topgun'. The school was equipped with a mix of A-4s, which were as maneuverable as a MiG-17, and T-38s, whose supersonic performance and small visual cross-section made them ideal 'surrogate' MiG-21s.

As mentioned earlier, Randy 'Duke' Cunningham and Willie Driscoll became the only Navy aces of the war on

10 May 1972 when they shot down an aggressively-flown MiG-17 (thought at the time to be piloted by 'Colonel Tomb'). Both crewmen categorically stated that they were only able to win because they had encountered the same sort of threat in training with US Navy adversary pilots flying the A-4.

The MiG-17 always remained a difficult opponent for the F-4 if fought on its own terms: in the 1973 War, the IDFAF lost an F-4E to a Syrian MiG-17. Other air arms looked to repeat this experience by also using smaller, more austere, fighters against a better-performing enemy. One of the most notable examples occurred within the RAF in the 1980s when a number of Hawk trainers were wired up to allow them to carry a single all-aspect Sidewinder AAM under each wing. Scheduled to be flown by instructors in a time of conflict, these Hawks would have worked with Tornado F.3 ADVs, which fulfilled the role of 'mini AWACS' by using their superior search radars to vector the small fighters against bombers attempting to attack RAF airfields.

Top: Carrying a full load of Mk 82 bombs fitted with fuze extenders, these two 388th TFW F-4Es head north into enemy territory from their base at Korat, in Thailand. This wing, comprising the 35th, 44th and 369th FSs, had earlier flown F-105s over Vietnam, prior to receiving the definitive E-model Phantom II.

Right: Although a very simple design, with relatively primitive radar and fire control systems, the MiG-21F was nevertheless a vast improvement over the NVAF's mainstay fighter, the MiG-17. It was able to operate at supersonic speeds and was far better equipped to launch AAMs.

1965-68 – The Enemy

The North Vietnamese fighter force evolved as part of a massive integrated air defense system created by Soviet aid and advisors in the 1965-68 period. The prime element in the system was not fighters, but radar directed anti-aircraft artillery of all calibres – 7,500 guns in mid-1967, compared with just 1,400 three years before. Because these weapons were being rapidly replaced by SAMs in the Soviet Union, they were could be supplied in great numbers, and at not cost, to the Vietnamese. New AAA batteries were purchased with Soviet aid, and the American government's reluctance to block sea or land routes into North Vietnam in 1965-68 made sure that a constant supply of weapons and ammunition was maintained throughout this period. Veteran pilots thought the anti-aircraft fire over Hanoi more intense than anything they had seen over Berlin or the Ruhr, despite the fact that German flak posed more of a threat to Allied aircraft in 1944-45 than the Me 262.

At this stage in the conflict, SA-2 SAMs and MiG-17 and -21 fighters, while limited in numbers, played an important synergistic role in air defense system. Their cost and operation were prohibitive when compared with an AAA battery, and they stretched the ability of the limited number of North Vietnamese technicians trained to service such equipment. As a result, the Soviets not only set up and helped operate the SAMs and MiGs, they also took them into action – as late as 1972, the Soviets reported that one of their pilots had had to eject from a two-seat MiG-21 caught by an F-4.

The North Vietnamese were under no illusions that the SAMs or fighters alone would be able to defeat the more powerful US attacks. Rather, they would combine with the overwhelming AAA network to make the total defense system more effective. For example, as early as 1965 the mere presence of NVAF MiG-17s forced the US to provide fighter escorts for each bombing attack, diverting aircraft which could otherwise have been employed also carrying bombs. Older aircraft such as the B-57 and F-100 simply could not venture into North Vietnam any more. The North Vietnamese fighter force operated not just by shooting down US aircraft (although they were happy to do this), but through virtual attrition and the diversion of effort away from

Simple to build and easy to maintain, the MiG-17F was the ideal fighter for the Soviet Union to export to its allies in the 1950s and 60s. It is estimated that no fewer than 8,000 MiG-17s were built in Poland and the USSR, with possibly as many as 12,000 constructed under licence in China. This particular F-model was flown to Homestead AFB, in Florida, by a defecting Cuban Air Force pilot on 5 October 1969.

purely bombing.

This emphasis on virtual attrition was also seen in their prime tactic – the forcing of US fighter-bombers to jettison their ordnance before reaching their target. Reflecting the Soviet origins of their integrated air defense system, the MiGs tended to operate under strict GCI.

As in Korea, there was no attempt to strike at airbases or carriers, nor at high-value targets such as EC-121s or KC-135s. Ground attacks by the regular North Vietnamese Army and the guerrilla-based Viet Cong ably supported the North Vietnamese defensive air campaign. Indeed, during the course of the war, ground forces were to destroy more US aircraft in their revetments through attacks on airbases than SAMs were to shoot down in action over North Vietnam!

Despite having little knowledge in the techniques of modern air warfare at the start of the conflict with the Americans in late 1964, the NVAF pilots swiftly learnt how to best exploit their MiG fighters in combat through a combination of firsthand experience and thorough instructing from Soviet and Chinese advisors.

The NVAF on the Offensive

The NVAF carried out its defensive fighter operations through the employment of offensive tactics. It protected targets in North Vietnam not by physically shooting down US jets, but by getting them to jettison their bombs whilst attempting to evade 'slashing' attacks similar to those performed by Soviet pilots attacking B-29s in Korea. In the last quarter of 1966, over half of the US strike aircraft sent north were forced to jettison their bombs before reaching their targets.

While the NVAF mainly reacted to incoming US strikes, there were times when it managed to go on the offensive and take the fight to the Americans. For example, MiGs were directed against a number of USAF aircraft standing off, supporting operations. The first incident occured on 29 July 1966 when an RC-47 of the 606th Air Commando Squadron (ACS), tasked with monitoring communications over North Vietnam, was shot down by a MiG-17.

Other MiG attacks were aimed at EB-66 tactical jammers, and although they often succeeded in driving these specialist jets off station, only one was ever lost – an EB-66C of the 41st Tactical Electronic Warfare Squadron, assigned to the 335th TFW, was shot down on 14 January 1968 reportedly by an AA-1 Alkali AAM fired from a MiG-17PFU 'Fresco-E'. A few weeks after this, on 3 February 1968, a MiG-21 used an AAM to shoot down a 509th FIS/405th FIW F-102A that had been flying a CAP mission between NVAF contacts and B-52s tasked with bombing the southern 'panhandle' of North Vietnam.

The NVAF would also often try and break up elaborate US rescue efforts staged to extricate downed airmen from enemy territory. In addition to forcing missions to be aborted, and thus leaving aircrewmen to their fate on their ground, the NVAF also managed to destroy a USAF HH-53 Jolly Green Giant helicopter (of the 40th Aerospace Rescue and Recovery Squadron on 28 January 1970), an F-8E, an A-1E (of the 602nd ACS/432nd ACW on 19 April 1967), two F-105Ds, one F-4D and an F-4E on RESCAP (rescue combat air patrol) or SAR (search and rescue) missions – another F-4D may have also been shot down by a MiG while covering the extraction of a special operations team from Laos. Such battles were not one-sided, however, and a number of NVAF jets were claimed by RESCAP and SAR aircraft, including three MiG-17s that fell the guns of US Navy A-1Hs.

The NVAF also made repeated attempts to intercept American reconnaissance aircraft, claiming a number of RF-101, RF-4 and RA-5 aircraft destroyed. However,

according to US records, the only losses officially attributed to MiGs were a 20th TRS/432nd TRW RF-101C on 16 September 1967 (flown by Major Bobby Bagley, rated as 'one of the best pilots ever to climb into a Voodoo' – he was made a PoW), and a RA-5C of RVAH-13, downed on 28 December 1972. The latter kill was the last victory attributed to MiGs during the Vietnam War, period.

Despite the missions detailed above, the NVAF was limited in its ability to undertake sustained offensive operations primarily because of the limited range of its aircraft. Political considerations had to also be taken into account, for although striking out from the protection of the integrated air defense network at US tankers, RC-121 and E-2A radar aircraft or even the carriers and airbases themselves – would have been militarily advantageous, it is unlikely that the escalation of the conflict would have sat comfortably with North Vietnam's crucial communist allies.

North Vietnamese Aces and Aerial Victories

The highest-ranking NVAF ace was reported during the war to be the mysterious 'Colonel Tomb' who had reportedly scored 13 victories before becoming the fifth victim of the US Navy's only aces of the conflict, Lieutenants Randy Cunningham and Willie Driscoll of VF-96. While the North Vietnamese do acknowledge that an experienced MiG-17 pilot was lost on 10 May 1972 (the day of Cunningham and Driscoll's fifth kill), they have made no mention of a 'Colonel Tomb'. For a number of years Western sources reported that a second ace was believed to have scored some 14 victories as a photo existed showing a MiG-21 with a matching tally of red stars on its nose, but this has since been proven to be a unit kill total.

The leading identifiable NVAF ace is Nguyen Van Coc who downed nine victories, although three of these were US reconnaissance drones, which the North Vietnamese treated as air-to-air kills – as over 200 of these were lost, they provided many opportunities for NVAF pilots to run up big scores with little threat of being shot down. Four North Vietnamese aces finished with eight kills each (again including drones). Postwar investigations by independent bodies have shown that the NVAF claims appear to have been rather exaggerated, which may account for many of these aces' scores – no less than 15 pilots were credited with scoring five or more kills by Vietnamese authorities.

Whatever the actual victory totals, a large percentage of the NVAF's air-air kills fell to a small percentage of pilots – a statistic consistent with the overall lessons derived from fighter operations over the decades. Most MiGs shot down by US aircraft were being flown by inexperienced pilots in their first few missions. The handful that survived were presented with a 'target rich' environment for the duration of the conflict, enabling them to run up substantial kill tallies.

Above: Although developed in the early 1950s as a fighter interceptor, the F-100 found effective employment over South Vietnam as a strike aircraft. Here it fires 2.75-in rockets.

Below: This MiG-21PF was seen at Phuc Yen in 1972 wearing red stars on its nose, denoting 14 kills. Some assumed this was the work of a single pilot, but it is now regarded as a unit total.

1965-68 – Elements of US Fighter Operations

A new element was now a vital part of fighter operations – tanker aircraft. The USAF had adopted air refueling in the late 1940s, first to extend the reach of bombers against the Soviet Union, followed soon after to aid in the deployment of fighters to distant theaters across the globe. In South-east Asia, it soon became apparent how important tankers were to fighter operations within a theater.

For the first time, the average fighter mission (especially those for USAF assets, whose bases were more distant from the heartland of North Vietnam than were USN carriers on Yankee Station) required air refueling. While the NVAF never used their MiGs to take the offensive to the highly-vulnerable tankers, protecting them nevertheless became as big a part of US fighter operations as defending airbases.

The importance of off-board sensors – those not carried on the fighters themselves – had been seen since the start of jet combat. For the US operations over North Vietnam, these sensors now became more significant as part of offensive operations as a counter to the potentially superior

situational awareness that the North Vietnamese radar network gave their fighters.

The US sensors supporting fighter operations over the North eventually included ground-based radars in Laos, plus radar-equipped piston-engined EC-121s codenamed College Eye – another recycled air defense asset – that also orbited over this neighboring country. Their naval counterpart was the E-2A aircraft and radars (and fighter controllers) based on cruisers in the Tonkin Gulf, codenamed Red Crown. As in Korea, ELINT was handled separately, and was not available to support fighter operations in a timely manner.

The lack of the latter proved costly, for US fighter operations conducted against an integrated air defense system increased the importance of electronic warfare. As in Korea, lessons from 1944-45 about the use of chaff and jammers to blot out enemy radar screens had to be relearned once again. Fighters acquired firstly radar homing and warning (RHAW) receivers and radar jammers, either internally or (especially in the USAF) in underwing pods. These were used primarily to

guard against SAMs and AAA, but soon became powerful enough to jam both GCI and fighter radars as well.

Wild Weasels – specialized two-seat F-100F and F-105F fighters that could take the offensive to the SAMs with sophisticated RHAW and anti-radiation missiles (ARMs) – joined the USAF order of battle as the war progressed, being matched aboard USN carriers by EA-6As and modified A-6s. EB-66s and EA-3s provided stand-off jamming support, which also proved effective against NVAF warning radars. Later, they would be joined by F-105F Combat Martins, which could jam NVAF GCI communications. Just as the North Vietnamese defenses comprised an integrated defense system of which fighters were only a part, US fighters were also becoming just one facet of an integrated offensive system. One problem that all this American technology could not overcome, however, was that the NVAF had the advantage of defending its own territory – its personnel had a more clear-cut strategic goal, even if their aircraft, tactics and technology remained inferior to those of the US forces.

Above: The KC-135 tanker became as vital a part of the USAF's strike package as the fighter-bombers themselves. A rendezvous with a Stratotanker took place both before and after the aircraft had hit their designated targets.

Right: The sheer proliferation of SAM sites across North Vietnam constituted the greatest danger to American aircrews. Here, an RF-4C is engulfed in flames after a SAM-2 had detonated nearby, peppering the underside of the jet with shrapnel. Both crewmen ejected and were made PoWs.

Left: Operating under the codename 'Big Eye' or 'College Eye' with the 522nd AEW&CW, EC-121D 'Rivet Top' 53-0555 was employed in the early warning mission during the 1960s over the Gulf of Tonkin. Indeed, on 24 October 1967 one of its controllers successfully guided a F-4D of the 433rd TFS/8th TFW onto a MiG-21 – the first time an enemy fighter had been intercepted and destroyed through directions given by airborne controller.

Rolling Thunder

Starting in March 1965, US airstrikes began to encounter MiG-17s over North Vietnam, and by 4 April the latter had scored their first combat kills. However, improved fighter escorts soon countered the MiG threat, and after losing six jets to US aircraft up to the end of July, the NVAF limited their fighter operations for some eight months as they chose instead to rely on the build-up of the air defense system – especially the SAMs. This stand-down also reflected the NVAF's shortage of trained personnel in general, and fighter pilots in particular.

By April 1966, after US countermeasures had been seen to limit the SA-2's effectiveness, the NVAF once again sent its jets into action, this time as part of the integrated air defense system – MiG-21s were also ushered into action. The Vietnamese pilots went to great efforts to target vulnerable USAF EB-66 EW aircraft, and the Americans were hard-pressed to counter the threat The MiG-21, in particular, proved very difficult to down in battle thanks as much to the limitations placed on US fighters as to the agility of the jet itself.

Operation Bolo

The US fighter force lacked a consistent response to the increasing North Vietnamese MiG threat primarily because of the political prohibition on offensive counter-air operations. Every fighter sortie had to be part of a strike against a pre-approved target, or acting as an escort for the bombers involved in the strike. By having to wait for the MiGs to come to them, US fighters had effectively conceded the initiative to the NVAF before they had even taken off .

Colonel Robin Olds, a USAAF ace in P-38s and P-51s over Europe in 1944-45, had not forgotten how to use fighters offensively, however. He was the commanding officer of the 8th Tactical Fighter Wing, based at Ubon in Thailand. His F-4C Phantom IIs had escorted the F-105s on their missions over the north for months, and he was becoming increasingly frustrated at the hit-and-run attacks being flown against his charges by MiG-21s based in sanctuaries near the Chinese border. He was determined to bring them if not to a decisive battle, then at least into a combat scenario of his choosing.

Operation Bolo, flown on 2 January 1967, was Robin Olds' response. He realized that the North Vietnamese had become as predictable and stereotyped in their attacks as the US strike forces had in their tactics. Through a simple change in the force make-up, and a more aggressive approach by F-4 crews from the 8th TFW once combat had been joined, seven MiG-21s were shot down. Four days later another similar operation netted another two NVAF fighters. Having lost half their operational MiG-21s in less than a week, the North Vietnamese fighter force scaled back its operations for a full month.

Robin Olds v. The NVAF MiG-21 Force

1. Colonel Olds leads West Force from Thailand to draw the MiGs into battle. East Force, more F-4Cs from Da Nang, will intercept in a 'pincer' attack.

2. Bad weather delays West Force's take off and prevents East Force from taking off at all. Not fearing an attack, the NVAF are on low alert state.

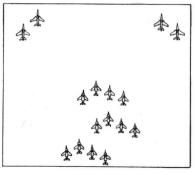

3. West Force uses routine F-105 flight patterns and even call signs, appearing to North Vietnamese radar just like another fighter-bomber formation.

A pair of F-4Ds from the 8th TFW are seen carrying a mix of ordnance, including LGBs and AIM-7 Sparrow IIs, as they set course for North Vietnam in early 1972.

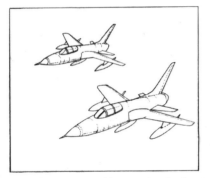

4. Olds' F-4s are supported by many other aircraft: F-105 Iron Hand defense suppression flights, RC-121s and EB-66s. F-104Cs will cover the withdrawal.

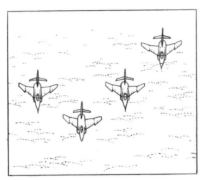

5. West Force passes the MiG-21 base at Phuc Yen, with flights of four F-4Cs following each other in five-minute trail. They find no MiGs above the overcast.

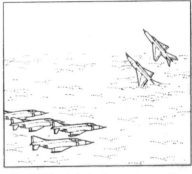

6. The MiG-21s take longer than usual to scramble, but GCI radar vectors them on to West Force. Pairs of MiGs suddenly pop up through the cloud.

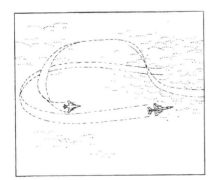

7. 12 F-4Cs dogfight with 9-12 MiG-21s for about 15 minutes. Olds uses a vector roll to turn inside a MiG despite its better horizontal maneuverability.

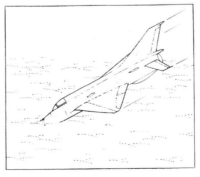

8. Seven MiGs are shot down, four hit by AIM-7s and three by Sidewinders, with no loss to the F-4s. The surviving MiGs dive through the cloud to Phuc Yen.

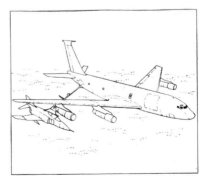

9. Colonel Olds reforms West Force and heads back to the RC-135 tankers waiting over Laos. The North Vietnamese do not challenge the forces's egress.

The Last Months of Rolling Thunder

Although Operation Bolo was a success, it was never repeated. Instead, the following month at last brought US air attacks against NVAF air defense targets, including most of the main Vietnamese airbases. In response to this change in tactics, the NVAF fighter force scrambled to protect their bases and destroyed seven US aircraft in April for the loss of nine MiGs. On 24 April, a co-ordinated US counter-air operation destroyed nine MiGs on the ground, and by the end of May, further attacks had resulted in the destruction of some 26 MiGs.

The NVAF fighter force reeled in the face of these new tactics, most of their MiGs being flown out to the sanctuary of Chinese airfields – shades of Korea. This meant that the NVAF could play only a limited role in the large-scale US air attacks of May-July 1967, which ushered into service USAF F-4Ds fitted with pod-mounted 20 mm cannon.

In August, NVAF fighters began to return in defence of Hanoi, their sortie frequency increasing in September. The NVAF had developed new tactics that exploited the limitations of US rules of engagement, and made full use of their expanded radar coverage. These tactics included using GCI coverage for 'slashing' climbing and diving attacks at the rear of US bomber formations, MiG-17s and MiG-21s making co-ordinated attacks from multiple directions.

These tactics gained initial successes, with even escorting F-4Ds falling victims to MiGs. In September, the MiGs doubled the expected 'virtual attrition' of USAF fighter-bombers forced to jettison bombs, and for a while it seemed that the MiG threat would neutralize US air superiority over North Vietnam.

The US responded by devoting increased resources to counter-air operations. For example, on 25 October a co-ordinated USAF/USN strike of previously unseen proportions hit the airfield and air defense system at Phuc Yen, destroying eight MiGs on the ground and another in the air.

By the time of the Christmas bombing halt, the NVAF fighter force had once again been driven into sanctuaries in China, although it remained active from these sites operating both MiG-17s and -21s. In the last months of Rolling Thunder up to March 1968, the NVAF fighters had limited capability to challenge US operations over North Vietnam.

Air combat during Rolling Thunder had resulted in some 120 claims for MiGs shot down, in exchange for 55 US aircraft. Like the air war against North Vietnam in general, the operation was marked with courage and adaptability by both sides. However, to US fighter crews brought up in the shadow of the 10-1 kill ratio achieved in Korea, it was an indication that deep changes were required in fighter operations.

Above: With its centerline weapons rack devoid of bombs, this F-105D from the 354th TFS/355th TFW heads back south to Takhli RTAFB, in Thailand during Rolling Thunder.

Left: Along with the F-105, TAC F-4Cs were the USAF's chief instrument of war during Rolling Thunder. The majority of the 583 C-models built by McDonnell Douglas saw action over South-east Asia.

1972 – Strategic Inputs

There was still much bitter fighting despite the bomb halt of 1968, although no mission were flown into North Vietnam. It was only after the NVA's spring offensive of 1972 that strike packages headed north over the border once again as part of Operation Linebacker I. The strategic goals of that year were much more limited than those of 1965-68, but ironically they allowed for more consistently effective fighter operations to be flown. Linebacker I was not so much concerned with the broader picture of South-east Asia, but simply to get the North Vietnamese to halt their offensive. This more limited goal, and the decreased chance of Chinese intervention, meant that many of the 1965-68 political constraints on fighter operations no longer applied.

1972 – Tactics, Training, Technology

The most successful Crusader unit in terms of MiG kills during Rolling Thunder was VF-211 'Red Checkertails', who destroyed eight MiG-17s in 1966-67 whilst on deployment with USS Hancock (1966) and USS Bon Homme Richard (1967). This F-8J was photographed during a later Hancock/VF-211 Tonkin Gulf cruise in 1972.

The most dramatic improvements over the campaign of 1968 centered around revised US tactics, training and technology. The lessons of Rolling Thunder had been clearly understood by those who flew fighters, even if they had eluded the political leaders. The improved US kill ratio in 1972-73 showed the effects of the improved tactics and training undertaken in the intervening four years. Allied with technological improvements in aircraft, missiles and electronic sensors, the final positive lessons learnt in the final months of the Vietnam War helped revive US and Allied fighter operations

in the latter years of the Cold War.

Most of the shortfalls of 1965-68 had been addressed prior to the commencement of Linebacker I. Improved aircraft would carry out fighter operations, the bulk of these missions falling to the new USAF F-4E, with its internal gun and slatted wings. The Navy F-4Js, although still lacking a gun, also offered superior performance when compared with the F-4Bs of 1965-68. With the F-105s now limited to Wild Weasel anti-radar tactics, bomb-carrying F-4s became the primary USAF strike aircraft of Linebacker I and II.

Short-Field MiG-21 Operations

The North Vietnamese Air Force (NVAF) demonstrated an ability to mount surprise attacks with MiG-21s from directions in which they were not expected. Even when US active and passive sensors were monitoring air bases around the clock, MiGs could still 'pop up' from dispersed locations previously unknown to the Americans. As a result of the MiG's limited endurance, and the comprehensive US sensor coverage across most of North Vietnam, being able to take-off quickly from hidden locations and then quickly climb to altitude (both important features of the MiG-21's design that reflected both Soviet experiences in Korea and the jet's primary employment in the USSR as an interceptor against strategic bombers) made the fighter ideally suited to NVAF operations.

MiG-21s were predominantly used in this fashion during the Linebacker II strikes of December 1972, when US attacks on their bases forced them to operate from camouflaged dirt strips. Due to the one-off nature of many of these runways, MiGs were flown in slung under Mi-6 helicopters, and then manhandled to the end of the strip. Mobile communications links with air defense fighter controllers were also brought to the site from more permanent facilities. When ordered to scramble, the MiG-21 would use SPRD-99 strap-on solid fuel rocket boosters to ensure that its take-off roll was as short as possible. The MiGs would then recover back to a conventional air base, where they were serviced before being re-lifted to another alert strip. Helicopters also provided logistics re-supply.

Here, as throughout the course of jet fighter operations, the NVAF had the option of an additional operational capability because an investment had been made in new technology by Mikoyan engineers back in the 1950s when the MiG-21 was first designed. Soviet fighters of the Cold War period often had features such as blow-in doors for jet inlet suction reduction, which cut down the chances of debris ingestion, and landing gear debris deflectors to allow the aircraft to operate from unpaved runways without the undercarriage propelling rocks and the like into the engine intakes. Both these features have been seen on later designs such as the MiG-29 and Su-27.

Another structural feature exploited by the NVAF was that all Soviet fighters were designed so as to allow their wings to be easily removed from the fuselage. This not only made it easier for the Vietnamese to recover MiGs stranded at dispersal fields, but also meant that unassembled jets could be fitted into standard shipping crates. This allowed the NVAF to keep airframes crated up and safely stored in reserve within small hardened facilities at Phuc Yen.

While the ability to perform boosted short or zero-length take-offs had also been developed by the USAF in the 1950s for their F-100 and F-104 'century series' fighters, the Soviets had been unique in committing both time and resources to ensuring its widespread operational use. This reflected the reality that had dawned on all 'superpower' strategists in the early 1960s – major fighter operating and dispersal bases were likely to be nuclear targets in any future global conflict. The Soviets believed that they would be able to keep intact a fair proportion of their Frontal Aviation fighters following a nuclear strike through dispersing them to unimproved strips. The adoption of this tactic also demonstrated that dispersed fighter operations were crucially reliant on heavy- and medium-lift helicopter support.

In addition to the arrival of the gun, other weapons had also improved. Better AIM-7E Sparrow missiles, with integrated electronics, benefited from new rules of engagement that allowed BVR attacks. Improved AIM-9H Sidewinders also made their service debut, this version of the AAM being the first designed to kill maneuvering fighters rather than just bombers or target drones. Accuracy in attacks on airfields drastically improved thanks to the advent of PGMs, with laser-guided bombs (LGBs) making a serious impact in aerial warfare.

Better ECM – pods for the USAF, internal jammers for USN fighters – allowed fighters to operate even in areas full of SAMs and AAA. New sensors provided improved situational awareness for crews, whilst Combat Tree (a then-secret system fitted to F-4Es) allowed them to detect airborne MiGs through their IFF, as had been done against Me 262s back in 1944-45. In 1972, another 1945 tactic of providing ELINT data and intercepted enemy communications information to fighters in near real-time was also re-instituted – data links now also connected EC-121 AWACS aircraft with fighters. Better communications and more secure-linked fighters also denied the NVAF source material for their situational awareness.

Although the USAF had dramatically upgraded the equipment on offer to its fighter wings, improved aircrew training was primarily a Navy initiative. Stung by the generally poor results of the 1965-68 period, they re-emphasized air combat training and established what would become the world-famous Topgun program. Dissimilar air combat was practised, with A-4s standing in for MiG-17s and T-38s for MiG-21s. The first instrumented air combat ranges were also set up to analyze the in-flight

data gleaned during training. The USAF Fighter Weapons School's syllabus at Nellis AFB was also drastically overhauled, and other USAF fighter tactical training was made more relevant. However, despite these measures, the USAF lagged behind at the start of Linebacker I. It compensated for this, however, by having one F-4E wing within a strike package specialize in air combat operations while the remainder concentrated on strike missions.

Linebacker started with the rapid return of many US fighters to Southeast Asia in March 1972. Improved rapid deployment techniques and the massive investment in improving airbases in the region quickly paid off. The strike packages committed to action were even more complex than those of Rolling Thunder, with some 60 to 80 per cent of the sorties generated purely devoted to supporting the strike aircraft tasked with bombing a target.

The North Vietnamese, meanwhile, had extended their integrated air defense system south during the four-year bombing halt. These forward sites did not last long as US strike aircraft peeled it back towards Hanoi by bombing airfields and destroying radars. As the bombing moved north, and without the Chinese sanctuaries of

1965-68 available to them, the NVAF was forced back into battle. It too had been enlarged, and now boasted more improved MiG-21s than MiG-17s, plus a small number of MiG-19s. Despite the much-vaunted training regimes and improved aircraft and weapons, the US fighter force was still pegged back to a near-even kill ratio with NVAF aircraft destroyed.

The Linebacker fighter operations included the most intense air battles of the war, with the mining of the approaches to Haiphong Harbor by the Navy in Operation Pocket Money in May resulting in strong NVAF resistance. The first US aces of the war (even Colonel Robin Olds only managed four MiGs, although he claims that he could have easily made ace if his F-4C had been equipped with a gun) were from the Navy, Lieutenants Randy 'Duke' Cunningham and William 'Willie' Driscoll bagging the magic five whilst assigned to VF-96 aboard USS Constellation – this F-4J crew were Topgun graduates. Their fifth kill, on 10 May 1972, came in a climactic dogfight against an expertly-flown MiG-17, its pilot purportedly being the ranking (and probably mythical) North Vietnamese ace 'Colonel Tomb'. A further 10 MiGs were claimed on the same day by other USN and USAF Phantom II crews.

A VF-2 'Bounty Hunters' F-14A launches from USS Enterprise in April 1975 at the start of a CAP over Saigon during the evacuation of the US Embassy. The Tomcat never got to test its mettle in combat over Vietnam, having to wait until 1981 to earn its 'battle spurs' off the coast of Libya.

US fighter operations over the north continued throughout 1972, with a trio of air force aircrew (one pilot and two Weapons System Officers) also finally making ace. In October, counter-air strikes on NVAF airfields were intensified, but despite this escalation, the North Vietnamese broke off the Paris negotiations aimed at ending the war in December. The focus of air operations was now clear – bomb them back to the conference table. This time, the bombardment of North Vietnam would involve the 'big stick' in the form of the B-52.

In the 11-day air campaign that raged over Christmas 1972, the B-52 raids had to face dense SA-2 defenses. They were supported in their endeavors by F-4 fighter escorts and dedicated defense suppression assets. The NVAF also came up to intercept them, but their numbers were limited by the effects of the fighting of previous months. The USAF claimed no B-52s lost to MiGs (while the NVAF claimed several), whilst the bomber gunners claimed two MiG-21s shot down.

The NVAF and the B-52s

The NVAF fighter force had to play a subordinate role to the SA-2 SAM (and a limited number of SA-3s and SA-4s) during Operation Linebacker II.

The USAF is adamant that not a single B-52 was lost to MiGs during the offensive, countering with claims that two MiG-21s were instead shot down by bomber gunners – some Air Force critics claim that at least one of these kills was actually an escorting F-4E that unwisely pointed its nose at a B-52, but SAC refused to entertain this speculation for fear of giving up its first MiG kills since Korea.

Alarmed at the B-52 losses to SAMs, USAF intelligence investigated the attack profiles utilized by the NVAF and found that MiG-21s were shadowing bomber cells at the same altitude, thus sending back accurate attack co-ordinates to the SA-2 sites on the ground. This made it easier for the SAM controllers to use optical guidance against B-52s jamming their radar screens with ECM. On 19 December 1972 the NVAF claimed that a MiG-21 had been hit be a missile from an escorting fighter whilst trying to get into the 'six o'clock' of a B-52. Forced to return to base badly damaged, the MiG crashed on landing after hitting a bomb crater.

The NVAF also stated that a pair of MiG-21s had in fact shot down two B-52s that the USAF had reported were lost to SA-2s. The first 'kill' occurred on 27 December 1972 when Pham Tuan (who later became the first Vietnamese cosmonaut) was vectored in his MiG-21 onto the tail of a B-52 by GCI. The pilot later claimed that he did not turn on his radar before firing so as to negate any attempts made by the B-52 crew to break his missile lock with ECM. However, the two bombers lost that night were reputedly hit by a hail of SA-2s, so it is

The US Navy's first frontline operational F-4 unit, VF-74 'Be-devilers' were heavily involved in Linebacker, Freedom Train and Linebacker II operations.

unlikely that Tuan did indeed get his kill. Less than 24 hours later another MiG-21 pilot got the posthumous credit for ramming a B-52, as the two blips merged and then vanished from NVAF radar screens. According to USAF records, what apparently happened was that the MiG was shot down by a Sparrow fired from an Air Force F-4D – no B-52s were lost on that mission.

NVAF figures admit that their fighter force was largely put out of action during Linebacker II through the sheer weight of the US defense suppression effort, rather than by the loss of aircraft shot down in fighter combat. In the 12 days of B-52 operations, the NVAF managed to launch just 27 MiG-21 and four MiG-17 sorties, which led to eight air-air engagements. In addition to the two B-52s destroyed, the NVAF claimed four Phantom IIs (USAF records suggest that the actual total was two F-4Es) and one RA-5C (although US Navy reports at the time stated that this jet was lost to a SAM, subsequent research has shown that it was indeed downed by a MiG-21 – see details mentioned earlier in the NVAF on the Offensive entry), while admitting the loss of three MiG-21s. F-4D pilots claimed four MiG-21s in addition to the two claimed by B-52 gunners.

Supporting strikes by F-4s and F-111s hit airfields and radars.

By the end of Linebacker II, the North Vietnamese had no option but to sign the Paris accords. The surviving MiGs had escaped to China, whilst virtually all the SAM sites had been either suppressed or exhausted of missiles. But this setback to the overall North Vietnamese strategy was just temporary.

In the period 1970-73 the US claimed 73 MiGs for the loss of 32 aircraft in air combat. However, the breakdown of this score between the services – 22-4

for the USN, and 51-28 for the USAF – showed how remarkable an impact the Topgun school had had on the results of air combat. Despite suffering higher casualties, the USAF had also made advances. They had become more proficient in the use of IFF, and had devised better Sparrow and Sidewinder launching techniques. Despite the poor technical record of AAMs in Rolling Thunder, about three-quarters of the MiG kills achieved in the eight years of war had fallen to missiles – the remainder had been claimed by guns,

thus earning the 20 mm cannon a place in the next two generations of fighters.

After Vietnam the USAF and USN spent the rest of the 1970s in the 'hollow forces' era – a military nadir suffered in the form of 'hangover' from the 'defeat' in Vietnam that was characterised by low funding and poor morale. Despite this, the importance of fighter operations was never forgotten, unlike in the 1950s. The stage was now set for a true revival of effective fighter operations.

Arab-Israeli Conflicts 1956-82

In the Middle East, fighters, and their operations, have shaped both the course of national policy and the Cold War itself. The Suez War of 1956, the Six Day War of 1967, the War of Attrition of 1969-70, the October War of 1973 and the Lebanon War of 1982 each had different participants, and provided different operational lessons. Combined, they have included some of the most intense fighter operations of the jet age.

The fighter operations in the Middle East also reflect the parallel evolution of the opposing air arms of Israel and the Arab world – particularly those of Egypt and Syria. The evolution of the Israeli fighter force from a rough and ready collection of surplus piston-engined aircraft in 1948 to one of the most technologically advanced air arms in the world, has been unmatched. The parallel evolutionary process of Israel's opponents – principally Egypt – has attracted less attention, but may be more significant as it provides a model of the potential successes and frustrations for Third World air arms trying to come to grips with modern fighter operations.

Fighters are not viewed simply as 'tactical' airpower in the tight confines of the Middle East. Fighter aircraft, and their operations, have achieved both a direct strategic impact in real terms, and shaped the orientation of national policy. Egyptian President Nasser's joint moves before the 1956 Suez Crisis against western interests and towards Moscow were driven, in part, by the need to acquire modern combat aircraft which the West had proven

Above: The IDFAF's first jet fighter squadrons were equipped with a mixed fleet of British Meteor F 8s and NF 13s and French Ouragans and Mystere IVs. This fine shot shows a Meteor F 8 at altitude in its original all-silver delivery scheme, equipped with a full complement of eight 5-in unguided rockets on the outer wing rails. Ironically, this particular jet had originally been part of a (cancelled) order for Egypt.

Left: The French equivalent of the Meteor F 8 was Dassault's MD.450 Ouragan, 20 of which were supplied to Israel in late 1955. These saw much use in both the 1956 Sinai crisis and over a decade later during the 1967 Six-Day War.

Above: The Mirage III was the first truly advanced fighter procured by the IDFAF, no less than 72 IIICJs being bought from Dassault in the mid-1960s. The Mirage's success in Israeli hands helped it achieve an enviable export record: it was adopted by over 20 air arms including, in this particular instance, the RAAF.

The 1967 conflict saw the IDFAF in combat with five Arab air arms, including Iraq. Again, superior tactics and a will to win prevailed over weight of numbers, the Iraqis for example, losing five of their 33 Hunter F 6s to Israeli fighters.

unwilling to provide. Similarly, Egypt's final break with the Soviets after the 1973 War came about principally because they would not provide upgraded replacements – on credit – for fighters lost in the struggle against Israel. The subsequent US provision of fighters to Egypt also became a key part of the Camp David Accords.

East across the Sinai Desert, the strong militaristic partnership between America and Israel started to emerge in its current form with the decision by the US government in 1968 to supply more modern aircraft. The largely French jet fighter forces was supplemented by A-4 fighter-bombers and then F-4s. Fighters have been the nexus of policy, prestige and operational power in the Middle East.

1956 – Sinai And Suez

The arrival of large shipments of Soviet-designed aircraft in Egypt was one of the main causes of the 1956 War. Sixty-five MiG-15 and -17 fighters and, most significantly, 40 Il-28 bombers (later to be reinforced with Tu-16 medium jet bombers) posed a threat to Israel and Western interests in the region. These aircraft further added to the shared motivations of Israel and the Anglo-French alliance to instigate military action to neutralize the Egyptians who, though still dependent on Soviet and Czechoslovak 'advisors' in 1956, were rapidly increasing their operational capabilities.

In 1956, the Israeli jet fighter force was comprised of just four-dozen Mystere IVAs, Ouragans and Meteors. The Il-28 threat made them anxious to invite French fighters and GCI radar to operate from Israeli bases in order to provide defence against attacks that their own fighters might be unable to handle. With French Mystere IVAs and F-84Fs deployed to carry out air defense and ground attack operations, Israeli fighters were able to concentrate on supporting the army's invasion of Sinai, starting on 29 October.

Israeli defensive counter-air missions successfully protected the advancing forces from repeated Egyptian air attacks until they arrived at the Suez Canal. In a number of dogfights, the Israelis maintained the upper hand, destroying 12 aircraft for the loss of just a solitary light liaison aircraft in air-to-air combat, although Arab groundfire accounted for 17 jets.

The most extensive counter-air fighter operations of 1956 were those flown by the Anglo-French forces. Their objective was the defeat of the Egyptian Air Force through the destruction of their airfields. As the few qualified Egyptian jet fighter pilots were already committed to opposing the Israeli thrust into Sinai, it was predicted that the Soviet and Czechoslovak 'advisors' would not come up to indulge in air combat.

The Anglo-French jet fighters were integrated into an operational framework that was basically identical to that employed during piston-engined era of the Second World War. They also used the same weapons – 20 mm cannon, rockets and 500- and 1,000-lb HE bombs (although the use of radar proximity fuzes for airbursts was a postwar innovation). No strategic targets were to be hit due to the

'Decapitation' By Meteor

A 'decapitation' attack is often one of the goals of the opening phase of an attack. Putting your opponent's command structure or, failing that, a commander out of action will delay their ability to react effectively to a rapidly-developing situation. In the main, fighters have not been effective at 'decapitation' missions with the odd exception such as the shoot-down of Admiral Yamamoto by USAAF P-38s in 1943.

The Israeli Air Force had a rare opportunity for air-to-air 'decapitation' on the first night of the 1956 War. As the crisis had developed, the Egyptian Chief of Staff, Marshal Abd al Hakim 'Amr, had gone to Damascus to sign a defense pact with Syria and Jordan in an attempt to enlist support against the expected Israeli/Anglo-French invasion. Word of the marshal's mission reached the Israelis too late for them to intercept him prior to his arrival in Damascus, but a plan was hastily formulated to engage his aircraft on its return leg to Egypt.

The aircraft chosen to undertake this crucial mission was the Meteor NF.13, the Israeli Air force's first jet nightfighter. Through a combination of even-handedness and profit motive, the British had sold equal numbers (six apiece) of Meteors to both Israel and its two major opponents in Egypt and Syria in 1953-56. While its origins were similar to those of its USAF F-94 counterpart (both were two-seat trainer versions of first-generation jet day fighters rushed into service as nightfighters to meet the emerging Soviet bomber threat), it was much less sophisticated, lacking the Starfire's high-technology fire control system.

Only two Israeli Meteor NF.13s were serviceable at the start of the 1956 War, and both were tasked with intercepting the marshal's aircraft. The mission was led by veteran squadron commander Major Yehoash Chatto Tzidon, who had shot down an Egyptian Vampire fighter in a border skirmish the previous year.

The Meteors were scrambled as soon as the Israelis got word that a Soviet-built Il-12 transport had left Damascus, bound for Cairo. Although the transport would fly around Israel, crossing the Mediterranean between Haifa and Cyprus, its route was well-within range of Israeli radar, and Chatto's Meteor was quickly vectored onto the aircraft by GCI – the Israelis had an experienced fighter controller (a former fighter squadron commander) running the intercept from the command center.

Chatto's navigator detected the target on the Meteor's radar at a distance of three miles, and ordered his pilot to close in to visually identify the target. Due to the latter's

The Republic F-105 Thunderchief ('Thud') fighter-bomber: primary target of the North Vietnamese air force.

The Shenyan J-6, the Chinese-built version of the Russian MiG-19 entered production in 1961.

The Hawker Hunter entered service with the RAF in 1954 and remained in service with Switzerland until the 1990s.

The distinctive Saab Draken entered service in 1960 and was flown by the Swedish, Danish and Austrian air forces.

The McDonnell Douglas F-4 Phantom saw extensive combat against Russian fighters in Vietnam and the Middle East. .

The delta-winged Mirage III proved highly successful in Israeli service during the 1967 'Six Day War'.

The US Navy's McDonnell Douglas F/A-18 Hornet fighter-bomber has a unique fighter/attack designation.

Armed with Phoenix radar-guided missiles, the F-14 was designed to destroy Soviet bombers at very long range.

The Royal Navy's modest force of BAe Sea Harriers achieved incredible success in the 1982 Falklands war.

Bear baiting: two USAF F-15 Eagles intercept a Soviet Tupolev Tu-95 in a typical Cold War confrontation.

The advent of the MiG-31 finally forced an end to overflights of the Soviet Union by USAF SR-71s.

Air defense of the UK: at last Tornado ADVs are directed by Boeing E-3s instead of the ancient Shackletons.

Prototype F-22s: the USAF's latest fighter is rated superior to any other interceptor in service.

The JAS 39 Gripen is the latest, highly-successful fighter design from Saab and is now entering service.

Egypt, like Israel, benefited from arms hand outs from Britain in the early 1950s, receiving a small number of Meteor F 8s and, seen here on the eve of their departure, Vampire FB 52 fighter-bombers.

limited nature of the Suez operation, and the counter-air operations would be swiftly followed by interdiction missions to seal off the Anglo-French amphibious invasion force from any Egyptian reinforcements or close-air support sorties generated by the remnants of its air force.

Starting on 30 October, repeated airstrikes on Egyptian airfields, which lacked the dense AAA defenses of their German counterparts of 1944-45, were made until the surviving aircraft were eventually flown out of range of the attacking jets. High-altitude bombing by RAF Valiants and Canberras (which suffered damage from the few MiG-17 interceptors that did get into action - protection from escorting interceptors was not a valid tactic in 1956) was less effective, and the more lethal strikes

were delivered by fighters and strike aircraft operating from Israel and aircraft carriers offshore.

The Anglo-French counter-air operations may not have been inspired, but they were effective. The gamble that advisors would not come up and fight

paid off, for they instead flew surviving Egyptian aircraft out of range. A total of 260 Egyptian aircraft were destroyed on the ground, while the only Anglo-Allied loss in air combat was an RAF PR Canberra intercepted over Damascus by a Syrian Air Force MiG-17.

much slower cruising speed, Chatto had to lower the Meteor's flaps and landing gear in order to stay astern of his piston-engined quarry. Reporting back to GCI that he had sighted the Egyptian Il-12, Chatto received authorization to open fire – the Meteor's four Hispano 20 mm cannon made quick work of the defenseless transport.

Upon their return to base, Chatto and his navigator were met on the tarmac by the Israeli Air Force chief of staff, but congratulations were somewhat subdued for it was quickly revealed to the crew that the marshal had arrived safely in Egypt. His aircraft had taken off later than scheduled, and the Il-12 that the Meteor had shot down in its place had been carrying a number of senior Egyptian officers and a contingent of Arab pressmen, which cynics suggested was evidence that it had been deliberately used as a decoy.

This episode clearly proved that even the most regimented form of fighter operation – GCI interception – can go wrong. If a target as precise as a single individual is being prosecuted, this places a tremendous burden on the accuracy of the intelligence pertaining to the movements of the person in question. Since the Il-12 shoot down in 1956, the difficulty in locating specific leadership figures in

the enemy camp has prevented repeats of the 'decapitation' mission. However, other high-value intercepts have been successfully performed by fighters without the need to resort to the shooting down of their targets. For example, in 1985 two US Navy F-14s that had launched from an aircraft carrier in the Mediterranean, intercepted an Egyptian airliner carrying terrorists who had participated in the hijacking of a US airliner in the Middle East, and managed to force it down in Sicily.

However, during the Gulf War USAF F-15E fighter-bombers were sent into Iraq on attempted 'decapitation' air-ground missions, their targets including a fleet of US-made recreational vehicles that were believed to be used by Saddam Hussein as his personal transport. Although these 'Winnebago-hunting' missions managed to place laser-guided bombs on a number of these elusive 'RVs', intelligence placing Saddam in a vehicle at any one time was never fresh enough to enable the F-15Es to kill the Iraqi leader in-situ. Despite the fighter having enjoyed limited success in this area over the decades, it may be that in future, frontline units will have to consider adopting techniques that will allow the ultimate in precision targeting – the need to kill or capture a single individual – to take place with a high degree of certainty.

Israeli Fighter Operations 1956-67

In the years between 1956 and 1967, Israel watched as its Arab opponents put sizeable forces, comprising in the main Soviet-designed aircraft, into service. In 1967 the Arabs had, on paper, a four to one advantage in combat aircraft over Israel. Most worrying were the Tu-16 and Il-28 jet bombers that were now flown by Egypt, Iraq and Syria (Il-28s only). The largest number of bombers was operated by the Egyptian Air Force which, despite a decade of Soviet influence, still had much of the faith in strategic counter-value bombing it inherited from the RAF in the 1940s. More disturbing still was the rumored Arab attainment of a chemical warfare capability.

The Israelis had a broad spectrum of responses to these actions (including a nuclear program), but the fighter force was the key through its development of a high-lethality offensive counter-air capability. The Israelis stressed this because of the limitations associated with passive defense. They were concerned that they would be unable to intercept a mass, escorted, jet bomber force before it struck Israeli cities and airbases. The answer was (as done so effectively in 1956) to take the offensive and put the Arab air arms out of action on the ground. This meant offensive – pre-emptive if possible – fighter operations. Once the air forces had been defeated, the fighters would turn their attention to supporting the army, as in 1956.

Using fighters to defeat enemy aircraft in air-to-ground operations rather than air-to-air was not new. In 1944-45, Allied fighters took the offensive against the Luftwaffe on the ground, even when they were defended by intense AAA. What was new, however, was the way

with which the Israelis approached this as an integrated response to the problem. They did not (unlike the USAF or USN) have to develop an operational approach that would be valid across a range of contingencies world-wide. Instead, the Israelis developed operations, weapons and tactics to solve this one specific task.

They were well aware that effective fighter operations depended on congruence between national strategy (focused by Nasser's immediate threat) tactics, technology and training. Israel stressed air-to-air combat tactics, using cannon as a primary weapon at a time when the USAF was relying on missiles alone and introducing fighters with no gun armament. at all. Increased numbers of advanced French-built fighters – most notably AAM-armed Mirage IIICJs – gave the Israelis parity with Arab MiG-21s.

Right: The most modern aircraft Israeli aircraft in 1956 were the 16 Mystere IVAs supplied from French Air Force stocks. These jets were used extensively to protect vulnerable C-47s tasked with dropping paratroopers deep into Egyptian territory on the opening morning of the War.

Left: Ouragans attacked Egyptian army positions with rockets, bombs and napalm. Three of the Dassault jets were lost to ground fire.

These all-silver Mystere IVAs hail from the IDFAF's most successful fighter unit, No 101 Sqn. This unit claimed to have shot down at least four MiG-15s (all with 30 mm cannon fire) for no losses during the Suez clash.

1967 – Fighter Operations Reshape a Region

The 1967 War opened with a perfect 1944 style offensive counter-air fighter operation that has since reshaped the geopolitics of the Middle East to this very day. Within 90 minutes, the backbone of Arab airpower had been broken. Yet, these minutes of victory for Israeli fighter pilots were the result of years of operational preparation.

All Israeli jets were used for the initial counter-air strike including the Mirage IIIs, which were the country's first-line

Above: By 1967 the Mystere IVAs had been replaced in the air defense role by Mirage IICJs and Super-Mystere B2s. A total of 36 of the latter were obtained in 1958, and they were responsible for the maintaining the integrity of Israeli airspace until the first Mirages arrived in the mid-1960s. Of the 24 involved in the Six-Day War, four were lost.

Left: Always sensitive about giving away specific details of their units and aircraft, the IDFAF have gone to great lengths to obscure serials and unit markings when their jets have come into contact with the world's press. This ferociously-marked Ouragan wore the badge of No 113 Sqn beneath the brown paper hastily taped to its fin.

fighter (and would claim 80 per cent of the air-to-air kills in 1967). Only 12 alert fighters were held back to defend Israel. The attackers understood that their targets were not just aeroplanes, but an overall offensive system. Thorough intelligence preparation had determined not only the extent of Arab radar coverage, but such things as the existence of a 'window of vulnerability' after the Egyptian dawn standing patrols had landed, but before senior officers had arrived on base. Another Israeli force multiplier was the availability of multiple pilots for each aircraft, who could replace returning crews in a rapid ground turn-around, thus boosting sortie rates. Everything was in place for the decisive strike.

When tensions increased in 1967 and Egypt closed the Gulf of Aqaba, the Israelis were ready. The blow was delivered against Egypt at 0745 on 5

June. The Tu-16 and Il-28 bombers were the main priority, followed by MiG-21 fighters, which were the most capable jets in the Arab air arms. After a few Syrian and Jordanian strikes against Israeli targets in response to the pre-emptive attack, Israel recovered its jets, rearmed them, and started the process on their airfields all over again. In total, some 500 Israeli sorties yielded over 300 aircraft destroyed on the ground on the first day, plus a small number of aircraft shot down in the few air combats that occurred.

After the first day the result of the fighter operations was a foregone conclusion. This tremendous success left the Israelis free to allocate sorties to support the army. Counter-air operations also continued, but longer-ranged interdiction and counter-infrastructure missions came to the fore in the closing days of the war. After the

first day, the surviving Arab fighters intercepted when they could (Arab radar sites had also been among the initial casualties), and not all the dogfights ended in Israeli victories.

1967, in retrospect, was the last old-style fighter operation. The Israeli jets used no precision guided munitions in their air-to-ground missions, nor AAMs in the air-to-air encounters. Keeping with the minimalist use of technology, Israeli fighters did not bother with electronic warfare either, the chaff barriers being left to transport aircraft – the Arabs' SA-2 SAM batteries were a nuisance rather than part of an integrated air defense system. Because of this, once the initial airstrike had put the Arab air forces largely out of action, almost all available Israeli fighter sorties could be devoted to interdiction and close air support. Few had to be diverted to undertake electronic

warfare, defense suppression or escort missions. Total Arab losses were estimated at around 450 aircraft, about 60 of which were downed in air-to-air combat. The Israelis lost just 46 aircraft, somewhere between three and ten in

air-to-air combat. The Israeli's substantial advantages in pilot skill, tactics and aircraft had been pulled together into a highly effective counter-air operation made possible by a coherent national strategy.

Demonstrating its ability to take-off from grass, a Mirage IIIC leaves a huge trail of dust in its wake during a press demonstration in France in the early 1960s. The IDFAF never had to worry about flying off anything but concrete, as Arab forces never succeeded in attacking any of their key fast jet bases.

Planning for the 1967 Offensive Counter-air Strike

Israeli planning for the OCA strike that changed the course of the 1967 War presented air force planners with the most severe challenge they had yet faced. The final operational order had to be as detailed as any of the nuclear warplans that dominated US Cold War thinking about fighter operations, without sacrificing the flexibility and reliance on low-level decision-making that the Israelis rightly prized as being one of their main advantages over their opponents.

They used effective planning as a force multiplier – crucial in light of the fact that their enemies always possessed greater numerical strength. The strike was intended not only to prevent Arab offensive air operations, and thus ensure air superiority, but also to make Israeli air resources available to support ground operations. The bombloads of Israeli fighters (mainly designed for air-air rather than air-ground missions, which the Israelis had stressed as the main criterion for future fighter operations when the aircraft were ordered) were limited, which meant that they could not rely on sheer weight of firepower. Pilots had to therefore be instructed in both accurate weapons delivery techniques (including classic strafing attacks) and the use of specialized weapons such as anti-runway 'dibber' bombs. On the ground, briefing officers compiled a highly-accurate intelligence picture of where the targets

– Arab aircraft – were likely to be. Full-scale mock-ups of Arab airbases were constructed in the Negev desert to further aid in the training process.

The Israelis had a number of advantages; they could count on blue skies, when other air forces had to plan for all-weather operations; they were carrying out a mission that had been planned since the early 1960s; they were able to take calculated risks; and they did not have to divert fighters away from air-ground attacks to fly escort missions for bombing strikes as the 'fighters' on this occasion were also the 'bombers'! It was calculated by strike planners that though making full use of the element of surprise, sufficient time would exist not only for the first fighters to drop their bombs, but also for them to climb to altitude in order to use their cannons to cover the withdrawal of the strike – this assessment proved to be correct in 1967.

Although the Israelis focused on a pre-planned strike, its execution was unique in that it did not lead to the participating crews' feeling stifled in their ability to deal with fast-evolving situations. This has since been ascribed to the make up of the Israeli Air Force of 1967 – a small number of highly-trained pilots led by young, but combat-experienced, fighter leaders, who had direct links to those making decisions at the highest level of the Israeli government.

1969-70 – The War of Attrition

The rest of 1967-68 saw a number of air battles, as the opponents eyed each other across the cease-fire lines (which meant the Suez Canal in the case of Egypt), but it was only with the supply of replacement Soviet-produced aircraft and SAMs (and advisors to go with them) that this confrontation began to escalate into a War of Attrition.

Artillery duels and commando raids – their tempo increasing after September 1968 – created a different type of war than that which had been fought in 1967. Strategy was no longer as clear-cut, for national survival was no longer at stake. Rather, it was a war of graduated response and controlled escalation. Increasingly, it also part of the Cold War, as the Soviets backed Egypt and the US backed Israel.

The Israeli Air Force had traditionally operated French-designed fighters since the mid-1950s, but had found itself cut off from new equipment due to French diplomatic priorities in the aftermath of the 1967 War. The US then offered to provide firstly A-4s and then F-4s to make good the shortfall in modern equipment. The Israelis, stressing self-sufficiency, not only had their own nuclear weapons but also an aircraft

industry that would soon produce indigenous fighters based on improved versions of the Mirage III and 5 designs (christened the Nesher and Kfir respectively, they would see extensive service in the 1973 and 1982 wars). They also installed a wide range of home-built electronic systems and warning devices that would make the new US aircraft more suited to Israeli requirements.

Due to the natural barrier of Suez Canal between the Israeli and Egyptian armies, and the latter's numerical superiority in respect to both its size and weight of artillery fire, the Israeli fighter force became the primary offensive weapon of the War of Attrition. However, for the first time its opponent possessed an integrated air defense system, with an emphasis placed on a massive SAM belt. The resurgent Egyptian fighter force was seen as a subordinate force in true Soviet fashion. Meanwhile, the 'hardening' of Arab airbases with individual aircraft shelters (HAS) – especially those in Egypt – proceeded apace under the watchful eye of an increasing number of Soviet advisors.

On 20 July 1969 the Egyptian Air

Force took the offensive with airstrikes in the Sinai. The Israelis responded through progressively escalating, and deeper, airstrikes that brought them up against the new integrated air defense system. As the F-4s arrived in Israel, so they shouldered the burden of these new strikes. In addition, the improving security relationship with the USA led to ECM equipment and tactics developed in South-east Asia being made available to Israeli fighter squadrons.

Despite this influx of American ideas, the latter continued to rely predominantly on their own tactics, stressing close-range air combat maneuvers, the use of the gun and the employment of a relatively small cadre of exceptionally well-trained aircrew. The USAF, rebuilding its own air combat capabilities after the frustrations of 1965-68 over North Vietnam, extracted many lessons from this Israeli experience.

The Israelis were able to carry out their missions during the War of Attrition despite the increasing numbers of SA-2 and SA-3 SAMs (which eventually moved forward to the canal itself), and eventually prevail in

Israelis v Soviets, 30 July 1970

1. After a Soviet MiG-21J attacked and damaged an Israeli A-4, a trap is set for the Soviets with four Mirage IIIs acting as 'live bait' off the Gulf of Suez.

2. Detecting them on radar, the Soivets scramble four alert flights of MiG-21s which are vectored against the Mirages by a female fighter controller.

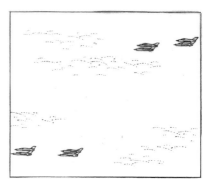

3. The Soviets flew in 'Kuban steps': two-plane elements in trail, stepped up in altitude. GCI vectored them on to the 'six o'clock' of the Mirages.

air combat as well. However, the political and diplomatic content of their fighter operations were often considered more significant than the missions themselves. Thus, there was no sustained attempt to defeat the Egyptian fighter force during the War of Attrition.

The Soviet advisors had largely taken over operational control of the Egyptian air defense system during the War of Attrition. In April 1970, the Soviets escalated their participation by committing an air regiment of upgraded MiG-21Js in an effort to halt increasingly deep Israeli penetrations, and at the

same time increase their own position in Egypt. However, after losing five MiGs to the Israelis in one dogfight, the Soviet fighters were withdrawn.

The War of Attrition ended on 7 August 1970. The Israelis claimed in excess of 110 Arab aircraft shot down for the loss of 16 of their own, although only two jets were lost in air combat. However, the strength of the SAM defenses, and the difficulty of putting together decisive fighter operations when there were political constraints to consider, negated the chance of a decisive victory being achieved on this occasion.

The IDFAF's ability to 'power project' in the Middle East was greatly enhanced when the US government agreed to sell Israel 50 F-4Es and six RF-4Es. These jets were immediately tasked with performing both fighter and bomber roles on the same sortie, thanks to the Phantom II's ability to simultaneously carry a wide range of air-to-air and air-to-ground ordnance.

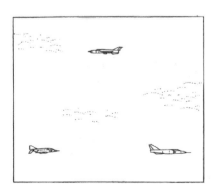

4. But the Mirages are trailed by two Israeli flights with 8 Mirages and four F-4Es flown by veteran pilots with a total of 59 victories between them.

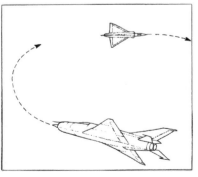

5. The F-4Es launched Sparrow missiles and the MiGs lost mutual support as they tried to evade, the Mirages then closed to attack with Sidewinders.

6. Five Soviets went down: one to a Sparrow, three to Sidewinders (two from an F-4, one from a Mirage) and one to a Mirage's cannon fire.

Israeli Long-Range Fighter Operations

Left: Undoubtedly the best fighter in the IDFAF since the first examples were delivered in the late 1970s, the F-15A has played a vital role in Israeli long-range fighter operations.

The fighter control for the F-15 on the majority of its sorties outside Israeli airspace has been provided by the hard-worked quartet of E-2Cs acquired in 1978. These AWACS aircraft have proven their worth again and again, particularly over the Bekaa Valley in 1982

Today, thanks to an improved international situation, Israel does not believe that its immediate neighbors, even a recalcitrant Syria, pose the greatest threat to its sovereignty. Since the 1980s the Israeli Defense Force Air Force (IDFAF) has been coming to grips with the need to conduct fighter operations against countries further afield such as Iraq, Iran or Libya. This has led them to invest in equipment that allows long-range fighter operations to be undertaken. In addition to the capability inherent in its force of F-15s and KC-707 tankers, the Israelis have also increased the long-range operability of their modernized and updated Phantom 2000s, plus procured 670-gallon drop tanks for their F-16s (which, for long-range strike missions, are empty on take-off and filled at altitude from a tanker) years before they were adopted by the USAF.

Israel's need for long-range fighter capability was first seen during the 1956 War when Soviet and Czechoslovakian advisors saved a number of Egyptian aircraft by ferrying them out of range of Anglo-French air attacks. This led to the Israeli decision to procure twin-jet French Vatour fighters (both air-air and air-ground versions), and these were instrumental in striking at more remote bomber bases in Egypt on the opening day of the 1967 war.

Later in the same conflict the Vatour force struck at airfields in western Iraq – especially H-3, which in 1991 was also repeatedly bombed. The second attack on H-3 on the third day of the war was performed by a flight of four Vatours, escorted by two Mirages. This strike force was intercepted by Jordanian Hunters as it closed on the target, the latter jets having been forced out of their airbases by Israeli attacks on the first day of the war. Because the IDFAF aircraft were at low altitude, the Jordanians were able to press home an improvized version of an attack used so successfully by North Vietnamese MiG-17s against American aircraft over SE Asia.

The Hunters used their superior low-altitude maneuverability to negate the defensive tactics of the Mirages – the delta wing of the Dassault fighter was optimized for high-altitude maneuverability. The Vatours, meanwhile, could do little to stave off repeated attacks from the Jordanian fighters for they were heavy with bombs and fuel, and the resulting engagement saw losses inflicted on both sides. The Israelis disclosed that the Jordanians had shot down one Mirage and two Vatours, and totally disrupted the attack – they claimed two Hunters destroyed in return. However, the Jordanians stated that three Mirages and three Vatours had been downed, all for the loss of a solitary Hunter.

Since this disastrous mission, the Israelis have stressed

the need to avoid air combat on their long-range missions at all cost. In order to achieve this, the IDFAF have applied both the high-level/top-down planning of the 1967 counter-air strikes, and the theory of decentralized execution, which has allowed those carrying out the mission to decide on the tactics employed. There has been no air-air combat associated with these operations for the same reasons that the initial strike on H-3 in 1967 avoided it – thorough intelligence gathering and planning, and effective use of the element of surprise.

Long-range missions undertaken by the IDFAF have also included the use of C-130s to rescue Israeli hostages at Entebbe airport, Uganda, in July 1976. The return of the C-130s required a long-range escort of tanker-supported F-4s, covering the laden Hercules as they boldly flew up the Red Sea past many of Israel's traditional Arab enemies. A more conventional strike staged on 7 June 1981 saw six F-15s and eight F-16s destroy the Iraqi nuclear reactor at Osirak, near Baghdad, whilst on 1 October 1985, F-15s were again used to strike at the PLO's headquarters in

Tunisia. Both of these attacks encountered no air opposition, but in either case the bombers were accompanied by escorts. The Tunisia strike was more complex, the F-15s being accompanied by tankers, which had to refuel them several times, an E-2C radar aircraft and, according to some reports, the same Boeing 707 airborne command post that had supported the Entebbe raid almost a decade earlier.

For a medium-sized power with region-wide adversaries, Israel's ability to conduct long-range fighter operations provides the national command authority with a capability that can have a greater impact on the politics of the Middle East than that associated with conventional warfare. Even countries such as the USA, which possesses the aircraft carriers and forward bases that Israel lacks, have found that they may be called upon to undertake long-range fighter operations – like the use of UK-based F-111s against Libya in 1986 – due to political or diplomatic considerations.

1973 – The Hardest War

Like the War of Attrition, air-to-air combat in the 1973 conflict was of secondary importance to the main battle fought between Israeli fighters and Arab integrated air defenses. This time, the Israelis did not stage a pre-emptive strike due to political and diplomatic constraints. This allowed the Egyptians to open the war on 6 October – commandos crossed the Suez Canal at the same time as Syrian troops launched a massive offensive against the Golan Heights.

In support of the troops on the ground, Egyptian airstrikes hit Israeli positions in Sinai in the opening days of the war. The Egyptian Air Force did not aim at using the initiative to put the Israeli fighter force out of action, however, nor were these strikes well

Above: Both the Egyptians and Syrians possessed large stocks of the Sukhoi Su-7BM fighter-bomber: it is estimated that 160+ were ranged against Israel in the 1973 campaign, during which it proved to be the hardest Arab fast jet to shoot down. This Egyptian example was seen at an undisclosed airfield near the Sinai border just prior to Yom Kippur.

Left: Despite a proliferation of more modern Soviet types entering service with the Arab air forces in the mid- to late 1960s, the venerable MiG-17 still remained a regular opponent of the IDFAF well into the 1970s. Some 210 were employed on ground attack missions during the 1973 war, and 84 were still serving in a similar role with the Syrian Air Force during the Lebanese conflict in the early 1980s.

co-ordinated with the fighter forces committed to defending Egypt. The latter, which had twice proven unable to effectively repulse the attacking Israeli aircraft, or defend its airbases, and had since become part of an integrated air defense network during the War of Attrition, effectively remained tied into that system.

The older Soviet-designed aircraft committed to the air-ground mission –

most notably MiG-17s and Su-7s – lacked range, PGM delivery capability and ECM. They were unlikely to have been able to put Israeli airbases out of action for long, and instead largely concentrated their attacks on reserve positions, artillery emplacements and command and control centers. The dedicated prosecution of these missions subjected them to heavy losses from Israeli fighters and SAMs.

Neither Egypt nor Syria could effectively use their fighter forces to take to the offensive in the first days of the war, in conjunction with their ground forces, as the Israelis had done in 1967. By integrating virtually all their air-to-air capable fighters within the air defense system, the Egyptians had secured a number of advantages, but also incurred substantial limitations that contributed to its ultimate defeat.

The reliance on ground-based radars and GCI interception gave the Egyptian MiGs a degree of situational awareness that would have been impossible with autonomous operations by their MiG-21s, fitted with small radars and possessing poor all-around visibility. Although the SAM belts meant that the MiGs did not have to secure the entire border, integrated air defense meant that they did have to keep up their commitment to defending the gaps in the SAM belts, and could not be concentrated where the national leadership needed them most. By doing this, the Egyptians not only gave up their offensive air-to-air capability against Israeli fighters (which, considering the latter's superiority in this domain was perhaps wise), but also the ability to defend their own troops when they advanced out of the range of the protective SAM umbrella. The Egyptians found out the hard way why flexibility is a necessary part of effective fighter operations.

The Israelis counted on their fighter force to maintain air superiority, defend them against airstrikes and slow down advancing troops as their ground forces mobilized. In the first three days, the fighters carried out all these tasks, but suffered heavy losses to self-propelled air defense weapons (most notably the SA-6 SP SAM and the ZSU-23-4 SP AAA vehicle) covering the Arab forward forces. The Israeli losses to SAMs and radar-directed AAA brought home the importance of effective EW for fighter operations, but it also became apparent that EW superiority was not limited to air-ground operations. If a GCI radar, or that on-board an enemy fighter, can be jammed and radio communications – voice or datalink – interfered with, EW can defeat an enemy's situational awareness.

Although the SAMs and AAA dominated the Arab air defenses, they could not take the offensive against the Israelis. However high their performance, they in effect conceded the initiative to the Israelis before the

first shots had been fired in the 1973 conflict. In addition, the Arabs suffered considerable losses to their own SAMs, underlining the difficulty of IFF even in a 'blue sky' environment like the Middle East. Having a multi-national force complicated the problem, and the losses were at their worst when Iraqi MiGs were committed to action over Syria as their IFF transponders proved to be incompatible with those used by their Arab neighbors. The Israelis, on the other hand, had invested both time

Above: A pair of Egyptian MiG-17Fs perform a border patrol over the Sinai Desert in the late 1950s. Although an effective fighter over North Vietnam when up against the rigid strike formations adopted by the Americans, the subsonic MiG fighter was totally outclassed by the more aggressively flown IDFAF fighters tasked exclusively with seeking out and destroying Arab combat aircraft

Below: Seen in 1981, this MiG-21R of No 26 Sqn, based at Inchas (north of Cairo), was one a number of late-model 'Fishbeds' supplied to the Egyptians as replacements after the Yom Kippur War.

and money in equipping all their combat aircraft with advanced IFF equipment that reduced their own losses to 'friendly fire'.

The 1973 war showed that it was easy to demand too much of fighter operations, for the Israelis had expected their air superiority to give them another victory like that experienced some six years before. But the Arab offensive, and the strength of their air defenses, made the Israeli Air Force interventions in the ground battles – on the Egyptian bridgehead on the 6th, on the Syrian armored columns and SAM sites on the 7th and against the Egyptian canal crossings on the 8th – costly affairs. Of the 115 to 120 aircraft the Israelis lost in the war, about 45 to 50 were lost in the first three days alone.

But neither the Egyptian nor the Syrian systems were able to prevent the Israeli Air Force pounding through defenses and hitting increasingly deeper

targets, including airbases, from on 9 October onwards. Over Syria, the Israelis also staged a counter-value campaign by hitting economic targets. In Egypt, however, the HAS program

The wreckage of a MiG-21PF shot down over the Golan Heights during the 1973 clash. The MiG-21, in its numerous versions, provided the bulk of the IDFAF's victories between 1967 and 1982 as it was flown by all Arab air arms except the Jordanians.

Foxbat Hunting

One of the sidelights to fighter operations in the Middle East during the 1970s and 80s centered around the repeated Israeli attempts to counter MiG-25 'Foxbat' operations – both the fighter and reconnaissance versions of this high-flying aircraft were operated within this time frame by the IDFAF's Arab opponents.

The first MiG-25 operations in the region were undertaken by a detachment of Soviet Air Force recce MiG-25R 'Foxbat-Bs', deployed to Egypt in October 1971 – their objective was to reconnoitre Israeli positions in the wake of the War of Attrition. Following a number of sorties along the Suez Canal, a MiG-25R made a provocative long-range overflight of Israel on 10 October which the IDFAF were unable to counter. However, when a Soviet 'Foxbat' attempted a repeat overflight on 6 November the Israelis were ready with a flight of stripped-down F-4Es, armed with Sparrows.

The MiG was attacked in a high-altitude snap attack – reportedly the F-4Es fired Sparrow missiles in a high-angle climb from 44,000 ft – head-on at the 'Foxbat', which was cruising at 76,000 ft. What apparently let the attack down was that the proximity fuze delay on the Sparrows (probably late AIM-7E models) could not cope with the Mach 3 speed of the 'Foxbat', and by the time they detonated, the MiG was out of their lethal radius.

Nevertheless, it was undoubtedly a sobering experience for the Soviet MiG-25 crews to see missiles tracking them at that height for the very first time.

Only two subsequent missions were flown (in March and May 1972), and these overflew the Sinai rather than Israel itself. It is believed that the photographs taken in these missions were later provided to the Egyptians, who found them invaluable in their planning for the 1973 War.

The Soviet 'Foxbats' were withdrawn in July 1972, only to return in the autumn of the following year after the cessation of the 1973 war. These aircraft would not penetrate Israeli airspace again, however, and as Egyptian relations with Moscow deteriorated, the detachment moved to Syria. There, both fighter and recce 'Foxbats' continued to fly regularly, and whilst originally a purely Soviet deployment, it eventually took on a Syrian component – the aircraft carried Syrian markings. Despite their 'arabification', the MiG-25s remained dependent on Soviet advisors and logistics support throughout – indeed, Syria's remaining 'Foxbats' are still reportedly maintained by Russian engineers today.

The Israelis were unable to counter the Syrian MiG-25 'Foxbat-A' fighters until the introduction of the F-15A into service. They then decided to 'defang' the Syrian 'Foxbat' threat once and for all by drawing them into a yielded results – the Israelis claimed to have destroyed 22 Egyptian aircraft on the ground, whilst the latter admitted just three. In either event, it provided a strong contrast with the results achieved in 1967.

Again, high sortie generation rates and multiple crews (although these were limited by Israeli insistence in emphasizing quality rather than quantity in aircrew ranks, an option not available to larger Arab air arms) proved a valuable force multiplier for the Israelis. Similarly, higher availability rates helped negate the Arab's two to one superiority in fighter numbers,

This war also demonstrated that airbase attack as a means of offensive counter-air assault did not eclipse air-to-air combat in non-nuclear warfare. More fighters were shot down in dogfights than were destroyed on the ground by each side, with the Israelis claiming 287 Arab aircraft destroyed for the loss of

between 10 and 21 of their own. These numbers represented almost two-thirds of the total Arab losses during the war, whilst for the Israelis it was just about a sixth of their overall figure. The combination of hardening and the proliferation of airbase defense systems, especially SAMs, had limited ground kills for both sides.

The Egyptian fighter force's limitations in carrying out offensive fighter operations became evident when, on 14 October, the Egyptian Army tried to advance from the bridgeheads over the Suez Canal towards the passes that led deeper into the Sinai. The bulk of the Egyptian fighter force, committed to the integrated air defense system, was heavily engaged defending against deep penetration Israeli attacks at the time, and lacked the flexibility to cover the advancing armor, which suffered heavy losses from Israeli airstrikes.

Once the Israelis took the offensive

and advanced over the Suez Canal into Africa, they started to put the SAM sites out of action. This brought the Egyptian Air Force into a battle for the bridgeheads, and again superior Israeli tactics and training resulted in lopsided victory ratios.

This conflict was in stark contrast to the 1967 war in that Israeli fighter operations in the latter campaign were successful because of brilliant operational planning, whereas in 1973 they succeed despite the absence of a coherent, over-arching, plan. Rather, the operational capability of the Israeli fighter force gave it an ability to improvise and adapt when the nation was subjected to a surprise attack. Because of the fundamental strengths of their fighter force, and the limitations of those of their opponents, the Israelis were able to overcome the assault in a way that their enemies were unable to do in 1967.

peacetime battle with F-15s. On 13 February 1981, two Israeli RF-4Es flew a high-altitude reconnaissance mission over the Lebanon to report on renewed Syrian offensive action. The Israelis thought that this mission was likely to evoke a Syrian response, and sure enough two MiG-25s were scrambled and climbed after the RF-4s. However, as they entered firing range on the rapidly fleeing Phantom IIs, they found that their targets had started to both dispense chaff and send out jamming signals from their ECM pods – a combination of the two had effectively obliterated the MiG-25s' radar picture. Meanwhile, a pair of patrolling F-15As that had been vectored onto the Syrian fighters by either an E-2C or ground-based radar, popped out of the clouds undetected and fired AIM-7F Sparrow AAMs at the 'blind' 'Foxbats'. One of the MiG-25s was destroyed, but the other escaped to retell the tale. Despite this loss, another MiG-25 attack was staged against RF-4Es over the Bekkaa Valley on 29 July 1981, and this again resulted in another 'Foxbat' falling victim to escorting F-15As.

Meanwhile, Syrian recce MiG-25s, which were capable of achieving faster speed and flying at higher altitudes than the fighter version, continued to overfly the Lebanon until 31 August 1983 when one was damaged by a modified Israeli HAWK SAM and forced down into the clutches of a waiting F-15A.

The hardest target tackled by the IDFAF in over 40 years of conflict, the MiG-25 remained untouchable for a decade until it was finally 'bested' by the F-15A.

1982 – The Battle for Lebanon

The most feared fighter over the Bekaa Valley in 1982, the F-15 Eagle cut swathes through the opposing Syrian MiG formations with their AIM-9L, Shafrir 2 and AIM-7F Sparrow III missiles. Around 50 A- and B-model Eagles have seen combat with the IDFAF over the past two decades.

Israeli fighter operations in 1982 were perhaps the most outstanding example of air-to-air success in the jet age. Eighty-two fighters – predominantly Syrian MiG-21s and MiG-23s – were destroyed without loss by Israeli fighters – predominantly F-15s and F-16s. As in 1967, operational planning by the Israelis (again, they saw the enemy as a system, not just fighters), backed up by superior aircraft, tactics, training and technology, assured the victory. It was apparent that the gap between the Israelis and their opponents had widened since 1973.

Achieving victory in 1982 was not as easy as it had been in 1967, however. The Syrian Air Force was part of an integrated air defense system in place in the Lebanon, which was basically an extension of that in place in the mother country itself. Following their heavy losses at the hands of Syrian SAMs during suppression missions in 1973, the Israelis had deployed long-range surface-to-surface systems such as US-

built Lance and Cricket missiles. The Israeli Air Force also possessed large numbers of ELINT and photo recon UAVs (some with real-time data links) and fighters with Shrike and Standard ARMs.

The Israeli ground advance into the Lebanon in 1982 included the extensive use of UAVs as both reconnaissance platforms, and targets to excite SAMs – the latter exposed the sites to air attack with ARMs. Israeli long-range artillery also forced some self-propelled SA-6 and SA-8 SAM units out of the southern Bekkaa Valley to be attacked whilst in travel mode by Israeli aircraft – this duly brought the Syrian fighter force into action over the Lebanon to try and cover the gaps in the SAM coverage, plus protect the retreating units.

Israeli fighter operations were, however, politically constrained, as neither Israel or Syria wanted the fighting to spread to the Golan – this restriction was overcome by the former through effective operational planning. By threatening the SAMs and Syrian forces in the Lebanon, the Israelis were able to draw enemy fighters out of their bases in Syria itself, which would otherwise have acted as sanctuaries. Once they were committed to battle, the Israeli fighters then had the ability to act in a way that a less operationally-proficient force would probably not have been able to.

They used all-aspect infrared guided missiles such as the US-designed AIM-9L Sidewinders and Israeli-designed Shafrirs. The Israelis did not have to maneuver into the attacking fighter's 'six o'clock position' for the first time in aerial combat. Sparrow BVR AAMs – now updated with state-of-the-art technology, and far advanced from those used over Vietnam and in the 1973 War – also accounted for several MiGs. The Syrian fighters were armed with AA-2 Atolls and AA-8 Aphids which, like all previous IR AAMs, were rear-aspect only missiles. They never got the chance to use them against the Israelis, for the combination of all-aspect missiles and superior situational awareness negated the Syrian fighter force as thoroughly as the well-planned operation had negated their SAMs and radars.

The Israelis again demonstrated the importance of situational awareness. Ground-based radars, E-2C AWACS aircraft and modified Boeing 707s doing stand-off jamming and real time ELINT all passed data to the fighters. The Israelis did not tie their fighters to strict GCI tactics, however, instead using their effective communications links (another key technological advance) to provide the situational awareness. Just as in previous battles with Arab air forces, the Israelis let the fighter leaders who were in the air, making use of their advanced radar, decide how the battle would be fought. The combination of combat experience and excellent training, guided by a coherent concept of operations, made them highly successful.

1982 – One-Sided Fighter Operations

The 1982 air battles over the Lebanon offered a model for future fighter operations – one-sided victory through air combat. Putting the Syrian fighter force out of action by attacking its bases was not seen as politically acceptable by the Israelis. Instead, their fighters had to operate over areas where the Syrians had strong SAM defenses, yet they were able to carry out their mission through the employment of an effective, integrated, operational response.

As has often been the case, successful Israeli fighter operations were made possible through the exploitation of failings in their opponents' force structure. Syrian expansion of its fighter force to confront Israel had manifested itself in a desire to deploy large numbers of aircraft, SAMs and radar sites, rather than improving the quality of its forces. The fact that the Syrians had little grasp on how to both integrate and operate all this hardware effectively was graphically shown in the way that he Syrian force was unable to survive, let alone prevail, against a world-class opponent. Their comprehensive defeat prefigured the equally one-sided annihilation of the Iraqi fighter force in 1991.

Returning to 1982, the Israelis cited the effectiveness of Syrian Army commanders in waging war against overwhelming numbers of attacking aircraft, but gave no praise to the totally ineffectual Air Force. Indeed, the only aircraft that had been able to inflict losses on the Israelis on the ground were Syrian anti-tank helicopters. The Syrians Air Force's initial response to this comprehensive defeat was to blame their Soviet-built aircraft and hardware, and they certainly had some justification for Arab fighters had managed to hit two or more Israeli jets with AAMs, but the enhanced survivability features of F-15s and F-16s got them back to base – this was a unique advantage that western fighters introduced in the 1970s had over their predecessors, which had been designed in the era of massive nuclear retaliation when hits were assumed to be fatal.

Despite an initial blaming of Soviet equipment, the Syrians were left with little choice but to rely almost exclusively on weapons provided by Moscow, for the acquisition of Western hardware was totally out of the question. Rebuilding their fighter force was the major priority, and to do this Syria's ties with the Soviet Union would have to become even more binding – demonstrating once again the ability of fighter operations to shape national policy in the Middle East. In order to achieve fighter protection as quickly as possible, Syria had to temporarily cede control of their air defenses to the Soviets. The latter swiftly rebuilt the force, focusing its emphasis more on offensive operations, rather than adopting the typically rigid defensive structure that had been synonymous with Soviet systems in the Middle East in the 1960s and 70s. For example, rather than just supply new squadrons with dozens of replacement MiG-21 and -23 air superiority fighters, the Soviets provided a mixed force of jets which also included the highly-capable Su-22 'Fitter-G' strike aircraft.

However, as has so often been the case when smaller countries have attempted to adopt 'superpower' solutions to military problems, Syria was thwarted in its attempt to create a new air force to rival the IDFAF not by a reversal in combat, but rather through non-payment of the bills – in 1987 the Soviets decided that the Syrians would receive no more MiGs on credit. They had proven to be poor opponents for the Israelis in the air in 1982, and were now unable to match them fiscally either.

Future Arab-Israeli Wars

Since 1982, there have been no major challenges to the Israeli fighter forces. On the rare occasions when they have encountered an airborne enemy – such as the 1986 Syrian MiG-23 shoot-downs over Lebanon – the ensuing engagements have been concluded quickly, and the results rather one-sided.

Today, the threat to Israeli security is no longer the conventional air attack, but rather the ballistic missile, which is soon to be joined by land-attack cruise missiles. The fighter force, which was forced to sit out the 1991 Iraqi missile attacks on Israel, may be back in the game with weapons such as the Moab missile – this weapon is supposed to be able to intercept ballistic missiles in their boost phase. As in 1967, pre-emptive strikes against such threats is likely to be seen as a valid policy option by the Israeli Defense Force.

Fighter operations in Israel have succeeded, in the main, because they rested on the solid foundation of world-class aircrew, excellent tactics and good aircraft. After 1969-70, they also had the advantage of the relationship with the US, which provided for a flow of technology and ideas (often both ways). While the provision of US fighters and missiles has been enough to win the Israelis the vast majority of the dogfights they have fought, it was not, by itself, enough to create effective fighter operations. That the Israelis have done themselves since 1956.

While Israel's Arab opponents – especially Egypt – could not measure up on a tactical level, they also failed to evolve an effective approach to fighter operations. After the defeat of 1967, their total embracing of the Soviet-style integrated air defense system seemed to provide both a coherent approach to fighter operations, and the advantage of a foreign patron. Neither proved to

Fighters And Countermeasures

In air-air operations, a fighter must not only defeat its opponent in the skies, but be able to do so in the face of a hostile integrated air defense system. The only exceptions to this rule are interceptors which are designed purely to operate over friendly territory.

The enthusiasm for light air-air fighters seen in the late 1970s and early 80s failed to come to grips with the changing nature of fighter operations. Making 'not a pound for air-to-ground' a design principle may seem a good idea when you are looking at producing a fighter to counter an enemy interceptor in a purely one-on-one dogfight. However, experience in combat over the decades has shown that the majority of air-to-air jet fighter operations do not exclusively center on the destruction of enemy aircraft – they are about securing air superiority in the face of an integrated air defense system.

The Israelis were exposed to the increasing technical and tactical nature of offensive fighter operations between 1967 and 73. They realized that their adversaries would look for ways to minimize the IDFAF's undoubted superiority in air combat, and so the Egyptian integrated air defense system was born. This forced the Israelis to initially improvize a response until they could procure the technology to effectively defeat it. The immediate measures adopted ranged in sophistication from the fitment of US-built radar homing and warning (RHAW) equipment to the stuffing of radar jamming chaff (aluminium strips cut to varying lengths) into the air brakes of fighter aircraft – when the brakes were deployed in combat, the chaff was discharged into the jet's slipstream.

Despite a quantitative increase in the effectiveness of the countermeasures adopted, the employment of new Soviet-designed SAMs like the SA-3 during the War of Attrition in 1969-70 and the SA-6 in the Yom Kippur War of 1973 claimed a number of Israeli fighters before a combination of US-sourced countermeasures (both passive RHAW and active jamming, usually carried in USAF-issue pods) and Israeli-developed evasive techniques effectively neutralized the SAM threat.

In the future, fighters will have to defeat both aerial and surface-based opponents at the same time. After the Gulf War the USAF, amid much criticism, disbanded its specialized 'Wild Weasel' SEAD units as a cost-cutting measure. Today, fighters such as USAF F-15C, F-16C and USN/USMC F/A-18Cs patrol the skies over Iraq and Bosnia armed with both air-to-air missiles and ARMs such as the AGM-88 HARM, this mix of ordnance being able to defeat enemy fighters and SAMs alike. Each of these aircraft also carries countermeasures needed against both fighters and SAMs – chaff, IR decoy flares and jammers. Considering the demands for near-zero losses that have dominated US military thinking at all levels in the post-Cold War era, it is hard to imagine an unsophisticated 'light fighter' being able to carry out this range of operations against both air and ground targets without sustaining casualties.

be the case. The Soviets turned out to be unwilling to sustain their security relationship with Arab air arms (even that with Syria faded after their credit was cut off in 1987), while the Soviet-model integrated air defense system, devised for homeland defense, did not prove adaptable to the Middle East. This latter concept of operations in 1973 and 1982 failed to maximize the inherent strengths of the fighter – speed and flexibility. Robbed of these advantages, all the Arab fighter forces were left with was the undoubted courage of their pilots, but in the modern age, this alone produces not victory, but long casualty lists.

Above: Although the Eagle has been the primary air superiority fighter in the IDFAF for 20 years, the F-16 Fighting Falcon has also acquitted itself well.

Below: Israel acquired the F-16 in the early 1980s and it was soon used in long range operations, attacking the Iraqi nuclear facility near Baghdad.

The Rebirth of Fighter Operations – The Last Decades of the Cold War

In the last 25 years of the Cold War (1967-91), the old certainties were gone. For a while the adversary appeared to be less evil than it had done in Stalin's time, until events as diverse as the Afghanistan War, the deployment of SS-20 missiles into Eastern Europe and the translation of Solzhenitsyn's works reminded us otherwise. For a while, in the 'low and dishonest' decade of the 1970s, it appeared that what Moscow called 'the correlation of forces' had indeed shifted in favor of the USSR. No one could assume the 'good guys' were going to win anymore.

By this stage in the Cold War, conflict no longer automatically meant nuclear destruction. The nuclear primacy that had shaped fighter tactics and operations in the 1950s and early 60s was inadequate to meet changes such as the NATO strategy of flexible response, adopted in the mid-1960s. In order to carry out this new style of warfare,

fighter operations would also have to be equally flexible. Motivating many of the changes were lessons emerging from conflicts fought in the Third World in the 1960s. Vietnam, the Middle East Wars and the conflicts between India and Pakistan in 1965 and 71 showed how different aspects of changing technologies were influencing fighter operations.

During the Cold War the closest NATO fighters got to engaging the 'enemy' was when they were vectored onto a patrolling 'Bear' or 'Badger' long-range bomber over the Atlantic or North Sea. This 'close encounter' occurred in the northern quick reaction alert area in February 1973 between a No 43 Sqn Phantom FG 1, scrambled from Leuchars in Scotland, and a Tu-95 'Bear-D'.

Changes East And West

Above: The MiG-23MF 'Flogger' was a prime example of the new multi-role fighter-bomber that the Soviet aerospace industry built in vast quantities in the early 1970s. At this time, the Communist bloc realized that it could probably defeat NATO in Europe without having to resort to nuclear weapons

Left: The Sukhoi Su-15 of just a few years earlier was very much a Cold War 'warrior' of the old school, built solely to intercept in-coming nuclear bombers at high speed and high altitude.

Soviet military aviation also changed its approach to fighter operations in the second half of the Cold War. The Communists now considered that an initial, non-nuclear, period of a war was possible. The need to prevail in such conditions led them to look at their own operational heritage from the Second World War and the immediate postwar years and, by the mid-1970s, the concept of theater air and air defenses operations, which had been eclipsed in the years of nuclear primacy was revived again.

The need to carry out these operations imposed new requirements for aircraft, tactics and training, and contributed to the Soviets carrying out the largest, and most prolonged, peacetime arms build-up ever seen. They were able to gain a formidable capability in conventional fighter operations, but their national economy was bankrupted in the process.

SR-71 – the Ultimate Target

During the Cold War the routine operations of one type of USAF aircraft proved more of an irritant to US adversaries than any other. The Lockheed SR-71 was capable of attaining higher speeds – over Mach 3 – and higher operational altitudes – up to 100,000 ft – than any contemporary reconnaissance aircraft, and both these attributes made it virtually untouchable. It was the ultimate product of the 'brute force' era (the late 1950s through to the early 1960s) in aeronautical engineering, with two huge turbo-ramjet engines driving a radically streamlined airframe. Indeed, it was only late in the SR-71's career when 'stealth technology' became watchwords for future combat aircraft that it dawned on aerospace engineers just how sophisticated the jet's shape really was. Not only could it withstand the heat stresses present when flying at Mach 3 in the upper atmosphere, but it also had a radar return far smaller than most modern fast jet types almost three decades its junior. This meant that most radars would either be unable to detect the SR-71 when flying at its operational cruising height and speed, or would simply filter out any return that may have been picked up as a spurious 'ghost in the machine'.

Most Soviet attempts to shoot down SR-71s were made by SAMs. Similarly, the North Koreans also fired off substantial number of SA-2s and SA-5s at the high flying jet over the years, as did the Cubans until regular USAF overflights were halted in 1977. Finally, in the 1973 Yom Kippur War, the Egyptians were reportedly planning (with Soviet cueing) to use SA-2s in an attempt to shoot down SR-71 overflights none of these launches met with success.

Indeed, the main threat to the SR-71 came not from ground-launched missiles, but from high-altitude interceptors such as the MiG-25 'Foxbat' and MiG-31 'Foxhound'. If these fighters could be vectored into the right position by GCI, they could make a zoom climb to maximum altitude and fire off long-range AAMs that could reach the altitude of even the highest-flying SR-71. In this case, the jet's two-man crew would have to defeat the missile through the use of their sophisticated on-board ECM equipment – this had proven effective against North Korean SA-5s, which could just about reach the SR-71's operational altitude.

Although the USAF never actual overflew the USSR in their SR-71s, the Soviets considered the jet to be a major annoyance simply because they could not intercept it. The arrival of the MiG-25 into service in 1972 went some way to assuaging Soviet fears about the invincibility of the Lockheed jet, and VVS units equipped with 'Foxbats' were strategically stationed on the eastern and western borders of the USSR to keep the SR-71 at bay – a fact spectacularly underlined when a disgruntled pilot from the Vladivostok detachment defected to Japan in 1976.

The Soviets continued to develop new anti-SR-71 tactics, and on 3 June 1986 these were demonstrated to a USAF

Above: Like the Su-15, the mighty MiG-25 was built to perform a specific function in true Soviet tradition – intercept and destroy the USAF's SR-71 recce platform. Although able to climb to almost 68,000 ft at speeds approaching Mach 3, the early versions of the 'Foxbat' were still unable to counter the SR-71 threat. This MiG-25P is equipped with its full complement of two IR-homing and two radar-homing AA-6 AAMs.

Left: With the introduction of the MiG-31 to PVO service in late 1982, the Soviets at last had an aircraft that could effectively combat the SR-71. Based on the MiG-25, the new interceptor featured a much better phased-array radar, coupled with more effective AAMs like the R-33.

Below: The 'Foxbat' was also modified into a dedicated recce platform, this particular MiG-25R relying on a SLAR (side-looking airborne radar) beneath the grey panel forward of the red number 50.

crew on a mission over the Barents Sea. Six MiG-31 'Foxhounds', vastly superior to the MiG-25 'Foxbat', performed a co-ordinated intercept that would have subjected the SR-71 to an all-angle AAM attack that even a combination of high-altitude maneuverability and ECM could not have defeated. Fortunately for the crew of the American jet, the interception took place over international waters, but the Soviets had nevertheless proved their point. It is uncertain whether this incident was a factor in the USAF's decision to retire the SR-71 three years later, although their flexible flying schedule and unmatched performance were sorely missed during Operation Desert Storm.

New Fighters in a New Age

A new generation of fighters emerged in the 1970s to accelerate the rebirth of air combat operations. In the US, these included the USAF's F-15 and F-16 and the Navy's F-14 and F/A-18; in Europe, the Mirage F1 and 2000 and Tornado; and in the 1980s, the MiG-29 and Su-27 in the Soviet Union. These fighters had greater capability and flexibility than those of earlier decades, but with a commensurate rise in unit price – the latter has had a detrimental effect on the numbers built.

There was less of the rapid succession of designs that marked the 1950s, caused by an unprecedented level of technological advancement. Longevity of

aircraft designs dominated the period, and by the end of the Cold War, new F-15Es coming off the production line were designed with a 27-year airframe life. But while the aircraft themselves may be longer lived, their components and weapons were more likely to be interchangeable and upgradeable. The new fighters continued the trend of moving to multi-role, multi-engine fighters from single role, single engine fighters. The USAF/USN and then the RAF had first come to grips with these problems in the 1950s and 60s. The rest of the world soon followed suit, although few air arms in the Third World had been able to afford the new

technologies by 1991.

US fighters increasingly began to dominate the air forces of the 'free world'. The F-4, operational throughout this period, set the standard for all fighters worldwide for a generation. Combat proven in Vietnam, the Middle East and, at the very end of its career with the USAF, the Gulf War, it was capable, upgradeable and effective in a range of air-air and air-ground missions. But, having entered service in 1962, it represented the culmination of the old designs rather than the start of the new ones.

The F-15 and F-16 were the first USAF aircraft designed primarily to

Above: Truly one of the great Cold War fighters, the F-4 Phantom II was passed down to ANG and reserve units within the USAF in the early 1980s

Left: The USAF's requirement for multi-role fighters rather than air superiority interceptors, led McDonnell Douglas to convert their F-15C prototype into the Strike Eagle. Capable of carrying a useful warload without the need of dedicated fighter protection, the F-15E began to enter service in the late 1980s

Below: Although a truly multi-role combat aircraft in the mould of the F-15E, this F/A-18A of the RAAF's No 3 Sqn is configured purely as fighter.

defeat enemy fighters since the mid-1950s. They represented the concept of a high-low mix that has been seen in fighter forces throughout the jet age, with the twin-engined F-15 being at the high, more expensive, end. Improved engines provided thrust-to-weight ratios that at last surpassed one to one at combat weights. Even though designed for air-to-air combat (the 'not a pound for air-to-ground'

motto that was used for post-Korea fighter designs was revived for the F-16), both of these fighters eventually evolved into highly-capable fighter-bombers.

Their main competition came from French-built Mirages and multi-national European designs such as the Jaguar and Tornado. The latter aircraft reflected the changing operational requirements of NATO, as well as the necessity to secure export sales. The Tornado's primary mission is air-to-ground, but the RAF, in need of a Phantom II replacement able to use BVR missiles to defend the UK and its Atlantic approaches, modified the airframe to carry both Skyflash (a British derivative of the Sparrow II) and an air-search-optimized radar. The resulting machine entered frontline service as the Tornado F.3 in the late 1980s.

The Mirage F1 of a decade earlier, and its Mirage 2000 successor, failed to recapture the export success of the Mirage III, but nevertheless remained mainstays of both the French Air Force and a small number of foreign operators.

The Soviets, and those countries supplied by them, relied on the MiG-21/-23/-27 and Su-7/-17/-22 series aircraft (with the swing-wing Su-24 as the high-end air-ground fighter) for their theater air-air and air-ground missions. In their country of origin, these machines were supplemented by specialized interceptors like the Su-15 and the massive Tu-128, which defended the Soviet Union well into the early 1980s.

It was only in the last decade of the Cold War that Soviet air-air operations benefited from new technology in the form of the MiG-29 and Su-27. These were twin-engined, all-weather fighters that could carry out autonomous air combat operations every bit as well as their western counterparts, due principally to advances in radars, long-range radar-guided missiles and fly-by-wire technology. Unlike previous Soviet fighters, they were no longer tied to GCI control for air combat.

The new fighters also blurred the distinction between air defense of the homeland and frontal aviation. For example, the Su-27, although apparently intended for air defense, also had obvious value in theater air operations – the strike-optimized derivatives of the jet that have appeared from Sukhoi over the past four years bear testament to this.

The proliferation of these fighters was very restricted when compared with their predecessors from the first half of the Cold War. This divergence was pronounced even in air arms relying on Soviet-designed fighters, MiG-29s being sold in modest numbers for export compared with MiG-21s or MiG-23s primarily because of the complexity and cost of the former type. Also, political changes within the Soviet Union meant that by the time the new MiG became eligible for export, its manufacturers were no longer able to afford to sell it to diplomatically-favored clients at discount rates.

Above: The Mirage F1C was Dassault's replacement for the hugely successful Mirage III/5 family, and like its predecessors, the new jet could tote a mind-boggling arsenal of weapons for both air-to-air and air-to-ground missions. This early-production jet is seen firing off a medium range Matra Super 530 AAM during weapons compatibility trials

Top left: As with their previous fighter designs, the Swedes went their own way when it came to producing a replacement multi-role aircraft for the excellent Draken of the late 1950s. The result was the Saab Viggen, whose close coupled-canard layout gives it a distinct appearance. It will remain operational well into the next century.

Left: The navalized MiG-29K completed carrier trials aboard the Admiral Kuznetsov in the early 1990s, prior to the Russian Navy opting for the bigger Su-33 instead. This choice may still prove to be academic, because funding problems have all but crippled the navy's ability to operate.

Air Defense

The air defense mission that dominated fighter operations in the 1950s and 60s diminished in importance in the latter decades of the Cold War. This reflected the rise of the ballistic missile and the decline of the manned bomber as the nuclear weapon delivery system of choice in the 1960s. By the 1970s, with the two superpowers agreeing to limited defense against ICBMs, it seemed irrational to invest in defending against bombers delivering the same nuclear weapons.

Impelled by this logic, the United States starting dismantling its national air defense capability during the Vietnam War. By the 1970s, it had been reduced to a fraction of its height of the Cold War. The USAF got out of the long-range SAM business in the

early 1970s with the retirement of US-based BOMARCs, followed by the RAF a decade later with the phasing out of UK-based Bloodhound batteries.

Yet, the air defense mission never went away. In the 1980s the cruise missile, which could be launched from submarines, ships or aircraft. brought it back into focus for the Americans. There were, however, few new resources allocated to the air defense mission in the US, but in the UK, the increasing range and capability of Soviet theater aircraft kept the air defense mission important right through to the end of the Cold War.

The Soviets had maintained a large numbers of fighters as part of their integrated air defense system right up to the end of the Cold War. This was

Right: Aerial refueling was a feature of almost every Lightning sortie thanks to the jet's chronically short 'legs' on internal fuel only. Photographed high over northern Germany in November 1973, this No 19 Sqn F 2A from Gutersloh (sited just 80 miles from the then East German border) is seen a matter of feet away from the port wing drogue trailed behind a No 57 Sqn Victor K 2.

Like the F-4 Phantom, the Lightning was in service for much of the Cold War, performing countless QRA scrambles over Germany and off the northern coast of Great Britain. It also saw limited service in the Middle East with the Saudi and Kuwaiti air forces – the aircraft closest to the camera is a Firestreak-equipped Kuwaiti Air Force T 55.

in response to the continued western bomber threat, especially from SAC, supplemented by that from US and NATO attack aircraft. Soviet air defense fighters were involved in some of the more newsworthy events of the later stages of the Cold War, including the destruction of a Korean Air Lines 747 in 1983 and, in an effort to avoid any such repetition of civilian death, the sparing of a West German youth who, in 1987, flew eastwards into the Soviet Union and landed his Cessna 172 in Red Square.

Force Reconstitution and Fighter Operations

One of the key determinants in the capacity of an air arm to sustain effective operations is the reconstitutional ability of its fighter force. Essentially this means how quickly can frontline units make good combat losses and continue to effectively take the fight to the enemy. A simple rule of aerial warfare dictates that an adversary's fighter force is unlikely to be put out of action unless it loses its force reconstitution capability.

In Korea and Vietnam the Americans fought opposing fighter forces which were able to continue air combat operations, despite unfavorable loss ratios, because of their substantial force reconstitution capabilities. The latter was achieved through a combination of the Soviet Union underpinning their efforts through its huge industrial resource, and China providing sanctuaries where both North Korean and North Vietnamese forces could regroup and refit. In the Middle East, however, the Arab fighter forces took years to reconstitute themselves after their defeats in 1956 and 1973. Today,

the Iraqi fighter force is still attempting to regain its pre-1991 capability some six years after Desert Storm. In these situations, the number of aircraft, aircrew and technicians available to the air forces in question were limited in their number, and as all had been committed to maintaining a large force structure that could not be funded (or manned) without heavy external support any losses incurred have proven difficult to replace.

During the Cold War, the Soviets invested in substantial force reconstitution capabilities for their fighters. This was reflected in their policy of keeping a large number of fighters in war reserve stocks, both in the Soviet Union and in eastern Europe. Many of these reserves were kept crated up in huge storage facilities, the Soviets believing that their relatively simple modular designs would allow these aircraft to be rapidly assembled as part of a massive force reconstitution program should most of their original fighter force be knocked out by NATO offensive counter-air operations. Large quantities of war reserve spares were also pre-positioned with the fighters.

Increasing the Pace of Change

There was now a new generation of leaders commanding fighter wings, planning operations and providing the necessary impetus for the development of aircraft, tactics, technology and training. Those fighter forces that were willing to train hard and come to grips with changing operational requirements could make these new men even more competent than the preceding generation (as the British demonstrated in the Falklands). This required substantial investments in both flying hours and large-scale exercises, which many air arms – already fiscally stretched by trying to procure the new technologies – were unable to afford.

The impact of the microchip revolution on fighter operations was widespread, making possible everything from the instrumented training ranges on which western pilots improved their skills, to the power-managed radar jammers which gave fighters the ability to defend themselves against both SAMs and BVR AAMs, to the fly-by-wire flight controls which helped give aircraft such as the F-16 their superb maneuverability. Fighter weapons, sensors and communications equipment all became more effective through the use of this technology.

The Operational Level of Fighter Combat

Air arms – especially English speaking air arms – have been late comers to embracing the realities of operational-level war. Historically speaking, they have been more concerned with developing and using aircraft and technology, whilst leaving strategy and doctrine to the 'bomber barons' who 'worshipped at the shrines' of Douhet and Trenchard.

Despite this apparent disinterest in strategies and tactics exhibited by 'frontline flyers', ever since the earliest years of fighter combat, squadron commanders have been making operational war-fighting decisions similar to those that confront their successors today. For example, in the summer of 1918 Group Captain Ludlow Hewitt of the RAF's 10th Brigade – a 'composite wing', in contemporary parlance – developed an operational plan for attacking German airfields with what would today be recognizable to a modern fighter pilot as a 'strike package'.

It comprized AAA suppression aircraft, dedicated bombers, close escort fighters and more escorts sweeping ahead of the main attacking force in likely areas of interception. Hewitt left the tactics of how to make the best use of the fighters to the individual flight and squadron leaders (the men who knew both the aircraft and their individual pilots the best), and instead concerned himself with melding the different types of aircraft, and their varying capabilities, together in sufficient strength to give the mission a fair chance of success.

Fighter tactics, the aces and the colorful aircraft themselves have often drawn the most attention from both professionals and enthusiasts alike when considering air combat. Yet repeatedly since 1945 (and back to the origins of air combat itself), sound operational concepts, implemented with skill and bravery, have either exploited or exposed the strengths and weakness inherent in both pilots and their aircraft.

Left: The arrival of the F-16 Fighting Falcon in 1978 gave the USAF a multi-role 'light fighter' replacement for its venerable F-4 Phantom II. This particular jet was one of the first pre-production F-16Bs built by General Dynamics, and although having a slightly reduced internal fuel capacity to allow for the fitment of a second seat, the 'twin stick' B-model is just as combat capable as the F-16A.

Right: The USAF learnt many lessons in Vietnam, one of which was the need for suitably modified aircraft to undertake specialized missions. The ability of the Phantom II to operate as both a fighter and a bomber made it a prime candidate and it duly fell to a handful of converted F-4Es to perform the hazardous 'Wild Weasel' tasking. Designated F-4Gs, these jets could employ a wide array of ordnance to complete their anti-radar mission, as ably demonstrated by this 37th TFW jet.

Fighter Operations in the 1980s

After their disappointing combat debut in the 1960s, the improved Sparrow AAM reaped much success over North Vietnam in 1972 and over the Middle East the following year. This drastic reversal in the missile's fortunes had at last underlined the increasing importance of the BVR weapon. As always, one of the primary practitioners of these type of fighter operations was the USN, whose F-14 Tomcat, armed with long-range Phoenix AAMs, was introduced in the 1970s. It was intended to defeat both missile-armed Soviet bombers and the weapons themselves when launched from submarines or warships against US carriers.

The British faced a similar threat in the North Atlantic, and in an attempt to compensate for their less than maneuverable Tornado fighter, they modified the Sparrow into the improved Skyflash BVR AAM, which transformed the F.3 into a potent long-range hunter-killer. The Soviets also provided the Su-27 and MiG-29 with improved BVR missiles. In America, the AIM-120 AMRAAM – a 'fire and forget' AAM developed to replace the Sparrow – required such a long development period that it only became operational in the post-Cold War era.

The rise of the BVR radar-homing missile meant that ECM was now no longer exclusively used against ground-based radars and SAMs. Systems controlling the pods and chaff carried by individual aircraft now had to be configured against AAMs as well.

In addition to radar-guided BVR AAMs, the emergence of the all-aspect IR-guided missile had the potential to revolutionize fighter tactics and, through them, operations. This technology was debuted with the introduction of the AIM-9L version of the Sidewinder in the late 1970s, and it meant that for the first

time since the introduction of the fixed, synchronized, machine-gun as fighter armament in 1915, pilots involved in air combat did not have to get into the enemy's 'six o' clock position' to be certain of attaining a kill. When these missiles were fired in action in the Lebanon, Falklands and Gulf Wars, they contributed heavily to the one-sided results secured by their users.

The US had first examined the potential impact of these new missiles in a series of tests known as the AIMVAL/ACEVAL trials in the late 1970s. Conducted using instrumented air combat ranges that had been put in place to test emerging defensive technologies, as well as to teach Vietnam-era lessons to new fighter pilots, these tests simulated the firing of all-aspect AAMs. The units involved found air operations resembled an eighteenth century land battle, with opposing flights charging at each other

and firing off their missiles, rather than the swirling dogfights of Vietnam, where fighters attempted to maneuver into the enemy's six o'clock. The results were disturbing, for the aggressors, flying small, cheap and hard to detect F-5Es and A-4s, were scoring an even number of kills as their opponents in the more advanced, and expensive, F-14s and F-15s.

In some industry circles, this was seen as evidence that the future of fighter design lay in the F-5E (this included its maker, Northrop, who designed the ultimate F-5E in the up-engined F-20, which sadly attracted no buyers when it was offered for sale in the early 1980s). The USAF and the USN, however, looked at the broader picture. The importance of not being seen in order to avoid the new AAMs meant that stealth would now be just as crucial for air-to-air combat as it was in the war against SAMs. This led to the USAF to

Although sharing the same tactical tasking, the F-14A (this one is from VF-14 'Tophatters', deployed aboard USS John F Kennedy) and the Sea Harrier FRS I (this is a No 801 Sqn jet from HMS Invincible) are very different. The former is a long range interceptor that will try and avoid having to go 'head-to-head' with an opponent through the employment of long range missiles guided by its huge AWG-9 radar and associated fire control system. The pilot of the Sea Harrier, on the other hand, has to rely on 'getting to the merge' to complete his task of carrier protection due to his jet's austere radar and short range AAMs.

Below: Demonstrating the difference in size between AAMs, this Mirage 2000 prototype has French-built Matra 550 Magic 'dogfighting' rounds fitted to its out wing pylons and two Matra Super 530 medium range weapons inboard.

start work on a new, stealthy, air-to-air fighter that would eventually become the F-22 of the 1990s.

They also realized that the only way to survive in the new, more lethal, world of fighter operations was to see the enemy first and shoot at him. This required a long-range missile (the AMRAAM) and superior situational awareness, the latter being more difficult to achieve. ECM and, increasingly, IRCM would be vital for survival against both AAMs and the new generation of SAMs.

The threat posed by the surface-launched missile had increased throughout the Cold War. Instead of the SA-2, SA-3 and SA-6 of Vietnam and the Arab-Israeli conflicts, new high-speed/highly maneuverable systems such as the SA-10 and SA-12, or the US Patriot, had entered service by the end of the Cold War. At the lower end of the spectrum, man-portable

infrared SAMs also proliferated. These were much more capable than the Soviet SA-7s of previous conflicts, and the US-designed Stinger (which proved highly effective in Afghanistan in the hands of the Mujaheddin) and the

Soviet SA-16 (the single weapon responsible for most of the coalition aircraft lost in the Gulf War) made fighter operations at altitudes between 500 and 10,000 ft increasingly hazardous.

The Need for Situational Awareness

The lethality of the new generation of fighters and SAMs made situational awareness an even more important ingredient to achieving effective fighter operations. Because of the capability of modern fighter weapons, even aircraft with the most capable on-board radars that emerged in the 1970s and 80s still need all the situational awareness they can get. Modern fighter operations required flexibility, and static ground-based radars used since 1940 would obviously not suffice.

Part of the answer was provided by additional on-aircraft sensors. These included passive radar detectors, originally intended for warning against SAMs, and infrared search and tracking (IRST) sensors. The radar detectors

became universal, whilst IRST was fitted to high-capability aircraft such as the F-14 and Su-27.

Soviet interceptors developed new tactics emphasizing these passive sensors in the 1980s. They had long had to deal with targets in the form of SAC bombers that would be using heavy ECM against them. In the 1960s, the Soviets had deployed the MiG-25 Foxbat-A interceptor against such threats, aiming to give it the capability to deal with jamming targets through the employment of an incredibly powerful search and fire control radar (known to microwave live rabbits that wandered anywhere near its test and calibration sites). Such brute-force solutions became less attractive as the

Above: All the essential ingredients for an effective ACM training sortie, US Navy style, are seen here over NAS Miramar in 1984. The E-2C would help guide the crew in the Tomcat to the point where it could visually acquire either the F-5E or TA-4J (both from the famed Topgun Fighter Weapons School), and a tortuous dogfight would then ensue. In real life, the Tomcat crew would be looking to 'splash' their adversaries at medium to long range with either an AIM-54 Phoenix or AIM-7M Sparrow III.

microchip revolution reached even Moscow.

Despite the arrival of new technologies, radar remained the main adjunct to the fighter pilot's eyeball. In the 1970s, the USAF's E-3 AWACS (Airborne Warning and Control System) replaced the Vietnam-vintage EC-121, whilst the USN's big carriers each deployed with four turboprop E-2B/Cs dedicated to air wing operations – although smaller than their USAF brethren, the Hawkeye is no less capable.

Since then, these aircraft have become a vital part of both offensive and defensive fighter operations. The value of the E-3, proven in training and exercises, led to the creation of a multinational NATO AWACS force, followed by the re-equipment of similar forces in the Royal Saudi Air Force, RAF and French Air Force. The E-2C, meanwhile, is used by Israel (where they were critical in the 1982 war), Japan and others.

The first Soviet AWACS was the 1960s Tupolev Tu-126 Moss, which was apparently optimized for the national air defense of the USSR. This was supplemented some years later by an AWACS version of the Ilyushin Il-76 transport known to NATO as the A-50 Mainstay, which had the potential to work with MiG-29 and Su-27 interceptors, and thus provide a formidable combination in theater fighter operations.

Above: The RAF's interceptor/AWACS combination takes the form of the Tornado F 3 and the E-3D Sentry, both of which usually operate out over the North Sea or northern Atlantic. The RAF's Sentry force numbers seven aircraft, and they are split between Nos 8 and 23 Sqns, both based at Waddington – this jet is a No 8 Sqn machine. The F 3s in this shot hail from No 5 Sqn, who operate a 13-strong fleet from Coningsby.

Maritime Fighter Operations in the Cold War

A VFA-125 F/A-18B is guided onto No 2 'bow cat' aboard USS Constellation whilst a VMFA-314 F/A-18A idles in its wake, awaiting its turn to launch.

Maritime fighter operations in the jet age have been exclusively oriented towards the projection of air power ashore from aircraft carriers. Only in the Falklands War has this been done both without the support of land-based aircraft and in the face of an actual, rather than potential, threat to the aircraft carriers themselves.

The one possible carrier-versus-carrier battle of the jet age was planned for the morning of 2 May 1982 off the Falkland Islands. The Argentine aircraft carrier 25 De Mayo was to have launched all eight of its A-4s in a bombing raid aimed at the British task-force, but this was called off due to the very real threat of submarine attack. If the Argentine Navy or Airforce had been able to co-ordinate this mission with a maximum effort raid by shore based aircraft (postwar studies have shown that the likelihood of this occurring would have been extremely rare, as the Argentine Air Force lacked any effective ground-based controllers in the area to direct strikes against the British), the potential 30-40 aircraft attack would have had

a better chance of penetrating the overstretched Sea Harrier CAP force than small individual raids made by flights of three or four jets

The US Navy retained sufficient investment – even in the 'hollow forces' era of the 1970s – for highly-capable carrier-based operations. As well as introducing greater numbers of force multiplying aircraft into carrier air wings, they also improved the operability of the radar and ECM aircraft that have now become an integral part of maritime fighter operations. The British, on the other hand, had to adapt fighter operations to compensate for the retirement of their conventional catapult-equipped carriers in the late 1970s.

As so often happens in the development of fighter operations, the course of this adaptation reflected internal defense politics rather than operational realities. The RAF had long sought to expand its role at the expense of the Navy's carriers – in one famous incident, the RAF disseminated a briefing showing how RAF F-111s (then on order, but subsequently cancelled) could cover the entire Indian Ocean from shore bases, whilst simultaneously not revealing that this feat simply required the continent of Australia to be moved 600 nautical miles to the west!

The British operational concept that emerged to compensate for the lack of aircraft carriers in the late 1970s and early 80s was for RAF interceptors – eventually Tornado F.3 ADVs – to be based at forward airfields in Scotland from where they could cover naval ships operating in the North Atlantic 'GIN (Greenland-Iceland-Norway) Gap'. The offensive maritime mission was taken over by shore-based ASM-armed Buccaneers, which were eventually replaced in 1994 by Tornado GR.1Bs and Nimrods armed with Sea Eagle and Harpoon ASMs respectively.

These aircraft were to be supported by long-range shore-based AWACS aircraft that would compensate for the withdrawal of FAA Gannet radar aircraft that had operated from the now-withdrawn carriers. The requirement for the new AWACS platform led to the development of the Nimrod AEW which, due to chronic radar software problems, eventually turned out to be one of the greatest British research and development disasters of the jet age. By the time the RAF's Boeing E-3 AWACS finally entered service in 1991, the Cold War was coming to an end!

In the interim, the decidedly obsolete fleet of piston-engined Shackleton AEWs had been formed to fill the radar mission (using radars removed from Fairey Gannets) whilst the RAF scrambled to find a replacement. This meant that the RAF could never truly fulfil the maritime defensive counter-air mission that it boasted it could in the early 1970s. Despite the purchase of a relatively large number of Tornado ADVs, there was never a substantial quantity of these jets available for frontline operations at any time in the late 1980s, principally because they were often delivered without the appropriate radar or fire control systems installed. The long-duration CAPs envisaged by the RAF's concept of operations would have also absorbed a large percentage of the flying time allocated to Strike Command's small tanker force.

As a worse case scenario, if the CAPs required by the Navy were at the Tornado's extreme flying range from their shore bases, a full squadron complement of 12 jets would have been required to keep a single two-aircraft CAP on station on a 24-hour basis. This operational concept of defending naval vessels with shore-based aircraft was also suspect when it came to dealing with an

escalating enemy threat. The likelihood of a massed Soviet attack using high-performance cruise missiles launched from submarines as well as bombers (the latter escorted by long-range Soviet fighters) began to look irresistible by the end of the Cold War. The flawed nature of the RAF's defensive maritime fighter operations was just one of the many elements of NATO's defense that was thankfully never put to the test

The British experience was repeated in a number of countries. In the later decades of the Cold War, Australia, Canada and the Netherlands were forced to retire their carriers due to a combination of increasing operating costs and the sheer expense involved in modernizing ageing vessels to enable them to survive in combat. However, the availability of V/STOL aircraft introduced

RAF fighter crews would often 'hand over' their 'Bear' contact to the F-15-equipped 57th FIS, based as NAS Keflavik, Iceland, once the Soviet bomber had passed out of their range.

other countries into the world of carrier aviation, with most notably the Soviet Union commencing operations in 1976. India also expanded its carrier force in this way, whilst new nations in the shape of Spain, Italy and Thailand acquired V/STOL carriers and AV-8s.

In the post-Cold War world, carrier-borne fighter operations retain unique advantages, as political sensitivities over the use of airbases on foreign soil remain. This was recently shown when Italy denied the USAF access to bases from which to operate F-117 stealth fighters against Serbian air defenses, and when Saudi Arabia refused to give the Americans permission to use similar facilities for a retaliatory strike against Iraq. Today, the carrier air wing is still the most flexible instrument of power projection available to any nation.

Offensive or Defensive?

Left: The Tornado GR 1 is arguably the most capable non-US strike aircraft in service with NATO today, and has proven its ability both in war and peace since the early 1980s. This jet belongs to the Germany-based No 15 Sqn, which was the first frontline unit to receive Tornados in late 1983.

Right: The arrival of the MiG-23/27 family in the frontline in the early to mid-1970s improved the communist bloc's chances of winning a non-nuclear conflict with NATO. The 'Flogger', in its many guises, proving highly capable in both the fighter and attack roles. Rather contradicting the low level strike role of their camouflaged MiG-23MLs, these VVS pilots are all kitted out in high altitude pressure suits and matching helmets.

Below: Although far less well-equipped than a Tornado or F-15E, the Warsaw Pact's MiG-21 force more than made up for it in sheer numbers — well over 2000 'Fishbeds' could be found in frontline use across eastern Europe from the early 1960s until the end of the Cold War. This early MiG-21F was operated by the Czechoslovakian Air Force.

A popular cartoon of the late Cold War years showed Soviet generals talking while reviewing their tanks parading through a conquered Paris. The accompanying caption read, 'By the way comrade, who did win the air superiority battle?' The question was not just to shoot down enemy fighters, but to make a difference in the central front balance, for that was at the very heart of the Cold War strategy devised by both sides in Europe.

The aim of fighter operations has always been to destroy or render ineffective enemy fighter aircraft which, in turn, removes obstacles to friendly use of the air. While there was broad agreement as to the goals by the East and West alike, there was much less of a consensus on how to carry it out. NATO diverged on whether limited resources would best be allocated to the offensive counter-air (OCA) or defensive counter-air (DCA).

The USAF stood strongly for investing in OCA fighter operations, with large forces able to take the war to the enemy (either in air combat or through attacking airfields) over their own

territory, even if the Soviet tank spearheads were advancing deep into West Germany.

The tactics with which these differing operational approaches were implemented reflected specific national requirements. The USAF saw offensive fighter operations as supporting penetrating strike packages — the evolution of those seen over North Vietnam — with massive support from SEAD or Wild Weasel aircraft, tankers, stand-off jammers, AWACS and RESCAP, all of which operated above the altitude of light AAA and man-

portable SAMs, and were protected by fighters from any interfering MiGs. In the 1970s, these strikes tended to be compact in order to allow mutual support between attacking aircraft — they were called 'gorillas'. By the 1980s, the increased range of sensors, communications and EW systems (especially defensive jammers) allowed these strikes to be more dispersed.

The US Navy differed from the USAF in that it was much more committed to the DCA mission. For an embarked air wing, the defense of its ships remained the priority mission, just as it had since

1945. F-4s carried out this mission until replaced by F-14s in the 1970s. For OCA tasks, including strike missions and offensive fighter operations, the introduction of the F/A-18 in the 1980s gave the Navy the ability to perform both tasks with a single aircraft type. Where air wings included both F-14s and F/A-18s, mission planners tended to reserve the DCA tasks for the former jet, whilst the F/A-18s carried out escort or OCA missions.

The RAF perceived the best OCA way to put enemy fighters out of action was not by shooting them down, but by putting their airbases out of action. Low-level attacks by small forces operating independently began the mission strategy of Bomber and then Strike Command, with aircraft types such as the Canberra, then Buccaneer and finally Tornado GR.1 undertaking this demanding role. These attacks were originally intended to deliver nuclear weapons, but the advent of the flexible response meant that conventional weapons had to also be used, including specialized anti-runway munitions. This OCA role was in effect thrust upon the RAF simply because it lacked the many specialized support aircraft available to its USAF ally. Lightning interceptors and BVR AAM-armed F-4s acted as 'backstops' both over the UK and Germany throughout this period, before being replaced in the late 1980s by the Tornado F.3.

With their homelands in striking range of Soviet Frontal Aviation, the French and Germans had to look more at the DCA mission. For the former, the problem was compounded by the fact that having invested in a small, but capable, national nuclear strike capability, they lacked resources for effective conventional airfield attack capability such as those possessed by the RAF and Germany. Both devoted a larger percentage of their fighter forces to the air defense of their homeland, whilst the Luftwaffe also maintained a long-range SAM force, integrated into the NATO air defense system.

The Soviets were also aware of the need for change, having seen the bulk of their 'clients' lose in conflict after conflict. Starting in the aftermath of the 1967 war, they had asked themselves 'how would we not lose in the same way?' They also realized that they would be unlikely to achieve a qualitative edge over their opponents, so the answer lay in improving frontline fighter operations. There, it was thought, the skills of commanders could compensate for any weaknesses in training or tactics.

The Soviet theater air operation would have probably included both strikes on NATO airbases and attempts to clear corridors through NATO air defenses. This would have required substantial numbers of escort fighters

Top: four jovial pilots pose in front of their MiG-21PFMs at a VVS base in the late 1960s.

Above: The Su-15 supersonic interceptor was built in typically Soviet quantities: over 1400 were produced exclusively for use by the APVO. Streaming a landing parachute, this is a two-seat Su-15UT trainer

Left: Built for the same role as the Su-15, the F-104 proved that it was more of an 'all-rounder'. Led by the Luftwaffe, a number of NATO states bought the Starfighter as an all-weather interceptor replacement for aircraft like the F-84, F-86, Hunter and Meteor.

accompanying strike aircraft in order to clear away NATO DCA aircraft. The theater air operation would not have been purely air-to-air, and would have included improved air-ground tactical aircraft like the Su-24 Fencer and MiG-27 Flogger – some armed with anti-radiation missiles against radars and SAM sites.

The attacks on NATO airbases would

have also included ballistic missiles with chemical, conventional or nuclear warheads. *Spetsnaz* (Special Forces) attacks would also have been a part of the theater air operation, for the Soviets recognized that the counter to NATO fighters was not just another fighter – the ultimate OCA weapon was, and still remains, a tank parked on a runway.

Realistic Operational and Tactical Training

Greater flexibility of late Cold War fighter operations was facilitated by improved, and more extensive, training. In the US, this was first seen in the upgrading of individual aircraft tactics and aircrew performance that eventually led to the improvement in kill ratios over the NVAF in 1972. The spread of instrumented air combat ranges, and their ability to aid in the development of operational as well as tactical skills, led to the start of the USAF's Red Flag exercises at Nellis AFB, Nevada, in 1975.

Red Flag took the ongoing process of improving aircrew and tactical skills and applied them in an operational context. Historically, it has been seen that if a pilot survives his first ten combat missions, he is less likely to be shot down and more likely to shoot down the enemy. The aim of Red Flag was to provide the equivalent of these ten missions in training.

However, the goal of Red Flag was more ambitious than just aircrew training, for it included the overall development of tactical and operational concepts that would be employed in the waging of future wars. Many of the ideas that would improve fighter operations in general, and go on to be so successful in

other allied nations benefiting from the Red Flag experience. The latter also provided their own insights into the development of operations, and gave all participants the experience of multi-national operations that would have been the norm in any conflict in Europe (and, as it turned out, the Gulf War as well).

What made these improvements significant was the increased investment in defence spending in the early 1980s, especially in the USA. This provided not only money to bring into service many of the systems improvement made possible by emerging technologies, but also for training to come to grips with the operational and technological problems of integrating the 1970s' generation of fighter aircraft into effective theater operations. This meant overcoming a whole host of problems ranging from the funding of sufficient flight hours for aircrew (always a key predictor of combat performance) to the procurement of an adequate overhead of replaceable components to prevent a repetition of the proliferation of cannibalized 'hangar queens' that were seen throughout the US services in the 1970s.

Little evidence exists that effective fighter operations can be had on the cheap. Even the Israelis, with their genius for improvisation and adaptation, have become more dependent on American aid to foot the defense bill. Unless those who pay for the provision of airpower are willing to continue to do so into the next century, the aircraft they buy to replace the present generation of frontline machinery will be either less effective or far fewer in number. The substantial investments of the early 1980s not only helped to keep the peace in the last decade of the Cold War, but also contributed to the successful fighter operations of the Gulf War.

Above: Like the French Rafale and the Anglo-British Eurofighter 2000, the JAS39 Grippen has been built using the very latest in fly-by-wire and composite structure technology. Despite having to operate on a much smaller budget than Dassault or British Aerospace/DASA, it has proven to be the first to reach the frontline.

Top right: The best all-weather fighter-bomber in the western world, the F-15E was tested in combat in the Gulf in 1991. The Strike Eagle is one of the most important aircraft in the USAF with 192 in service. This particular jet saw action over Iraq with the 335th FS/4th FW, whose markings it wears here.

Bottom right: Despite looking less than war-like in its garish paint scheme, this F-16A is currently the most effective combat aircraft in the Indonesian Air Force. A modest fleet of eight single-seat and four two-seat Fighting Falcons have equipped a solitary unit (No 14 Sqn) since 1989

the Gulf War, first appeared as improvisations to meet a Red Flag scenario, and were then evaluated, tested and standardized. These exercises also trained both fighter leaders and staff planners in the complexities of modern fighter operations.

The introduction of Red Flag was followed by Green Flag exercises, stressing realistic EW exercises, and Blue Flag, which focused on air-ground operations and made more use of simulation. The US improvements realized in these exercises were spread through multi-national participation. Allied air forces soon started playing in Red Flag, with firstly the RAF and then

Sea Harriers and Skyhawks – Fighter Operations in the Falklands War

Argentina's invasion of the Falklands Islands on 2 April 1982 started a war where fighter combat operations would be no less decisive despite their limited scale. The British campaign in many ways depended on a true 'Few', for the handful of fighter pilots flying the FAA's Sea Harriers would be responsible for performing all the air-to-air missions generated against the attacking aircraft of the numerically-superior Argentine Air Force and Navy.

The fighter operations on both sides were shaped by the aircraft, technology and tactics involved, as well as the progress of the military campaign into which the fighter missions had to be integrated. The British were more successful because their investment in all these areas far outweighed their shortage of numbers. The opposite was true for their opponents: Argentine fighter crews were, in the words of one RAF pilot 'great stick-and-rudder men', They demonstrated tremendous courage, but gallantry alone has not been able to deliver successful fighter operations since 1917.

The decommissioning of HMS Ark Royal in 1978. and the loss of its air group (30 fixed-wing aircraft) gave the idea that Britain was no longer prepared to defend its remaining territories outside Europe.

Below: BAe Sea Harier FRS 1s are shown wearing the pre-war grey and white scheme, complemented with full colour units markings – No 800 Sqn on the jet in the foreground and the 'flying fist' of No 899 Sqn on the Sea Harrier hovering in the distance.

Fighting Outnumbered to Win – the British Experience in the Falklan

The great Prussian strategist Carl von Clausewitz once wrote 'superiority in numbers is the most common element in victory'. British fighter operations in the Falklands demonstrated both the strengths (in their one-sided kill ratio) as well as the limitations of a numerically inferior, yet highly capable, fighter force. In the words of Admiral Sir John Woodward, who commanded the British task force, 'with the elements of surprise and maneuver by this time largely lost, we were into a strictly attrition war'. Yet the Sea Harriers in the Falklands prevailed in a one-sided battle of attrition fought against a numerically superior enemy.

The Ark Royal's replacement in the Royal Navy of the 1980s was the Invincible class 'through-deck cruiser' of 18,000 tons, which could embark six to eight Sea Harriers and up to a dozen Sea king helicopters

British operations in the Falklands show that despite the importance of 'maneuver warfare', the Leninist motto of 'quantity has a quality all of its own' is still valid today. The entire British campaign found itself depending on a relatively small number of jets and pilots for air superiority, just as the UN had been forced to make do over Korea for most of 1951 with a solitary wing of F-86s. While the force multipliers working in favor of the Sea Harriers included a much greater ability to generate sorties (there were almost five times as many British fighter sorties over the Falklands as Argentine), the near-impossible workload needed to maintain this tempo of operations for any great period of time placed considerable demands on air- and ground-crews alike.

The FAA Sea Harrier pilots, like most fast jet multi-role NATO crews in 1982, thought that future air combat operations would be 'multi-bogey affairs in an outnumbered environment' against the Soviets. In the Falklands, the Argentine limitations in putting together co-ordinated strikes, or in challenging the Sea Harriers in air combat after 1 May, did not really stretch the numerically-limited British force to its limit.

As mentioned earlier in this volume, a concentrated Argentine strike might have had a much greater effect on the task force. In Red Flag exercises staged in the late 1970s, the USAF would put into the air the sort of concentrated air attacks – 50 to 60 aircraft – that the Soviets would be expected to utilize to force corridors through NATO air defenses. Even when 12 to 16 F-15s and F-16s were committed to repelling these attacks, they could not prevent a number of jets from getting through and hitting their chosen targets – even though they were able to exact heavy losses. However, over the Falklands, Argentine aircraft were usually engaged in two- to four-ship flights, which made the combats similar to the '1-v-1'

and '2-v-2' engagements that the Sea Harrier pilots had routinely practised back in European skies. This Falklands lesson is likely to be highly applicable in future combat scenarios.

With the cost of procuring modern fighters continuing to increase, there is renewed interest in purchasing small, but highly effective, air-air fighter aircraft. For example, it has been proposed that the USAF deploy only a single wing of F-22 fighters because of their high cost, this 'silver bullet' outfit of air-air 'specialists' emulating the role of the 4th FIW in 1951 or the 432nd TFW in 1972 in any future conflict. The Falklands experience suggests that this operational concept may eventually see a highly-limited, yet numerically superior, opponent prevail. In the words of USAF general T R Milton, 'The best fighter pilot in the world . . . flying the best airplane, is still "going down" if he is sufficiently outnumbered by almost any sort of aircraft armed with a reliable missile'. In the late 1990s, as advanced fighter aircraft and long-range all-aspect AAMs proliferate on a worldwide scale, it is unlikely that there will be any low-capability threats encountered in the next major conflict. Thus, such a 'silver bullet' force may run up high kill ratios, but still be vulnerable to attrition.

'I counted them all out, and I counted them all back' – Brian Hanrahan, BBC correspondent during the Falklands War, commenting on the first Sea Harrier strike mission of the conflict flown from HMS Hermes on 1 May 1982.

Sea Harriers Go South

As the British task force headed south in April 1982, it was faced with the same problem as their Argentine foes had encountered earlier that same month – how to prepare fighter forces for the coming conflict that were not designed to fight each other over the Falklands.

The FAA's Sea Harrier FRS.1 was the only British fighter in the conflict to

carry out pure air combat operations (RAF Harrier GR.3s to joined the task force off the Falklands, but were tasked principally with the air-ground role). It was a single-seat aircraft that differed from all previous jet fighters in being able to land and take-off vertically (although for heavily-loaded aircraft, the combination of a rolling take-off over a bow-mounted 'ski jump' was

Aside from SAMs and radar-guided AAA (which ultimately proved to be more deadly), the Sea Harrier's main protagonist was the Mirage IIIEA, of which roughly ten were based within flying distance of the Falklands with Grupo 8 de Caza at Rio Gallegos. It is estimated by British sources that at least two (possibly three) Mirages were lost on the first Argentine raid on the task force on the evening of 1 May, and after that the sleek Dassault fighter was relegated to protecting the mainland from potential Vulcan bomber strikes

preferable). The Sea Harriers had received new all-aspect AIM-9Ls from the Americans just prior to the task force setting sail, and also carried twin 30 mm Aden cannon in pods beneath the centre fuselage.

Despite these advantages in weaponry, the Sea Harrier's small size and V/STOL operations limited its range and ordnance capability to below that which can be anticipated from fighters operating conventionally from ships such as the USN's fleet carriers.

The scrapping of the last British conventional carrier, HMS *Ark Royal*, in the late 1970s seemed to put an end to the need for naval fighter operations for the RN. The RAF claimed that they would be able to provide shore-based fighter CAPs (combat air patrols) over British warships in their most likely

areas of operations – the North Sea and the North Atlantic.

Ark Royal's successors were the new 'through-deck cruiser HMS *Invincible*, and the modified conventional carrier HMS *Hermes*. Both were optimized to perform the anti-submarine warfare (ASW) role, which was consistent with the overall commitment of the RN to function as part of the NATO force opposing Soviet submarines in the North Atlantic. The Sea Harrier fighters were seen as providing a secondary capability, being intended to despatch Soviet Bear and Badger snoopers or bombers that got too close to a task force, or to carry out the tactical nuclear delivery mission on NATO's northern flank. While classic air-to-air combat was seen as unlikely to occur in these missions, both the Sea Harrier (and its thoroughly-trained pilots) was flexible enough to be adapted to the role of defeating enemy fighters and fighter-bombers as would be seen in the Falklands.

This change in mission emphasis soon led to a shortage of both Sea Harriers and trained pilots, which in turn helped create a lack of flexibility in its use (especially at the operational level, where no one had considered using Sea Harriers to perform a number of the mission taskings now required of it), as well an inability to sustain extensive losses. In fighter operations, quantity has a quality all of its own.

Throughout the Falklands War improvisation was the order of the day, and the FAA were fortunate in possessing fighter leaders of the caliber of Sea Harrier squadron commanders Andy Auld and 'Sharkey' Ward, both of whom had had a thorough grounding in both the jet and its capabilities, as well as the requirements of the operations facing them. Despite the FAA's air-to-air jet combat experience comprising just a single MiG-15 kill over Korea, the

principal problem facing the FAA squadron leaders in the build up to the Falklands conflict was not the lack of operational experience, but the difficulty in getting their capabilities effectively integrated into the overall theater operation because those in charge were not experts in fighter operations. As a result, the aircrew often felt frustrated when the Sea Harriers were not used in ways which best allowed them to carry out their missions effectively – this included the incorrect positioning of the vital CAP (combat air patrol) stations by fighter directors. These lapses led to some of the most costly Argentine successes of the conflict.

Effective fighter operations – like tactics – are often the result of literally 'learning on the job'. In both World

Wars, the willingness of those in combat to adapt to changing frontline conditions was often tempered by the insistence of those making operational decisions that these be consistent with what was then perceived to be effective (or at least politically or bureaucratically valuable) doctrine. The FAA benefited from input received from the USMC (also Harrier operators), who had developed improved air-to-air tactics. One of their main innovations was vectoring in forward flight (VIFF), using the moveable nozzles of the Kestrel engine in air combat maneuvering. However, despite contemporary press reports at the time claiming its successful employment in the Falklands War, the FAA did not use 'VIFFing' in action in 1982.

An irresistible combination, the pairing of the Sea Harrier FRS 1 and the AIM-9L Sidewinder proved to be the undoing of the Argentine Air Force in 1982. This 'barley grey' jet (XZ458) was one of eight FRS 1s issued to the hastily-formed No 809 Sqn from No 899 Sqn stocks at RNAS Yeovilton in May 1982 and shipped down to the task force aboard the merchantman Atlantic Conveyor. Issued to No 801 Sqn upon its arrival, the jet flew 45 sorties from the deck of HMS Invincible before to returning to Britain. Like many Falklands War Sea Harrier FRS 1s, this jet was subsequently written off in a flying accident, suffering a bird strike off the Scottish coast on 1 December 1984 whilst serving with No 800 Sqn.

The Argentines Prepare

Posing a threat far greater than their numerical strength suggested, the Argentine Navy's five Super Etendards of 2 Escuadrilla de Caza y Ataque were charged exclusively with attacking the British fleet with the small stock of Exocet missiles supplied with the French jets. Usually operating singularly or in pairs at ultra low-level to avoid detection, the Dassault fighter-bombers managed to sink two vessels with ASMs, despite the fact that neither one exploded properly.

As alluded to earlier, neither the Argentine Air Force or Navy were prepared to take on an opponent such as the FAA's Sea Harriers. The former's fighter units used a mixture of Mirage IIIs, Israeli Neshers and A-4s, whilst the Navy had carrier-based A-4s (although these only ever operated from land) and a few shore-based Super Etendards, which were capable of firing Exocet ASMs.

Operational readiness and pilot training had suffered in the years preceding the war due to limited monies available for flight training, and a chronic spares shortage because of international sanctions aimed at

Argentina's military government. Support aircraft for missions such as reconnaissance, combat search and rescue and air refueling were few, whilst equipment such as chaff, ECM and modern AAMs were all absent. Realizing that it was easier to have role-specific squadrons rather than multi-role aircraft, the Argentines had specialized in their organizational structure. For example, one Mirage III squadron would do interception whilst a combination of air force A-4s and naval aircraft handled anti-ship missions. For all their government's posturing against Chile and the UK, fighter tactics were not considered a priority.

Above: The bulk of the air strikes flown against the task force were undertaken by ex-US A-4P Skyhawks, approximately 49 of which were shared between air force Grupos 4 and 5, and eight navy A-4Qs assigned to 3 Escuadrilla de Caza y Ataque. Despite performing their mission with much gusto, the Skyhawk was no match for the Sea Harrier or the array of SAMs that protected their intended targets, and 25 were lost. However, they did manage to sink a number of Royal Navy warships with'iron' bombs, relying on skill and bravery rather than modern technology.

Left: The Skyhawks suffered such appalling losses primarily because they had no effective fighter cover to protect them from British Sea Harriers – despite the small Mirage IIIEA force flying some 45 combat sorties over the Falklands. This jet was the first Mirage delivered to Argentina, and was photographed in France prior to heading to South America in mid-1972.

In late April the Argentines belatedly tried to train pilots in air-to-air and anti-ship tactics, but they lacked the tanker aircraft that would allow their aircraft to operate over the Falklands for any extended period of time. They had not made the upgrading of Port Stanley airport, on the Falklands, their main priority – this precluded its use by air defense fighters. As with the USAF in Korea in 1951, the lack of suitable base improvements had drastically reduced the effectiveness of subsequent fighter operations.

Despite real limitations, the legacy of successive defense cuts in the 1960s and 70s, the British had the advantages in the aircraft, tactics, training, and technology on which effective jet fighter operations are always based. The Falklands War underscored the need to have both an adaptable fighter force and operational concepts that are not wedded to specific scenarios.

Environmental Conditions and Fighter Combat

Left: FAA Sea Harriers had trained to defend British naval units against Soviet air attack in the unforgiving seas off Norway. Thus they were better prepared to fly and fight in the south Atlantic than their opponents.

Right: While the astonishing capabilities of the Sea Harrier had been recognized by 1982, the small size of the Harrier force left no room for error against a numerically far larger air force.

A major contributing factor to the British success in fighter operations in the Falklands was their ability to operate in the marginal environmental conditions of the sub-Antarctic autumn encountered around the islands. On a number of occasions, Sea Harriers were able to make vertical landings on completely 'socked-in' carriers which simply would not have been possible with even the most capable of conventional aircraft. While these operations were not without cost (amongst the first Sea Harriers lost were two that collided in cloud whilst attempting to intercept an Argentine Canberra bomber), without the ability to operate in all weathers the Sea Harriers would have left the task force at the mercy of radar-equipped, Exocet-firing, Etendards. The latter could take off in good weather on the mainland and head towards a radar contact regardless of the cloud cover.

Here again, the British commitment to NATO furnished them with capabilities that were directly applicable to the Falklands. Sea Harrier pilots had trained for operations off northern Norway, whilst RAF Harrier crews were used to flying missions over the central German front, where the cloud base is regularly below 3,000 ft and visibility restricted to three miles for 40 per cent of the year.

The bad weather on the central front was a major reason why, until the late 1970s and early 1980s (and, in some cases, until the end of the Cold War), most NATO air arms perceived that 'fighter operations' almost always meant simply intercepting enemy aircraft. They relied

heavily on accurate GCI, and did not train their flight leaders to be able to deal with rapidly-evolving situations (which the FAA had to counter in the Falklands). By 1982, the Europeans had begun to adopt multi-role techniques thanks to the superbly-maneuverable F-16, which had been purchased as a replacement for the fast, but decidedly unmanueverable, F-104. To help facilitate this change, many of their pilots went through US and NATO schools and participated in Red Flag exercises, but even by the mid-1980s, they had still not acquired the level of skill in air-air fighting in bad weather that the British had demonstrated in the Falklands.

As with so many facets of the British success in 1982, the degree of operational flexibility shown by pilots in the frontline was due to the improvization and skill of individual aircrew, rather than an institutional understanding of the importance of fighter tactics by their superiors. The British services had often de-emphasized air-air fighter operations, instead shifting the emphasis to air-ground missions. Training costs, and the desire to minimize accidents in peacetime, also limited the number of pure air combat sorties flown. While this had been slowly changing in the late 1970s and early 80s, fortunately for the Falkland Islanders, the individual RAF and FAA aircrews at the 'pointy end' learned faster than the institutions that commanded them.

Although British fighter doctrine had provided its pilots with a less than ideal grounding in the tactics to be

employed in the Falklands War, their opposite numbers in the Argentine Air Force and Navy were unprepared for the defence of their recent territorial acquisition. Their operational doctrine, such as it was, was also improvized. They had not trained for combat with other fighters, and like the British, the weather compounded their problems. Due to the vast distances involved in flying sorties between the Argentine mainland and the Falkland Islands, all offensive operations required the use of aerial refueling. Peacetime flying had not emphasized this crucial aspect of modern fighter operations, hence the fact that most fast jet pilots had strictly limited experience in operating with the Air Force's modest tanker force.

Operating at extreme range, where fuel consumption was all-important, Argentine fighter pilots could only fly below the weather when they got to the target area itself as purely tactical flying on low-level bombing runs usually involved keeping engines at higher power settings, with resulting higher fuel consumption. This often meant that they had to penetrate the airspace around the

Falklands at medium altitude, making them ideal targets for British naval and shore-based SAMs. The problems associated with first locating targets and then staging co-ordinated attacks with other aircraft (both greatly complicated by the weather) was a powerful 'force divider' for the Argentines over the Falklands, and these factors effectively negated the majority of the sorties that actually made it into the airspace around the islands.

Even outside the central and northern fronts of Europe, weather conditions continue to shape fighter operations. In the Gulf War, the worst winter weather in many years limited coalition air operations, whilst more recently, NATO fighter operations over Bosnia have been adversely affected by atmospheric conditions, especially during the winter months. When the opportunity to achieve visual target identification is compromised by adverse weather (especially during peacekeeping operations), any problems associated with securing reliable IFF information in place of a confirmed sighting assume critical importance when attempting to enforce effective fighter operations.

Fighter Operations Begin

Fighting in the Falklands commenced on 1 May when an RAF Vulcan bomber, flying from Ascension Island with multiple in-flight refuelings along the way, attacked Port Stanley airport. This was the first of five Vulcan attacks against the islands, three of which saw ordnance dropped on the airport (although only one bomb actually cratered the runway) and two resulted in ARMs being fired against Argentine radar. The main effect of these raids

was not measured in material destruction, however. Rather, they clearly showed that a long-range bombing campaign could be unleashed on mainland targets in Argentina. After 1 May, the Argentines had to pull fighters away from the airbases in the south and hold them in the north of the country defending their cities. This demonstrated once again that the positive effect of counter-air bomber strikes on fighter operations can be

considerable, even if the physical damage is limited.

Fighter operations opened in earnest after the first Vulcan raid when Sea Harriers attacked both the Port Stanley airport and the airfield at Goose Green, destroying armed trainers and Pucara turboprop counter-insurgency aircraft which had been forward deployed to the islands. The Argentines responded with airstrikes on the British taskforce, and in one of the most intense days of

air fighting (the only one in which Argentine fighters carried out real air combat), three aircraft were shot down by Sea Harriers (a fourth was finished of by the Port Stanley airport defenses as an 'own goal') without loss.

In the days that followed, the Argentine aircraft carrier was pulled back into port due to British submarine action, whilst its A-4s went into action from shore bases. The Argentines soon scored a success with the sinking of a British destroyer through the use of an Exocet ASM fired from a Super Etendard – Sea Harrier pilots blamed this loss on mishandled CAPs by the task force command.

The weeks leading up to the British amphibious invasion were punctuated by attacks on RN warships by the Argentines, the Sea Harriers keeping up their CAPs as well as striking at land and sea targets – both sides suffered operational losses in the difficult operational environment. The landings on 21 May brought the Argentine air force, including the surviving Falklands-based Pucaras, into action, flying no less than 56 sorties. While the British carriers stood off at long range, the 25 Sea Harriers then available were able to sustain two two-aircraft CAPs for most of the day. In addition, Argentine helicopters, which could have participated in the ground battle, were

destroyed by British fighter attacks. In response, the Argentine air attacks sank a British frigate and damaged others, but they lost 12 aircraft in the process, 9 (plus a single kill shared) falling to the Sea Harriers.

The following days and weeks saw these types of operations continue, the Sea Harriers (reinforced by RAF Harrier GR.3s) both striking at surface targets and keeping CAPs over ships while the Argentines tried, time and again, to hit these vessels with bombs and Exocet missiles. While they had successes (a container ship, a destroyer and a frigate were lost), the Sea Harriers maintained their one-sided record of victories whenever they managed to intercept the attackers. They also managed to intercept and destroy an Argentine C-130 resupplying Port Stanley.

The British fighters continued to suffer losses from ground-based air defenses and operational conditions, however, and operations began to suffer due to a shortage of aircraft – one of the results of this was the loss of two British landing ships with heavy loss of life due to the absence of a CAP. Fortunately, the air-ground mission became easier with the establishment of a landing pad ashore and the introduction of laser-guided bombs on RAF GR.3s before the Argentine surrender on 14 June.

The Argentine Air Force's Grupo 6 de Caza had 37 ex-Israeli Daggers. This famous shot was taken on 24 May 1982 during an early afternoon strike on the task force in San Carlos Water: it shows 'Plata-I', flown by a Capt Dellepiane, passing along the port side of HMS Fearless below mast head height, having just dropped two 500-lb parachute retarded bombs. Neither weapon hit its intended target, and although his flight of three Daggers was engaged by Sea Dart SAMs whilst egressing, they escaped without loss.

Right: The task force suffered its first serious casualties on 4 May when the destroyer HMS Sheffield was struck by one of two Exocets fired at it from a pair of Super Etendards – 21 sailors were killed in the fire that engulfed the ship.

V/STOL and 'VIFFing'

The Falklands War was not the first time V/STOL aircraft had been used in combat – the Soviet Navy claimed that distinction with the unsuccessful employment of the Yak-38 'Forger' in Afghanistan in 1980. However, it was the first – and only – conflict where one side relied totally on this type of fighter aircraft, and the only action where they have engaged in air-air combat.

The Sea Harrier that went into action in 1982 was the end product of a developmental process involving both airframe and engine that could trace their origins to the mid-1950s, and had seen the first operational Harrier GR.1s entering RAF service in 1969. In the late 1950s and early 60s, it was envisaged that V/STOL would revolutionize fighter operations because of the threat posed to conventional airfields by nuclear attack – strategists believed that runways at all major bases would be rendered inoperable within 24 hours of any major conflict in Europe .

By the time the Harrier had been developed and was on the cusp of entering service, its role within the frontline force structure had became more specialized. With NATO's emphasis having now shifted from all out nuclear strikes to a more flexible response to any enemy action

This excellent postwar shot of XZ457 (the highest scoring FRS 1 in the Falklands with four kills) shows it fitted with dual Sidewinder rails under each wing – unfortunately for the FAA pilots involved in the 1982 conflict, only single round rails were available then, and they were limited to just two AIM-9Ls.

through the deployment of conventional weapons, the RAF's Harriers became close air support specialists. To effectively perform this task, Harrier units were initially based in camouflaged 'hides' near to the frontline, where full use was made of their V/STOL capability. However, keeping these dispersed sites well-stocked with associated consumables like fuel, weapons and spare parts proved to be a logistical nightmare, so a new centralized forward basing concept was adopted instead.

The Harrier achieves vertical take-off and landing by vectoring thrust from its centrally-mounted Pegasus engine through four moveable nozzles. Vectoring in Forward Flight ('VIFF') entails using the Pegasus' nozzles in lift mode to improve a Harrier's maneuverability. It can allow the jet to rapidly decelerate, thus forcing a chasing opponent to either overshoot, turn inside the now-stationary Harrier or pitch the nose up very rapidly in order to avoid a collision.

Developed by the USMC in the 1970s, 'VIFFing' was proven in a number of guns-only dogfights with F-14As. Despite the excellent low-speed maneuverability provided by the latter's variable-geometry wing, the AV-8s enjoyed great success. This was also partly derived from the Harrier's low fuel consumption in a dogfight – only about 12 per cent of the fuel flow figure of a thirsty F-4, for example.

The RAF and FAA learned of this tactic through their pilot exchange program with the Marine Corps. Prior to this, the FAA had concentrated more on engaging Soviet long-range bombers, rather than stressing aspects of air-air fighter combat. The adoption of true fighter tactics by the FAA after encountering 'VIFFing' is a good example of the benefits of cross-fertilization of ideas between air arms through the medium of exchange tours – this was a key element in the revival of fighter operations in the 1970s and 80s.

Although naval aviators had had little chance to really become familiar with 'dogfighting' in the Sea Harrier prior the Falklands War, their lack of air-air expertise was largely offset by the inclusion of senior FAA pilots who had flown F-4s (as well as a handful of RAF Harrier pilots with experience in flying Lightning interceptors) within the ranks of the aircrew that accompanied the task force to the South Atlantic. This ability to draw on a pool of experienced pilots (and operational planners) with a broad range of frontline flying is a major advantage enjoyed by larger, or more diverse, fighter force over smaller, or single-type, air arms.

Because of the lack of concerted air-air opposition after 1 May in the Falklands, Sea Harriers never got to use 'VIFFing'. Most of their successful combats were described as 'pre-Battle of Britain' type engagements, meaning that Sea Harrier CAPs had to rely on visual sightings to ensure the successful interception of low-flying targets because the jets were often deployed outside effective radar coverage of ships, or the threat had approached the patrol line below the radar coverage provided by the fighters' onboard systems. This led to high speed, low-level, high-g intercepts, rather than the type of close-in

dogfights (similar to the MiG-17-v-F-4 battles over Vietnam) regularly undertaken by the USMC. Sea Harriers would simply roll in from above and behind their chosen targets and launch their Sidewinders.

Despite it not being used in air combat in the Falklands (or subsequent USMC, RAF and FAA Harrier operations in the Gulf and Bosnia), 'VIFFing' remains a valid tactic, and other Harrier operators like the Spanish, Indian and Italian navies have also adopted it.

What have had more of an effect than 'VIFFing' in the recent formulation of fighter tactics are the number of design innovations built into conventional take-off and landing fighters. These have demonstrated improvements

No 800 Sqn's XZ499 is marshalled forward on Hermes prior to launch. This jet flew 38 sorties during the Falklands war, and was credited with destroying a Skyhawk and a patrol boat.

in high-g control and high angle of attack maneuvers, both of which have been made possible through a combination of fly-by-wire and computerized control systems and high thrust-weight ratios. This has meant more than just spectacular maneuvers at airshows — most notably the MiG-29's 'tail slide' or the 'cobra' flown by the Su-27. By increasing the pilot's ability to get his all-aspect missiles (and cannon) pointing at a target faster than was previously achievable, air combat had become less-survivable than ever before by the end of the Cold War.

Situational Awareness

The situational awareness gap was one of the most significant British limitations in the Falklands. The Sea Harrier – for all its strengths – was often reduced to 'pre-1940' tactics, with CAPs having to search visually for the enemy. Its radar had limited performance over land, and when CAPs were mis-positioned, many Argentine strikes got through unscathed.

The conventional carrier's airborne early warning (AEW) radar aircraft was also badly missed. The Royal Navy was forced to rely on radar picket destroyers to both direct Sea Harriers and provide radar warnings of incoming aircraft – much as the US Navy had done off Okinawa in 1945. As then, detached ships, whether radar pickets or 'air traps' paid a heavy price in losses to enemy bombing.

As a response to this, the British rushed into service an AEW version of the Sea King helicopter which, although not comparable to a fixed-wing aircraft in terms of its performance, still provided Sea Harriers and task force commanders alike with vital situational awareness. Although made operational

in an incredible 11 weeks, the first Sea King AEWs arrived just too to late to participate in the war.

Despite lacking an AWACS element embarked with the task force, the British did have some sort of covert early warning of attacks being launched – in some instance, they were able to alert Sea Harriers when Argentine aircraft took off from mainline bases. It is uncertain whether this warning was provided by submarines with radar or ELINT antennas above the surface, or by special operations forces on the

Argentina obtained refurbished ex-US Navy Skyhawks as early as 1966, this shot showing former A-4B BuNo 142788 on the ramp outside the Douglas plant at Tulsa, Oklahoma, prior to delivery.

ground in Argentina, or through the use of other sensors, including those provided to friendly countries in the immediate vicinity. Still, such warning were unable to completely close the British situational awareness gap.

ASW Sea Kings patrolled around the task force in search of Argentine submarines. The helicopter later served as the platform for a hasty AEW conversion that finally allowed the Sea Harriers to gain vital 'situational awareness' when aloft.

Sortie Generation

Above: Some 3256 nautical miles from the closest British air base at Ascension Island, the Falklands were too remote even for the long-legged Nimrod MR 2s to overfly on ASW and fighter control sorties. However, No 206 Sqn did fly a very limited number of record-breaking distance flights in an effort to monitor the movements of the Argentine Navy.

Left: Some of the most intensive strikes of the war were flown on 21 May in response to the British landings in San Carlos Bay, and although 17 Argentine aircraft (Daggers, Skyhawks and Pucarás) were reportedly downed, separate flights of Daggers and Navy Skyhawks still managed to penetrate the AAM/SAM umbrella and sink HMS Ardent.

Fighter operations in the Falklands again emphasized the importance of logistics support. The Sea Harriers were at the end of an 8,000-mile supply line, which meant that every pound of jet fuel and every Sidewinder missile expended was difficult to replace, limiting sortie generation rates. Despite this, between 21-25 May the FAA generated about 300 Sea Harrier and Harrier sorties.

By comparison, despite their huge numerical advantage, the Argentines were able to launch only 180 sorties against the Falklands over the same time frame, and less than half of these reached their target. Increasing the number of sorties is, as ever, a vital force multiplier for fighter operations.

Why the British won

The air-to-air operations of the Falklands War were incredibly one-sided. Sea Harriers destroyed 25 aircraft (including 19 downed with 27 AIM-9L shots, the remainder by cannon) without loss, and accomplished their mission of protecting British ships. They also completed many of their air-to-ground tasks, although five jets were lost to ground defenses. The Argentine fighters had failed miserably in their mission to challenge them in this role.

While British fighter operations in the Falklands must obviously be considered a success, their victory was only a limited one, as evidenced by the loss of seven ships to Argentine air attacks, which accounted for the majority of those killed in the conflict. The British fighter force was so small, and pushed to its limits, that even a reduced Argentine fighter force remained a threat. Operationally speaking, both sides were weak. The British perhaps had less excuse for such weakness, as they had been trained to meet world-

class opponents, but the threat that they met was so limited that the superior British pilots, tactics, training and weapons won the day – despite their operational weakness – because the enemy was weaker still.

Argentina's complete lack of air combat training and tactics was a crucial factor in their defeat. After 1 May, no Argentine fighter tried to dogfight with a Sea Harrier – they were either shot down or refused to engage the enemy. No Argentine AAMs were fired after 1 May – a big factor in this lack of enthusiasm for air combat with the Sea Harriers was the limited fuel carried by the Mirage fighters, which were operating at maximum range (reflecting a lack of tankers). Whatever the reasons for the overwhelming superiority of the Sea Harrier force, this conflict graphically underscored that even good 'stick and rudder men' do not automatically become combat-effective fighter pilots when up against world-class opposition.

Below left: Only five or six air-launched Exocets were available to the Argentine forces and these had been exhausted by 1 June.

Above: One of 9 Super Etendards delivered after the war. Had all 14 been operational, and the Exocets available, Argentina might have won the war.

Below: The Dagger was essentially an illegal Israeli copy of the Mirage 5, which had been dubbed the Nesher in IDFAF service.

The Gulf War and Post-Cold War Fighter Operations

The end of the Cold War changed the rules just in time for the Gulf War as without a Soviet threat, coalition airpower could concentrate solely on Iraq. The absence of Soviet support for the latter country also meant that airpower did not have to be constrained by concepts of graduated escalation – as had been the case throughout the jet age – to avoid a Cold War crisis. The Iraqis also faced fighter forces still enjoying the benefits of the boosts in spending lavished upon them in the early 1980s – new aircraft, better weapons and systems, better trained aircrew and fighter leaders and staff planners who had been taking the business of air-to-air fighter operations seriously for many years. Forces configured to stand up against a Soviet theater air operation subsequently proved capable of achieving a quick knockout blow against the Iraqi fighter force.

Right: The chief rival to the F-15C is the Su-35 'Flanker', which has impressed many observers thanks to the spirited displays performed by Sukhoi test pilots at airshows across the world.

Following the Iraqi invasion of Kuwait in August 1990, a massive coalition air armada gathered on airbases throughout the Middle East over the next six months. The numbers and types of fighters involved gave the coalition an unprecedented operational capability. The vast majority of these fighters came from NATO countries, and as a result they enjoyed the benefit of pre-existing operational concepts

(refined during the years of the 'flexible response' strategy) that they applied to the upcoming conflict. Those countries that were not NATO members – such as the Kingdom of Saudi Arabia (KSA) and other Arab coalition members – had months to adapt to the new operational concepts. This transition was aided by the fact that they used the same aircraft as their NATO allies, and had often trained with them.

Above: The F-15C Eagle proved itself to be the best air superiority fighter in the world during the brief time it got to engage the enemy over the Gulf, shooting down 34 enemy aircraft in 25 days.

Right: Another possible threat to the Eagle is offered by the Eurofighter 2000, although one hopes that the two jets will only ever encounter each other in ACM exercises rather than in a genuine 'shooting' war. Unlike the F-15, the Eurofighter has been designed from the outset with a strike capability very much in mind.

Operational Concepts – Gulf War Air Combat

While fighter operations were carried out during the Gulf War by a number of the Coalition partner air arms, the concepts which bound them into an effective fighting unit were predominantly those routinely employed by the USAF. Planning staffs from this organization structured all sorties so that they would be consistent with their 'centralized control – decentralized execution' philosophy, as practised during Red Flag exercises over the previous years.

The second part of this operational doctrine was accomplished through the issuing of Air Tasking Orders (ATOs). While criticised by other Coalition partners for being little more than daily versions of the USAF's SIOP (the warplans for nuclear attack on the Soviet Union, which obviously had to be finely detailed in advance), therefore dictating that much of the operational flexibility that could have been tailored in to deal with specific

Fighter Sweep 17 January 1991

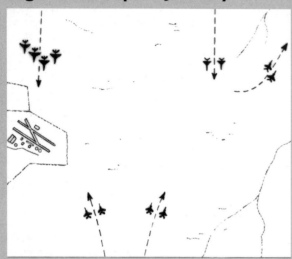

1. Four F-15Cs of Penzoil flight approach Mudaysis airfield. A USAF E-3 reports 'bandits' then identifies a pop-up contact at 35 miles. Penzoil 3 and 4 engage.

2. Penzoil 3 and 4 close with the enemy. The E-3 reported no friendlies present, so Penzoil 3 fires an AIM-7M, destroying an Iraqi MiG-29.

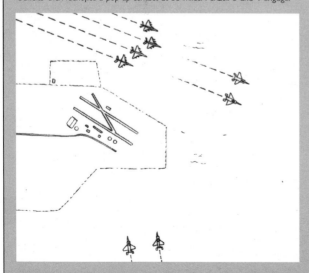

4. Citgo flight watched Penzoil's kill but was then alerted by the E-3 that Iraqi fighters were now 40-45 miles ahead, following the egressing F-15s.

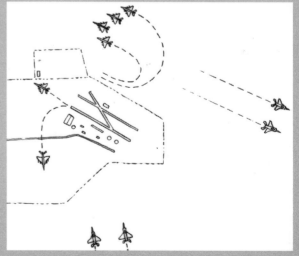

5. Alerted by their GCI, the Iraqis break off, but two more Iraqis take off from Mudaysis. Under GCI control, one Mirage F.1 climbs towards Citgo flight.

threats was ignored, the ATOs did allow for the optimal use of airpower throughout the duration of the conflict.

Coalition offensive fighter operations were mounted in response to objectives and priorities issued by the JFACC (Joint Force Air Component Commander) in the 'black hole' in Riyadh. The JFACC also set the Rules of Engagement (RoE) that would govern fighter operations, and unlike those employed during Operation Rolling

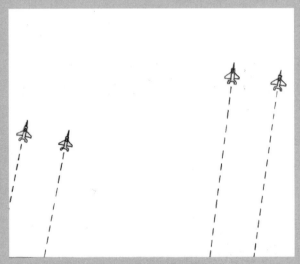

3. Trailing Penzoil flight by 60 miles, Citgo flight (four more F-15cs) was at 25-30,000 ft, with one element 20-25 miles in trail from the lead.

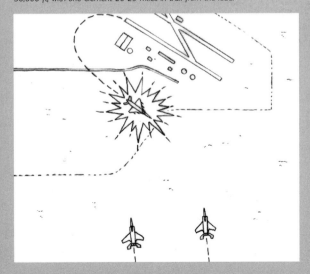

6. Citgo 1 fired a single AIM-7M, destroying the Mirage which attempted no defensive maneuvers. No more Iraqi aircraft were located that night.

Thunder back in the 1960s, they proved effective. Few Iraqi aircraft that could have been engaged escaped and, most importantly, there were no coalition shoot-downs of friendly aircraft which, considering the vast number of sorties, and the number of countries involved, was an incredible achievement in itself. When undertaking effective fighter operations, there is no harder a component to achieve than combat identification. This was helped in Desert Storm by the lack of Iraqi offensive air operations in response to Coalition attacks.

As has been the case since the First World War, it is the responsibility of the flight or mission lead pilot to sort out targets, and then direct and co-ordinate the actions of his fighters with other friendly forces – be they airborne or ground-based. Placing this command authority in the cockpit, rather than back in the Pentagon, prevented the loss of flexibility that crippled Rolling Thunder re-occurring in Desert Storm.

Since the advent of GCI in 1940, the lead pilot has had to co-ordinate with a 'battle manager'. Originally, this was a GCI controller, but by the time of the Gulf War, the 'battle manager' for air-air operations was usually in an E-3 AWACS, E-2 Hawkeye or an airborne command post such as a USAF EC-130 ABCCC (airborne command, control, communications), making full use of the situational awareness generated through a wide range of sensors.

The 'battle manager' needs to have the best possible knowledge pertaining to both the threat and opposing friendly forces. Although the AWACS controller has allocated the pilot a target (sometimes preferentially picking a friendly fighter in deference to any number of competing claimants as was the case when an AWACS designated an RSAF F-15C to splash two Iraqi Mirage F1EQs, thus strengthening the bond of the Coalition in the process) and provided the initial cueing for the fighter, as always it is up to the fighters to re-acquire the target themselves, using either the 'Mark I Eyeball' or on-board sensors. While flight or mission leaders can assign targets, prosecution of the intercept remains at cockpit level with the individual fighter crews.

Gulf War operations did not bring into question the need for manned fighters. This was just as well, for in future conflicts the enemy may trying to jam the voice UHF radio links (datalinks suffered from incompatibility in Desert Storm) on which fighter operations so depended in 1991. Further complicating the fighter pilot's lot may be the appearance of enemy interceptors hell-bent on neutralizing the all-important AWACS and ABCCCs. Should they succeed, then the skill of individual pilots will again be the most significant factor in determining the outcome of any aerial conflict.

The Iraqi Threat

Facing this force was the Iraqi Air Force of some 600 aircraft – the sixth largest in the world, its capabilities were much less impressive than its numbers, however. Having grown during the Iran-Iraq war, its aircrew and technical skills were spread too thinly over too large, and diverse, a fast jet force (which included Soviet-built MiG-29s, Su-24s, MiG-25s, MiG-23s, Su-25s, French-built Mirage F1s and Chinese-built F-7s) to be sustained in combat. Despite the huge investment in weaponry, the Iraqi Air Force had achieved only limited success in the Iran-Iraq War.

The Iraqi fighter force of 1991 was part of an integrated air defense system (the French-designed KARI) which, like its Soviet counterparts in Egypt and Syria in 1973, emphasized the use of SAMs and AAA. This was a very modern system, using computers, datalinks, redundant fibre optics and UHF communications links. n addition to ground-based radar, the Iraqis used French equipment on home-made AEW aircraft – modified Il-76 transport airframes. Reflecting the tightly-held

top-down command and control of all Iraqi forces, fighters were highly dependent on centralized control and execution, and relied on GCI tactics.

Reflecting the weakness of the Iraqi fighter force in actuality (though not in numbers), only 12 per cent of total coalition offensive sorties would be devoted to air-to-air fighter operations. Because the chief opponent of coalition air-to-air fighter operations was an integrated air-ground system, the destruction of ground targets would be as vital as the shooting down of aeroplanes. The Iraqi fighter force would be defeated not only by their opposite numbers in the skies, but also by the whole range of air-ground missions carried out by coalition strike and bomber aircraft. Of the air-ground efforts that helped defeat the Iraqi fighter force, the most notable in the opening days of the war were the undetected attacks on radars, and similar high-value targets, by F-117 stealth fighters.

During the war, Iraqi fighter pilots demonstrated limited air combat skills which reflected their poor training. At

an operational level, Iraq had little willingness to take the offensive against coalition aircraft, yet the potential remained for such operations. Indeed, until the latter stages of the conflict, the coalition had to plan for a last-ditch counter-air strike by surviving Iraqi aircraft. This required substantial DCA activity by aircraft such as USN F-14s, RAF Tornado F.3s (restricted to friendly airspace because of their limited air combat capability) and French and Arab Mirage 2000s. There was no enemy air offensive, however.

Iraq relied exclusively on their force of Scud ballistic missiles for attacks on KSA, Bahrain and Israel, these weapons being crudely targeted at population centers (especially in Israel) with the hope of gaining political impact, rather than being used against coalition airbases to reduce the sortie generation rate. However, the massive Scud-hunting efforts ordered as a result of these strikes diverted more coalition air sorties away from the specified aim of the air campaign than any Scud attack on coalition airfields could have achieved.

Left: Although two MiG-25s were destroyed by USAF F-15Cs, it is now unofficially believed that the very first aerial kill of the Gulf War was actually achieved by an Iraqi 'Foxbat' which shot down a VFA-81 F/A-18C with an AAM on 17 January 1991.

Right: Iraq, like all Arab states supplied with arms from the USSR relied heavily on the MiG-23/27 in both fighter and strike roles. These MiG-23UMs belong to a Soviet training unit based in the Ukraine.

Below: A dozen US Navy Hornet units were involved in the action of Desert Storm, including VFA-15 'Valions', embarked aboard USS Theodore Roosevelt.

Fighter Combat and Doctrine in the Gulf

Doctrine, in the view of eminent military historian Sir Michael Howard, is always wrong. No military force has ever been able to predict in advance the concepts needed for effective operations in future war. He went on to say, however, 'that it really doesn't matter as long as the military has the capacity to quickly correct it when needed'.

The American approach to operational doctrine, in the opinion of F-15 pilot Major 'Mike' Holmes, varies within the services. 'In the Army, it's a bible – it tells you how to do things. In the Air Force, it's a set of considerations that you might want to think about as you plan or conduct operations. The Navy has only recently felt a need to even have any written doctrine outside of tactical procedures.'

While there is much truth in these descriptions of the different approaches to doctrine followed by the various branches of the US military both during and after the Gulf War, doctrine has certainly been more than just simply a

'set of considerations' when applied to fighter operations throughout the jet age. Rather, doctrine has shaped the success or failure of fighter operations, proving to be more important than either of the quotes from Sir Michael or 'Major Mike' might suggest.

Doctrine is difficult to change, and many air arms have failed Sir Michael's requirement for rapid doctrinal response. For example, the USAF had not fully recovered from its doctrinal devaluing of air-air fighter operations in the late 1950s and early 60s by 1972, as the difference between Air Force and Navy kill ratios from that year clearly show – 2-to-1 for the former and 13-to-1 for the latter. The rebirth of effective fighter operations in the last decade of the Cold War was essentially a change in doctrine, as well as aircraft.

Since even the best, and most professional, air arms have often stuck to their established doctrine rather than evolving, air forces of the 1990s need to build on the

Left: Although the IDFAF had proven the Eagle's ability in its designed role as early 1979, the closest USAF examples had got to a potential enemy was escorting snooping 'Bears' across the North Atlantic.

Right: Built as a 'light fighter', the F-16's ability to carry ordnance, including Maverick ASMs (seen here) has made it one of the USAF's primary weapons. The F-16 formed the backbone of the strike force in the Gulf, losing 5 to AAA and SAMs.

Below: One of the first aircraft to deploy to Saudi Arabia in response to the invasion of Kuwait, the RAF's Tornado F 3s had a frustrating war once the shooting started. Deemed unsuitable to accompany strikes into enemy territory, it therefore spent the war flying uneventful patrols over Saudi Arabia.

lessons of the Gulf (and other recent conflicts), or in the future face the return of doctrinal irrelevance, which will exact a heavy cost in battle.

The USAF and US Navy, like the RAF, have often failed to clearly explain their operational doctrines for all types of air combat to those who must carry them out (or those who must organize and pay for their forces). They lack viable capstone doctrinal publications that explain just how different types of operations should be undertaken.

While frontline conflict remains the catalyst in war around which campaigns and major operations are planned and executed in any medium, in the air the boundaries that separate tactical, operational and strategic levels of warfare are not so apparent as they are on land or at sea. Rather, tactical and strategic considerations basically inhabit the same space as routine operations. Thus, an examination of one level of war in terms of the

employment of fighter assets is likely to also involve the others elements as well. For example, the distinction between 'tactical' and 'strategic' airpower, blurring as early as Vietnam, became further indistinct in the Gulf. The merger of the USAF's SAC and TAC into Air Combat Command (ACC) – almost 25 years after RAF Strike Command had been produced by the merger of Bomber and Fighter Commands – was an organizational reflection of operational reality.

In the past, when doctrine has not proven effective in guiding operations, it has usually been because it was unrealistic or too divorced from actual military experience. Today, with the lessons of 50 years of jet fighter combat to draw upon, the potential exists for forces such as the USAF, US Navy and RAF to put in place effective concepts of operability that will not only guide those services' daily operations, but joint and multi-national endeavours as a whole.

Fighter Operations in Desert Storm

The majority of coalition fighter operations (with the notable exception of USN and other DCA sorties, and USMC close air support) were centrally tasked under a unified Air Tasking Order. With over 2,500 sorties being flown in each daily ATO, and with a maximum of 1,000 aircraft from a number of different countries in the air at any one time, strong control mechanisms were obviously required. Often criticized in past conflicts for being over-centralized and a hindrance to the flexible application of airpower, in the conditions of the Gulf War the ATO provided an efficient allocation of airpower simply because the Iraqis soon lost any active ability to interfere with the progression of the coalition battle plan.

The Iraqi fighter force was first rendered both 'sightless' and 'brainless' by the destruction of its radars,

command centers and headquarters. Its communications links were severed, both by F-117 precision attacks on switching nodes and through special operations forces cutting through fibre optic cables in the desert. When the Iraqi air defense system switched to backup UHF communications, these too were put out of action. The Iraqi air defenses could not cope with stand-off jammers employed by aircraft like the EF-111, EA-6B or EC-130, whilst the use of ARMs by USAF Wild Weasels and a broad range of coalition strike aircraft effectively wiped out a large percentage of the radar and SAM sites in-theater. The use of self-defense jammers and RHAW equipment was also near-universal among coalition aircraft sent on offensive missions.

The few Iraqi jets that came up to challenge the air offensive stood little

power diminished by 70 per cent.

Following these initial attacks, the Iraqi Air Force was pinned down by repeated counter-air strikes against them on their airfields. This was done in the opening days through attacks on runways and taxiways. Aircraft such as RAF and RSAF Tornados used low-level strike tactics with JP233 munitions, while French Air Force Jaguars attacked with Beluga and Durandel munitions. USAF F-111s and USN A-6Es employed stand-off PGMs from medium altitude: a tactic later adopted by RAF Tornados after their low-level tactics (that had been developed for European contingencies) proved too costly in operational losses to ground fire and SAMs. B-52s also added their bomb tonnage to airfield attacks. Some 90 aircraft, including the bombers and AEW aircraft which had not fled the country, were caught outside the HASs during these raids and destroyed.

Over one hundred Iraqi aircraft were chased to Iran, where they flew to intern themselves, rather than face inevitable destruction either in the air or on their bases. Many of these aircraft, often flying at night, were shot down en route by coalition fighters which had positioned BARCAPs (barrier combat air patrols) deep in Iraq, often close to the Iranian border. USAF F-15Cs with improved Sparrow BVR AAMs were highly lethal in all weathers, and were responsible for most of the kills during this phase of the war.

The coalition cause was helped significantly by the excellent situational awareness of its fighter pilots. A line of E-3s and E-2Cs stood off from Iraqi airspace, co-ordinating strikes and passing information. They were supplemented by terrestrial radars including the RSAF's Peace Shield system and USN Aegis missile cruisers in the northern Gulf. Near real-time ELINT

The USAF even unleashed the 'big stick' during Desert Storm, B-52Gs based literally on the other side of the globe delivering an overwhelming tonnage of ordnance against strategic targets in northern Iraq and dug-in elements of the Republican Guard.

chance of doing any damage to the attacking aircraft, and virtually zero chance of surviving a combat engagement with a coalition fighter. Attacks on the Iraqi infrastructure also affected fighter operations, with raids on power stations literally 'pulling the plug' on much of the air defense system. Within three days 85 per cent of Iraq's radar network was out of action and its ability to generate electric

Undoubtedly one of the 'stars' of Desert Storm, Lockheed's F-117 stealth 'fighter' belied its designation and attacked strategic targets in Baghdad using GBU-27 2000-lb Paveway LGBs. Two of these weapons could be carried in the Night Hawk's bomb bay.

was often available from sources such as USAF RC-135 Rivet Joint aircraft, also patrolling outside Iraqi airspace. EC-130 airborne command posts further helped co-ordinate fighters and strikes. Supporting all these operations was a massive tanker fleet. Together, these aircraft played an important role in the success of Gulf War fighter operations (and have probably made themselves prime targets for any future opponents in the process).

Finally, any Iraqi fighters that had survived this onslaught were destroyed by more counter-air attacks, the cratering of runways and the systematic destruction of their hardened aircraft shelters. F-117s, F-111s and Tornados (hastily re-equipped with PGMs) cracked 375 HASs and destroyed 141 aircraft.

In air combat the toll was one-sided, with 45 Iraqi aircraft being destroyed (requiring the expenditure of about 178 AAMs). The vast majority of these kills were scored by USAF F-15Cs who, as air-to-air specialists, were tasked with

carrying out the job of 'using scouts offensively'. Some of the other kills showed the wide range of air combat capabilities in the coalition forces. Navy F/A-18s on a strike mission disposed of a pair of Chinese-built F-7s without having to jettison their bombs (a far cry from the Vietnam experience), whilst one of the few Iraqi offensive missions came to an end when an RSAF F-15C was vectored onto two Mirage F1s by an AWACS, and subsequently 'splashed' them both. Included amongst the more unusual kills was an Iraqi Mirage F1 that was maneuvered into high ground by a fleeing, and unarmed, EF-111, and an F-15E on an air-ground mission that dropped a laser guided bomb on a hovering Iraqi helicopter (the recommended tactic against such targets).

On the debit side, the Iraqi Air Force may have destroyed one coalition aircraft – the first loss of the war in the shape of a USN F/A-18. It is uncertain whether a missile from a MiG-25 Foxbat

or an SA-6 SAM brought it down. A further 37 jets were shot down by Iraqi ground-based air defenses.

The Gulf War was also marked by effective IFF. Despite the massive offensive and defensive coalition air operations, no aircraft were confirmed as lost to friendly fire. Following years of NATO problems with IFF interoperability, this reflected a combination of the lack of offensive operations by the Iraqis, good planning and good luck. This last factor preserved a B-52 hit by a F-4G Wild Weasel's ARM, which had deduced that the fire control radar in the bomber's tail turret was in fact from an Iraqi AAA battery!

Doctrine and Fighter Operations in the Gulf – RAF Tornado Operations

The RAF participated at the highest levels in the planning of the air campaign against Iraq. Their tasking in the offensive counter-air mission in the opening days of the war (in the absence of a true fighter capability) was to use their force of air-ground Tornado GR.1s to help put Iraqi airfields out of action through low-altitude attacks with Hunting JP.233 anti-runway weapons. They were joined in this mission by similarly-equipped Italian and Saudi Tornado IDSs.

These hazardous strikes, performed throughout the first week of the war, were in the main successful. They were instrumental in limiting the number of Iraqi aircraft which could be launched to either challenge the air offensive, or later escape to Iran. Those that remained in the HASs were systematically destroyed as the war progressed by attack aircraft using LGBs from medium-altitude. When Coalition commander General Norman Schwarzkopf praised RSAF Tornados for putting bomb craters in an Iraqi runway 'as accurately as if they had been delivered by a pickup truck', he was paying tribute not only to the coming-of-age of a Third World fighter force, but also to the effectiveness of the Tornado OCA attacks.

Yet these attacks raised serious questions in respect to the applicability of tactics designed for the central front in Europe being utilized against Iraq. The sheer size of the runways and percentage of redundant taxyways that made up typical Iraqi airbases was greater than had ever been seen in the main operating bases (MOBs) sited in the former East Germany – the primary targets for RAF Tornado units during the Cold War. For example, Talil airbase was twice the size of London-Heathrow International! A further problem was caused by the fact that the runways were built over a sand base, rather than earth. This meant that the 'heaving' of densely-packed foundation that the JP.223's submunitions were specially designed to create did not occur when detonated within sand.

Operational planning for Tornado sorties in a central European conflict also assumed that heavy losses were inevitable – it was projected that half the force would be shot down within the first days of heavy operations. In the Gulf War, where the Coalition operated in the unremitting glare of a sceptical media, there was an increased sensitivity to losses. While the shooting down of seven Tornados (including one Italian jet) on OCA sorties in the first week of the war caused great concern, only one was lost while carrying out a JP.233 attack pattern. Indeed, just 106 Hunting canisters were used by the RAF in the low-level phase of operations.

Fighter sweeps in the first week of the air campaign effectively cleared the Iraqi Air Force from the skies, allowing RAF Tornados to switch to far less hazardous medium altitude attack profiles using LGBs. Another factor that allowed the Air Force to change roles so effectively was that they could quickly deploy ageing Buccaneer attack aircraft to the Gulf to serve as laser designator platforms. Despite the unusually bad weather that troubled fighter operations on a number of days, medium altitude attacks remained feasible to a greater degree than would have been the case in a European conflict due to the fact that the cloud cover was never total – enemy air defenses were also less effective.

The RAF's use of Tornados in the OCA mission showed both the strengths and weaknesses of modern fighter operations. One strength was the skill and adaptability of the individual Tornado aircrews, which. allowed them to switch from low-level attacks using JP.223s to medium level LGB delivery without even 'breaking stride'. However, despite this seemingly flexible attitude towards prosecuting the Gulf War the RAF has since been accused of doctrinal rigidity in its execution of OCA operations, most notably by the British supreme commander during Desert Storm, General Sir Peter de la Billiere. He has claimed that RAF commanders in the Gulf came under high level pressure from superiors back in the UK to adhere to their institutionally-preferred operational concept of low-level attacks with JP.223, no matter what the cost.

However, in this case it appears that rigidity flowed, at least in part, from a shortage of resources that stemmed back some 15 years to when the Tornado was conceived, rather than from a desire to see peacetime doctrine vindicated by wartime operations. A fiscally-strapped RAF had been forced to invest in a single multi-role design to fill both the fighter and attack roles for the 1980s, and the resulting Tornado proved to be a much better 'bomber' than it was a 'fighter'.

The proof of this came in the Gulf War when the RAF's Tornado F.3s ADVs in-theatre were kept solely on the DCA mission because of their inferiority to Iraqi MiG-29s in air combat. This meant that the RAF's contribution to the OCA mission exclusively took the form of Tornado GR.1s undertaking air-ground strikes. The fiscal criterion that saw all the money in the 'pot' spent on a single 'fighter' type was also applied when the RAF chose a single type of weapon (the JP.223) and a single mission (conventional low-level OCA against airbases in East Germany) for the resulting Tornado GR.1. This allowed it

Designed to fight at low level over central Europe, the Tornado GR 1 won its 'battle spurs' against in equally dangerous environment over Kuwait and Iraq. This particular jet is a recce-optimized GR 1A of No II Sqn.

to retain an element of operational viability as a 'niche competitor' within NATO.

Had there been more resources and more weapons types available, as well as more training hours, the RAF Tornado force would have had more options – it is cheaper, and easier, to have multi-role fighters than multi-role fighter pilots. One solution to this problem is that adopted by the Israelis, who have trained individual squadrons (especially in the late 1970s) to specialize in the delivery of a single type of weapon – one unit with Walleye LGBs, another with Maverick ASMs, another with Standard ARMs and so on.

The ability of the RAF's strike crews to change mission profiles so easily in the Gulf was greatly facilitated by the plethora of resources available to them, including integration in Coalition air strikes and a permissive air defense environment. In a conflict in Europe, the RAF would not have been able to offer them penetrating AAM-armed fighters to escort their Tornados, or specialized Wild Weasels and ECM aircraft to neutralize the SAM threat, or, in a Cold War scenario, AWACS to cover and co-ordinate their strikes. Therefore, the RAF's approach to OCA operations early on in Desert Storm reflected the limited resources that would have been available to them in a general war.

The controversy surrounding Tornado operations in 1991 also served to underline how the gulf in effectiveness between first rank and second rank fighter

forces has grown bigger in recent years. In the 1970s, the RAF, the Luftwaffe or the French Air Force would have claimed that despite lacking the USAF or the US Navy's power projection capabilities, specialized support aircraft or training facilities, they were comparable in effectiveness thanks to up to date tactics and a proven ability to adapt to specific environments. The Gulf War, however, showed that American investment in its fighter forces during the 1980s had gave it a superior capability across the board. Only possibly Israel could now make the claim of being a true 'niche competitor'.

The RAF has strongly refuted charges of doctrinal rigidity in its Gulf War operations. However, the claims still raise vital issues. The key to successful operations is flexibility, and rigidity in doctrine, or in the missions guided by it, defeats this crucial aspect of fighter operability. The importance of doctrine is to provide guidance – not direction – for those making the operational decisions and directing training.

An effective fighter force is more than just 'a bunch' of squadrons and aircrew. It requires a level of investment in training and weapons that far exceeds the cost of acquiring a modern fighter. However, without this investment in operational flexibility, a fighter force is giving up one of its most important assets.

Fighter Operations – Iraq and Bosnia

Fighter operations in the years since the end of both the Gulf and Cold Wars in 1991 have been limited in scope and purpose – but no less challenging to those who must plan and execute them. These factors, plus their multi-national composition, may offer a preview of what future air-to-air fighter operations may look like.

Because these operations have been part of 'operations other than war', the option of removing aircraft that might violate a cease-fire, UN Security Council Resolution or other limitations on their operations through OCA airstrikes is limited. While allied operations against both Iraq and Bosnian Serbs since 1991 have included airstrikes, these have not targeted airfields and air defense systems on a sustained basis. Because these

Right: Like the F 3, the Mirage 2000C was also frustrated in its attempts to see action in its chosen interceptor role during Desert Storm. This aircraft is from 5 Escadre de Chasse, who sent 14 jets to Al Ahsa air base in October 1990. Like RAF and USAF fighter units that have since spent time patrolling the 'No Fly' zone over Iraq, E/C 5 have also returned to Saudi Arabia on numerous occasions.

Below: The US Navy has also carried out its fair share of missions over the exclusion zones of Iraq and Bosnia. Indeed, it has been called upon to attack ground targets in former Yugoslavia, the F/A-18 performing the tasks with a minimum of fuss.

operations are, by definition, 'retail' responses to individual aircraft violating them, they require an equally limited response – that of fighters shooting down the violators.

The ability of fighter aircraft to visually inspect, warn and, if required, destroy airborne violators with precision means that this is another mission where the fighter is likely to be irreplaceable. They provide a visible deterrent presence that the threat of SAM use or retaliatory OCA attacks does not possess. Fighters are a visible indication of political will in such operations.

Because the fighters carrying out these missions must often operate over territory where there are hostile SAMs, RHAW, ECM and stealth capabilities are certainly required. Situational awareness is also vital in such operations, and the E-3s and E-2s from a number of coalition partners have made it possible for fighters to prevent hostile flight operations. As a result of this international 'policing' role assumed by the Americans, the USAF's E-3 force is today stretched thinner than it ever was in the Cold War.

Of course, a fighter's situational awareness will not compensate for an itchy trigger finger. There has been a succession of tragic instances where fighters (and often their ground- or air-controllers) 'saw' what they expected to see, rather than what was in front of them. In 1974 Israeli fighters attacked and shot down a Libyan 727, while USAF F-15s destroyed two US Army helicopters over northern Iraq in 1993.

The Future of Fighter Operations

Left: Grandly dubbed the 'world's first light weight multi-role combat aircraft' by its manufacturer, the Grippen combines the best of Swedish aeronautical engineering with an American powerplant and AAMs. Saab are pinning great hopes on this jet winning export abroad, and have gone into partnership with seasoned exporters British Aerospace.

Right: One of Grippen's main competitors is the stylish Dassault Rafale, which has been ordered in good quantities by both the French Air Force and Navy. This is the Rafale B 01 prototype two-seater, which first flew in April 1993. Although planned as a single-seater, the two-seat Rafale has now emerged as the preferred option for the French Air Force due to crew overload in the Gulf War.

Below: The effectiveness of a two-man crew was graphically shown in the results achieved by 'two-holers' like the F-111, A-6 and F-15E. With defensive weapons systems getting more and more effective, it will take an adept crew to prosecute the mission tasking and survive to fight another day.

The question remains as to whether fighter operations have a future and, if the answer to that is affirmative, whether a new generation of fighters is required to carry them out. The record of jet fighter operations since 1945 appear that the answers to both questions is in the affirmative.

The jet fighter thrives on its flexibility. Its advocates have never had the strength of a rigid doctrinal framework, as have advocates of strategic airpower, but have instead had to point that a flexible, competent and well-equipped fighter force should be able to deal with threats that the planners have not anticipated. Effective fighter operations cannot simply be described as the use of 'tactical' airpower. Fighter aircraft have demonstrated throughout the jet age that they can have far-reaching effects in warfare, and have become a pre-requisite for effective overall theater fighting.

To do this in the future will likely require improved fighter aircraft, rather than improved SAMs or the improved AAMs fitted to today's fighters. Throughout the jet age, effective operations have had to rest on the basic foundations of aircraft, tactics, training and technology. These factors all require continued investment in pilot training, new weapons and active thinking in terms of improvement. One cannot rest on one's laurels, or fret about accidental losses in training. All of this requires money and flexibility – two quantities in short supply in the West, as budget cuts and the re-emergence of a peacetime 'garrison mentality' become widespread.

Any predictions about the form that next generation air-to-air fighter operations will take are unlikely to be accurate. The prudent solution is to invest in sufficient numbers of high quality fighters and aircrew (the brittleness of small 'silver bullet' forces has also been seen throughout the last 50 years), and to make sure they have a coherent operational approach to guide their use.

Fighter Directory

Dassault Mirage 111

Type: fighter   **Accommodation:** one pilot

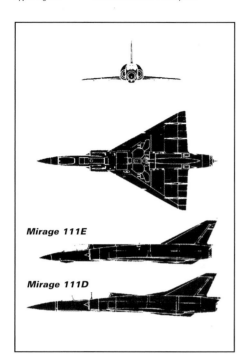

Mirage 111E

Mirage 111D

Dimensions:
Length: 49 ft 3 in (15.03 m);
IIIR 50 ft 10 in (15.50 m)
Wingspan: 26 ft 11 in (8.22 m)
Height: 14 ft 9 in (4.5 m)

Weights:
Empty: 15 540 lb (7050 kg);
IIIR 14 550 lb (6600 kg)
Max T/O: 30 200 lb (13 700 kg)

Performance:
Max Speed: Mach 2.2; 863
mph at sea level
Range: 1294 nm (2400 km)
Powerplant: one SNECMA
Atar 9C turbojet
Thrust: 13 670 lb (60.8 kN)
with afterburner

Armament:
two 30 mm DEFA 552A
cannon; five hardpoints; 8818
lb (4000 kg) warload; Matra
R.530, Magic AAMs; AS.30
ASM; bombs; rockets

Variants:
IIIB/D two-seat ground
attack/training aircraft; IIIR
reconnaissance version

Notes: IIIR has a longer nose with five camera lenses. Brazilian, Swiss and
other upgraded models have canards aft of air intakes.

Dassault Mirage 5

Type: multi-role fighter   **Accommodation:** one pilot

Dimensions:
Length: 51 ft (15.55 m)
Wingspan: 26 ft 11 in (8.22 m)
Height: 14 ft 9 in (4.5 m)

Weights:
Empty: 14 550 lb (6600 kg)
Max T/O: 30 200 lb (13 700 kg)

Performance:
Max Speed: Mach 2.2; 863
mph at sea level

Range: 1400 nm (2600 km);
700 nm (1300 km) at low level
Powerplant: one SNECMA
Atar 9C turbojet
Thrust: 13 670 lb (60.8 kN)
with afterburner

Armament:
two 30 mm DEFA 552A
cannon; seven hardpoints;
8818 lb (4000 kg) warload;
Matra R.530, Magic, AIM-9

Sidewinder AAMs; AS.30 ASM;
bombs; rockets

Variants:
5D two-seat ground
attack/training aircraft; 5R
reconnaissance version; 5PA4
Agave radar and Exocet; Elkan
SABCA upgrade with canards
and new avionics fitted into
ex-Belgian aircraft sold to
Chile

Dassault Mirage 50

Type: multi-role fighter   **Accommodation:** one pilot

Dimensions:
Length: 51 ft (15.56 m)
Wingspan: 26 ft 11 in (8.22 m)
Height: 14 ft 9 in (4.5 m)

Weights:
Empty: 15 765 lb (7150 kg)
Max T/O: 30 200 lb (13 700 kg)

Performance:
Max Speed: Mach 2.2
Range: 1330 nm (2410 km);
740 nm (1370 km) low level
Powerplant: one SNECMA
Atar 9K-50 turbojet
Thrust: 15 873 lb (70.6 kN)
with afterburner

Armament:
two 30 mm DEFA cannon;
seven hardpoints; Matra
R.530, Magic, AIM-9
Sidewinder AAMs; Exocet,
AS.30 ASM; bombs; rockets

Variants:
operational trainer; Pantera (IAI
upgrade of Chilean Mirage 50)

Notes: Re-engined Mirage 5 with additional fuel and a higher payload, Mirage 50s can be equipped with Agave radar and Exocet missile. Both Dassault and IAI are offering upgrades, the latter product featuring a Kfir-style nose plug, whilst the former boasts a Mirage F1-type IFR probe.

Dassault Mirage F1C

Type: multi-role fighter   **Accommodation:** one pilot

Dimensions:
Length: 49 ft 11 in (15.23 m);
F1C-200 50 ft 2 in (15.30 m)
Wingspan: 27 ft 6 in (8.4 m)
Height: 14 ft 9 in (4.5 m)

Weights:
Empty: 16 314 lb (7400 kg)
Max T/O: 35 715 lb (16 200 kg)

Performance:
Max Speed: Mach 2.2; Mach
1.2 low level
Range: 756 nm (1400 km) low
level

Powerplant: one SNECMA
Atar 9K-50 turbojet
Thrust: 15 873 lb (70.6 kN)
with afterburner

Armament:
two 30 mm DEFA 553 cannon;
seven hardpoints; 8818 lb
(4000 kg) warload; Super 530,
550 Magic, AIM-9 Sidewinder
AAMs; AM 39 Exocet, AS.30L
ASMs; reconnaissance pod;
bombs; rockets

Variants:
F1A attack version without
radar, with undernose laser,
used by South Africa and
Libya; F1B operational trainer;
F1C air defence version with
Cyrano IV radar; F1CR
reconnaissance version; F1C-
200 with in-flight refuelling
boom; F1CT as above,
converted to air-to-ground
role; F1E export version

Dassault Mirage 2000C

Type: multi-role fighter   **Accommodation:** one pilot

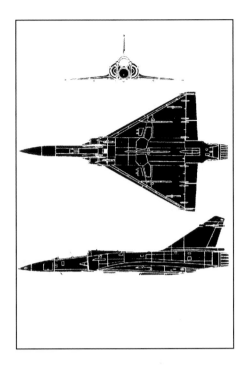

Dimensions:
Length: 47 ft 1 in (14.36 m)
Wingspan: 29 ft 11 in (9.13 m)
Height: 17 ft (5.2 m)

Weights:
Empty: 16 534 lb (7500 kg)
Max T/O: 37 480 lb (17 000 kg)

Performance:
Max Speed: Mach 2.2 (Mach 1.2 at sea level)
Range: 2000 nm (3704 km); 1000 nm (1850 km) at low level
Powerplant: one SNECMA M53-P2 turbofans
Thrust: 14 462 lb (21 385 lb with afterburner)

Armament:
two 30 mm DEFA 554 cannon; nine hardpoints; 13 890 lb (6300 kg) warload; Super 530D, 530F, 550 Magic, Magic 2 AAMs; bombs; rockets

Variants:
Mirage 2000 RDM
Mirage 2000 RDI
Mirage 2000-5
Mirage 2000B two-seat operational trainer

Dassault Rafale

Type: multi-purpose fighter   **Accommodation:** one pilot

Dimensions:
Length: 50 ft 2 in (15.30 m)
Wingspan: 35 ft 9 in (10.9 m)
Height: 17 ft 6 in (5.34 m)

Weights:
Empty: 19 973 lb (9060 kg); 21 319 lb (9800 kg) Rafale M
Max T/O: 47 399 lb (21 500 kg)

Performance:
Max Speed: Mach 2

Range: 2000 nm (3706 km) air-to-air; 1180 nm (2186 km) ground attack
Powerplant: two SNECMA M88-2 augmented turbofans
Thrust: 21 900 lb (97.4 kN) - 32 800 lb (145.8 kN) with afterburner

Armament:
one 30 mm DEFA 791B cannon; Maximum of 14 hardpoints; 13 228 lb (6000 kg) warload; ASMP stand-off nuclear weapon; Mica AAMs; Apache stand-off weapon dispenser; Exocet ASMs; bombs

Variants:
Rafale A proof of concept demonstrator; Rafale B two-seat operational trainer; Rafale C for French Air Force; Rafale M carrier borne fighter

Notes: 250 planned for French Air Force and 86 for French Navy. In an attempt to replace the ageing F-8 Crusader as soon as possible, the first naval aircraft will lack the full avionics suite to bring them into service earlier.

Eurofighter EF2000

Type: multi-role fighter   **Accommodation:** one pilot

Dimensions:
Length: 47 ft 7 in (14.5 m)
Wingspan: 34 ft 5 in (10.5 m)
Height: approx 13 ft 1 in (4 m)

Weights:
Empty: 21 495 lb (9750 kg)
Max T/O: 46 297 lb (21 000 kg)

Performance:
Max Speed: Mach 2
Range: 600 nm (1112 km)
Powerplant: two Eurojet
EJ200 advanced turbojets in
production models
Thrust: 26 980 lb (120 kN) –
40 500 lb (180 kN) with
afterburner

Armament:
one 27 mm Mauser cannon;
total of 13 hardpoints; 14 330
lb (6500 kg); AIM-120
AMRAAM, Aspide, ASRAAM
AAMs; a range of stand-off
weapons; bombs; rockets

Variants:
operational trainer

Notes: The EF2000 continues to suffer from political decision-making concerning its future, particularly in Germany. However, several prototypes are now flying, including a two-seat trainer version.

Panavia Tornado ADV

Type: interceptor   **Accommodation:** one pilot, one weapon systems officer in tandem

Dimensions:
Length: 61ft 3in (18.68m)
Wingspan: spread 45ft 7in
(13.91m); swept 28ft 2in (8.6m)
Height: 19ft 6in (5.95m)

Weights:
Empty: 31 970lb (14 500kg)

Max T/O: 61 700lb (27 986kg)

Performance:
Max Speed: Mach 2.2
Range: 2000nm (3704km)
Powerplant: two Turbo Union
RB199-34R Mk104 turbofans
Thrust: 18 200lb (81kN)

Armament:
one 27mm IWKA-Mauser
cannon; two hardpoints; four
Skyflash, four Sidewinder
AAMs

Variants:
none

Notes: called F3 in UK service. Italy has leased 24 ex-RAF aircraft as an interim measure before introduction of the EF2000.

Mikoyan MiG-17 Fresco

Type: Type: fighter bomber   **Accommodation:** one pilot

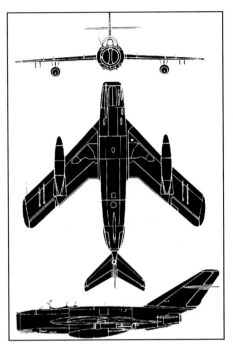

Dimensions:
Length: 37 ft 3 in (11.36 m)
Wingspan: 31 ft 7 in (9.63 m)
Height: 12 ft 5 in (3.8 m)

Weights:
Empty: 8664 lb (3930 kg)
Max T/O: 13 379 lb (6069 kg)

Performance:
Max Speed: 711 mph (1145 kmh)
Range: 755 nm (1400 km)
Powerplant: one Klimov VK-1A turbojet
Thrust: 7605 lb (33.83 kN)

Armament:
one 37 mm Nudelmann-Suranov NS-37 cannon and two 23 mm NR-23 cannon; two hardpoints; bombs; rockets

Variants:
J-5 Chinese built version; JJ-5 Chinese trainer; FT-5 for export; LIM-6 Polish-built with brake chute fairing

Notes: Also built under licence by China, Czechoslovakia and Poland, a total of 9000 are believed to have been produced.

Mikoyan MiG-19 Farmer

Type: interceptor   **Accommodation:** one pilot

Dimensions:
Length: 37 ft 6 in (11.43 m)
Wingspan: 32 ft (9.75 in)
Height: 12 ft 9 in (3.885 m)

Weights:
Empty: 12 698 lb (5760 kg)
Max T/O: 19 840 lb (9000 kg)

Performance:
Max Speed: Mach 1.4
Range: 370 nm (685 km)
Powerplant: two axial flow turbojets
Thrust: 8818 lb (4000 kg)

Armament:
two 37 mm cannon and two 23 mm cannon; AAMs; air-to-air rockets

Variants:
Shenyang J-6 Chinese-built version; F-6 export version; JJ-6 two-seat trainer; FT-6 for export; various radar-equipped sub-variants

Notes: The Chinese version proved to be more popular. Export success for the F-6 was followed by large exports of the A-5 on which it was based (for A-5 see separate entry).

Mikoyan MiG-21 Fishbed

Type: multi-role fighter   **Accommodation:** one pilot

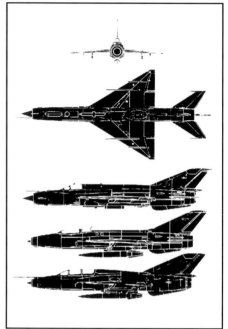

Dimensions:
Length: 51 ft 8 in (15.76 m)
Wingspan: 23ft 5in (7.15 m)
Height: 13 ft 5 ft (4.1 m)

Weights:
Empty: 12 882 lb (5843 kg)
Max T/O: 21 605 lb (9800 kg)

Performance:
Max Speed: Mach 2, Mach 1 at low level
Range: 971 nm (1800 km)
Powerplant: one Tumansky R-13-300 turbojet
Thrust: 9340 lb (41.55 kN), 14 550 lb (64.73 kN)

Armament:
one twin 23 mm GSh-23 cannon; four hardpoints; K-13A Atoll, AA-2C Atoll, AAMs; rockets; bombs

Variants:
MiG-21U/UM trainer

Notes: Fighter versions progressively improved, with increased avionics, armament and better radar. Characterised by increases in spine, tailfin area and nose size. Upgrades offered for the hundreds of MiG-21s still in service.

Mikoyan MiG-23 Flogger

Type: multi-role fighter   **Accommodation:** one pilot

Dimensions:
Length: 51 ft 4 in (15.6 m)
Wingspan: spread 45 ft 10 in (13.96 m), swept 25 ft 6 in (7.78 m)
Height: 15 ft 9 in (4.82 m)

Weights:
Empty: 22 485 lb (10 200 kg)
Max T/O: 39 250 lb (17 800 kg)
Performance:
Max Speed: Mach 2.35
Range: 1050 nm (1950 km)

Powerplant: one Soyuz/Khachaturov R-35-300 turbojet
Thrust: 28 660 lb (127.5 kN) with afterburner

Armament:
one 23 mm GSh-23L cannon; six hardpoints; R-23R Apex, R-23T Apex, R-60T Aphid, weapons dispensers, bombs, rockets

Variants:
MiG-23U trainer; MiG-23B series (hybrid fighter-bomber with MiG-27-type nose and MiG-23B intakes); MiG-23ML/MLD lightweight fighter version with improved avionics; MiG-23MS downgraded export version with Jay Bird radar in smaller radome

Mikoyan MiG-27 Flogger-D and -J

Type: ground attack fighter   **Accommodation:** one pilot

Dimensions:
Length: 56 ft (17.076 m)
Wingspan: spread 45 ft 10 in (13.96 m), swept 25 ft 6 in (7.78 m)
Height: 15 ft 9 in (4.82 m)

Weights:
Empty: 26 252 lb (11 908 kg)
Max T/O: 44 750 lb (20 300 kg)

Performance:
Max Speed: Mach 1.7
Range: 582 nm (1080 km)
Powerplant: one Soyuz/Khachaturov R-29B-300 turbojet
Thrust: 17 625 lb (78.40 kN), 23 335 lb (112.7 kN) with afterburner

Armament:
one 23 mm GSh-23l cannon; 30 mm GSh-6-30 gun pod; seven hardpoints; 8818 lb (4000 kg) warload; tactical nuclear bombs; R-3S Atoll-D, R-13M AAMs; Kh-23 Kerry, Kh-29, AS-14 Kedge ASM; bombs; rockets

Variants:
numerous sub-variants

Notes: Redesigned MiG-23 for ground attack role, 'Flogger-J' has LERXes, improved avionics and a laser rangefinder.

Mikoyan MiG-25 Foxbat

Type:

Dimensions:
Length: 78 ft 1 in (23.82 m)
Wingspan: 45 ft 11 in (14.01 m)
Height: 20 ft (6.1 m)

Weights:
Empty: n\a
Max T/O: 80 950 lb (36 720 kg)

Performance:
Max Speed: Mach 2.83
Range: 675 nm (1250 km) supersonic; 933 nm (1730 km) subsonic
Powerplant: two Soyuz/Tumansky R-12BD-300 single shaft turbojets
Thrust: 49 400 lb (220 kN)

Armament:
four hardpoints; R-23 Apex, R-73A Archer, R-60T Aphid AAMs; Kh-58 Kitler ASM - MiG-25BM

Variants:
MiG-25PU/RU trainer; MiG-25BM defence suppression; MiG-25R/RB/RBSh tactical reconnaissance aircraft

Notes: Designed to intercept high-flying high-speed bombers, the MiG-25 has been adapted to a number of roles mainly tactical high-altitude recce.

Mikoyan MiG-29 Fulcrum

Type: multi-role fighter   **Accommodation:** one pilot

Dimensions:
Length: 48 ft 9 in (14.87 m)
Wingspan: 37 ft 3 in (11.36 m)
Height: 15 ft 6 in (4.73 m)

Weights:
Empty: 24 030 lb (10 900 kg)
Max T/O: 40 785 lb (18 500 kg)

Performance:
Max Speed: Mach 2.3
Range: 1133 nm (2100 km)
Powerplant: two
Klimov/Sarkisov RD-33
turbofans
Thrust: 22 220 lb (98.8 kN)

Armament:
one 30 mm GSh-301 cannon;
seven hardpoints; R-77, R-
60MK, R-27R1, AAMs; weapons
dispensers; bombs; rockets

Variants:
MiG-29UB trainer; MiG-29K
carrier borne fighter

Notes: The 'Fulcrum-C' and MiG-29S have a larger curved spine housing an
active jammer and fuel. MiG-29M with FBW controls, sharp LERX, new spine,
broad-chord tailplanes and PGM capability. The MiG-29K did extensive trials
aboard the aircraft carrier Kuznetsov.

Mikoyan MiG-31 Foxhound

Type: interceptor   **Accommodation:** one pilot, one weapon systems officer in tandem

Dimensions:
Length: 74 ft 5 in (22.7 m)
Wingspan: 44 ft 2 in (13.464 m)
Height: 20 ft 2 in (6.15 m)

Weights:
Empty: 48 115 lb (21 825 kg)
Max T/O: 101 850 lb
(46 200 kg)

Performance:
Max Speed: Mach 2.83
Range: 1700 nm (3300 km)
Powerplant: two Aviadvigatel
D-30F6 turbofans
Thrust: 68 340 lb (303.8 kN)

Armament:
one 23 mm GSh-23 cannon;
four R-33 Amos, two R-40T

Acrid, four R-60 Aphid AAMs;
also cleared for R-77
AMRAAMski

Variants:
MiG-31B/D improved variants
with refuelling probes (retractable); MiG-31M new canopy,
frameless windscreen, R-37
missiles, wingtip ESM pods

Sukhoi Su-27 Flanker

Type: multi-role fighter   **Accommodation:** one pilot

Dimensions:
Length: 71ft 11in (21.935m)
Wingspan: 48ft 2in (14.70m)
Height: 19ft 5in (5.932m)

Weights:
Empty: 39 021lb (17 700kg)
Max T/O: 48 500lb (22 00kg)

Performance:
Max Speed: Mach 2.35
Range: 2160nm (4000km)
Powerplant: two Saturn/
Lyulka AL-31F turbofans
Thrust: 55 114lb (245.4kN)

Armament:
one 30mm GSh-301 cannon;
ten hardpoints; R-72R Alamo-

A, R-27T Alamo-B, R-27ER
Alamo-D, R-73A Archer, R-60
Aphid, R-33 Amos; rockets

Variants:
Su-27UB operational trainer;
Su-27K carrier-borne fighter
(now Su-33) with canards and
folding wings; Su-27P
interceptor for PVO

Notes: the Su-27K was the prototype Su-33 which was to be the standard
carrier-borne fighter for the Russian Navy. Some 20 Su-33s were delivered
and are now used from shore-bases.

Sukhoi Su-35 Flanker

Type: multi-role fighter   **Accommodation:** one pilot

Dimensions:
Length: 72ft 2in (22m)
Wingspan: 49ft 2in (15m)
Height: 19ft 8in (6m)

Weights:
Empty: 40 564lb (17 500kg)
Max T/O: 74 956lb (34 000kg)

Performance:
Max Speed: Mach 2.35; Mach
1.18 low level
Range: 2160nm (4000km)
Powerplant: two
Saturn/Lyulka AL-32FM
turbofans
Thrust: 61 730lb (274.6kN)

Armament:
one 30mm GSh-301 cannon;
14 hardpoints; 17 635lb
(8000kg) warload; R-27
Alamo, R-40 Acrid, R-60
Aphid, R-73A Archer, R-77
AMRAAMski AAMs; Kh-25ML
Karen Kh-25MP Kegler, Kh-29
Kedge, Kh-31 Krypton ASMs;
guided bombs; bombs, rockets

Saab J35 Draken

Type: interceptor   **Accommodation:** one pilot

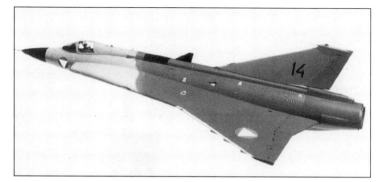

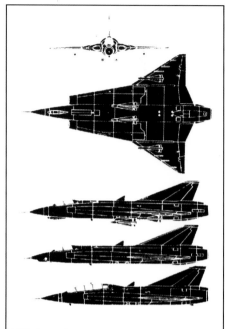

Dimensions:
Length: 50ft 4in (15.35m)
Wingspan: 30ft 10in (9.4m)
Height: 12ft 9in (3.89m)

Weights:
T/O: 23 956lb (10 354kg)

Performance:
Max Speed: Mach 2

Range: 1754nm (3250km)
Powerplant: one licence built
Rolls-Royce Avon 300 turbojet
Thrust: 12 790lb (5800kN);
17 650lb (8000kg) with
afterburner

Armament:
one 30mm ADEN cannon; six
hardpoints; RB27 (Falcon),

RB24 (Sidewinder) AAMs;
bombs; rockets

Variants:
J35C trainer; S35E
reconnaissance version; J35J
upgraded fighter version
(Sweden & Austria)

Notes: To be replaced by Gripen in Swedish service by next century. S35E has
a notch below the nose cone and camera lens' along the side.

Saab J37 Viggen

Type: multi-role fighter   **Accommodation:** one pilot

Dimensions:
Length: 51ft 1in (15.58m)
Wingspan: 34ft 9in (10.6m)
Height: 19ft 4in (5.9m)

Weights:
Empty: 26 014lb (11 800kg)
Max T/O: 37 478lb (17 000kg)

Performance:
Max Speed: above Mach 2;
Mach 1.2 low level
Range: 1080nm (2000km)
Powerplant: one Volvo
Flygmotor RM8B turbofan
Thrust: 16 203lb (72.1kN), 28
108lb (125kN) with
afterburner

Armament:
one 30mm Oerlikon KCA
cannon; seven hardpoints;
RB71 (Skyflash), RB74
(Sidewinder) AAMs; bombs;
rockets

Variants:
SK37 trainer; SF37
reconnaissance aircraft

Notes: The Swedish Viggen fleet is undergoing modernization to create a full
multi-role capability with weapons designed for the Gripen.

Saab JAS-39A Gripen

SWEDEN

Type: multi-role fighter   **Accommodation:** one pilot

Dimensions:
Length: 46ft 3in (14.1m)
Wingspan: 27ft 6in (8.4m)
Height: 14ft 9in (4.5m)

Weights:
Empty: 14 600lb (6622kg)
Max T/O: 27 560lb (12 500kg)

Performance:
Max Speed: over Mach 2
Range: n\a
Powerplant: one General
Electric Volvo Flygmotor
RM12 turbofan
Thrust: 12 140lb (54kN); 18
100lb (80.5kN) with
afterburner

Armament:
one 27mm BK27 cannon;
seven hardpoints; RB74
(Sidewinder), AIM-120
AMRAAM AAMs; RB75
(Maverick), RB15F ASMs;
munitions dispensers; bombs;
rockets

Variants:
JAS-39B trainer

Notes: Hungary and the Czech republic have shown an interest in the Gripen, and an export version is now being marketed through British Aerospace.

BAe Sea Harrier FRS Mk 1/51

UK

Type: carrier-borne multi-role fighter   **Accommodation:** one pilot

Dimensions:
Length: 47 ft 7 in (14.50 m)
Wingspan: 25 ft 3 in (7.7 m)
Height: 12 ft 2 in (3.71 m)

Weights:
Empty: 14 052 lb (6374 kg)
Max T/O: 26 200 lb (11 880 kg)

Performance:
Max Speed: Mach 1.25; 736
mph (1185 km/h) low level
Range: 800 nm (1500 km)
Powerplant: one Rolls-Royce
Pegasus Mk104 vectored
Thrust turbofan
Thrust: 21 500 lb (95.6 kN)

Armament:
two 30 mm ADEN cannon;
five hardpoints; 8000 lb (3630
kg) warload - 5000 lb (2270
kg) with vertical take off;
Matra Magic AAMs

Notes: In service with Indian Navy only (FRS Mk 51), as virtually all Royal Navy FRS Mk 1s (illustrated) are being converted to the more advanced F/A Mk 2 standard.

Grumman F-14 Tomcat

Type: carrier-borne interceptor   **Accommodation:** one pilot, one weapon systems officer in tandem

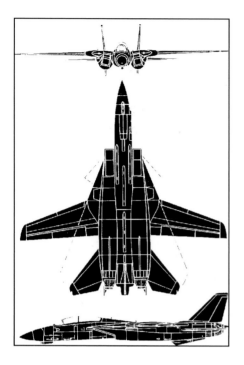

Dimensions:
Length: 62 ft 8 in (19.10 m)
Wingspan: spread 64 ft 1 in (19.54 m) - swept 38 ft 2 in (11.65 m)
Height: 16 ft (4.88 m)

Weights:
Empty: 41 780 lb (18 951 kg)
Max T/O: 74 349 lb (33 724 kg)

Performance:
Max Speed: Mach 1.88
Range: 1600 nm (2965 km)

Powerplant: two General Electric F110-GE-400 turbofans
Thrust: 32 176 lb (143.12 kN) - 54 000 lb (240.2 kN) with afterburner

Armament:
one 20 mm M61A1 Vulcan cannon; four AIM-7 Sparrow or four AIM-54 Phoenix under fuselage; four AIM-9 Sidewinder or two AIM-9 and two AIM-7/AIM-54 on wing pylons

Variants:
F-14A - basic TF30-engined fleet fighter
F-14B - F110 engines by retrofit (originally designated F-14A Plus)
F-14D - new-build and by retrofit with upgraded engines, dual undernose TCS/IRST fairings and strike capability

General Dynamics F-16 Fighting Falcon

Type: multi-role fighter   **Accommodation:** one pilot

Dimensions:
Length: 49 ft 4 in (15.03 m)
Wingspan: 31 ft (9.45 m)
Height: 16 ft 4 in (5.09 m)

Weights:
Empty: GE - 19 517 lb (8853 kg); PW - 18 726 lb (8494 kg)
Max T/O: 37 500 lb (17 010 kg)

Performance:
Max Speed: above Mach 2

Range: 1480 nm (2642 km)
Powerplant: one General Electric F100-GE-100 or one Pratt & Whitney F100-PW-220 turbofan
Thrust: GE - 29 588 lb (131.6 kN); PW - 29 100 lb (129.4 kN)

Armament:
one 20 mm M61A1 Vulcan cannon; six hardpoints, two wingtip rails; 12 000 lb (5443kg) warload; AIM-120 AMRAAM, AIM-7, AIM-9, Rafael Python 3 AAMs; 30 mm gun pod; AGM-65A; AGM-88 HARM; Harpoon, Penguin; LGBs; bombs; rockets

Variants:
F-16A single-seater; F-16A (ADF); F-16B/D operational trainer; FS-X Japanese licence built derivative

Notes: Specification applies to F-16C. Israeli F-16Ds have a box-like spine fairing housing additional ECM equipment.

Lockheed F-104S Starfighter

Type: multi-role fighter   **Accommodation:** one pilot

Dimensions:
Length: 54 ft 9 in (16.69 m)
Wingspan: 21 ft 11 in (6.68 m)
Height: 13 ft 6 in (4.11 m)

Weights:
Empty: 14 900 lb (6700 kg)
Max T/O: 31 000 lb (14 060 kg)

Performance:
Max Speed: Mach 2.2 - Mach 1.2 at sea level
Range: 1576 nm (2920 km)
Powerplant: one General Electric J79-GE-19 turbojet
Thrust: 11 870 lb (52.8 kN) - 17 900 lb (79.62 kN) with afterburner

Armament:
one 20 mm M61 Vulcan cannon; maximum of nine hardpoints; 7500 lb (3402 kg) warload; Alenia Aspide AIM-7 Sparrow, AIM-9 Sidewinder AAMs; bombs; rockets

Variants:
F-104G mutli-role fighter-bomber; RF-104G dedicated recce jet; TF-104G operational trainer; RF-104G(T) Taiwanese conversion with LOROP camera in lengthened nose; F-104ASA Alenia-built upgrade of Italian F-104S interceptor

Lockheed F-22 Lightning 11

Type: advanced tactical fighter   **Accommodation:** one pilot

Dimensions: production model
Length: 62 ft 1 in (18.92 m)
Wingspan: 43 ft 0 in (13.11 m)
Height: 16 ft 5 in (5 m)

Weights:
Empty: YF-22 30 000 lb (13 608 kg)
Max T/O: F-22 60 000 lb (27 216 kg)

Performance: YF-22
Max Speed: supercruise Mach 1.58 - Mach 1.7 with afterburner
Range: unknown
Powerplant: two Pratt & Whitney F119-PW-100 advanced technology engines with vectoring exhaust nozzles
Thrust: 70 000 lb (310 kN)

Armament:
one long-barrel 20mm gun; three internal bays, four external hardpoints for ferry tanks only; AIM-120 AMRAAM, AIM-9L Sidewinder AAMs

Variants:
YF-22 prototype and proof of concept aircraft
F-22A enlarged, refined production fighter

McDonnell Douglas F-4 Phantom

USA

Type: multi-role fighter   **Accommodation:** one pilot, one weapon systems officer in tandem

Dimensions:
Length: 63 ft (19.20 m)
Wingspan: 38 ft 7 in (11.77 m)
Height: 16 ft 5 in (5.02 m)

Weights:
Empty: 30 328 lb (13 757 kg)
Max T/O: 61 795 lb (28 030 kg)

Performance:
Max Speed: Mach 2
Range: 1718 nm (3184 km)
Powerplant: two General

Electric J79-GE-17A
Thrust: 35 800 lb (159.2 kN)
with afterburner

Armament:
one 20 mm M61A1 cannon
(not in Wild Weasel); nine
hardpoints; 16 000 lb (7250
kg) warload; AIM-7 Sparrow,
AIM-9 Sidewinder AAMs;
B57/B61 free fall nuclear
weapons; bombs; rockets

Variants:
RF-4C/E tactical
reconnaissance aircraft; F-4E
basic tactical fighter with
undernose cannon; F-4EJ Kai
Japanese update with APG-66
radar and improved RHAWS;
F-4F ICE German air defence
update with APG-65 and
AMRAAM; F-4G Wild Weasel
air defence suppression
fighter; Kurnass 2000 Israeli
upgrade with new avionics

McDonnell Douglas F-15C Eagle

USA

Type: air superiority fighter   **Accommodation:** one pilot

Dimensions:
Length: 63 ft 9 in (19.43 m)
Wingspan: 42 ft 9 in (13.05 m)
Height: 18 ft 5 in (5.63 m)

Weights:
Empty: 28 600 lb (12 973 kg)
Max T/O: 68 000 lb (30 845 kg)

Performance:
Max Speed: Mach 2.5+

Range: 2500 nm (4631 km)
Powerplant: two Pratt &
Whitney F100-PW-220
turbofans
Thrust: 47 540 lb (211.4 kN)
with afterburner

Armament:
one 20 mm M61A1 Vulcan
cannon; 11 hardpoints; four
AIM-7 Sparrow or AIM-120

AMRAAM; four AIM-9
Sidewinder

Variants:
F-15D twin-seat operational
trainer
F-15J version for Japan
F-15DJ two-seater for Japan

Notes: Can be configured to carry conformal fuel tanks and extra ECM kit

McDonnell Douglas F/A-18C Hornet

Type: multi-role fighter   **Accommodation:** one pilot

Dimensions:
Length: 56 ft (17.07 m)
Wingspan: 37 ft 6 in (11.43 m)
Height: 15 ft 3 in (4.66 m)

Weights:
Empty: 23 050 lb (10 455 kg)
Max T/O: 56 000 lb (25 401 kg)

Performance:
Max Speed: Mach 1.8

Range: 1800 nm (3336 km)
Powerplant: two General Electric F404-GE-400 low bypass turbofans
Thrust: 32 000 lb (142.4 kN) with afterburner

Armament:
one 20 mm M61A1 Vulcan cannon; nine hardpoints; 15 500 lb (7031 kg); AIM-7, AIM-

120 AMRAAM, AIM-9; SLAM, Harpoon, AGM-65; AGM-88 HARM; guided weapons; bombs; rockets

Variants:
F/A-18D operational trainer; F/A-18D night attack with FLIR; F/A-18E/F advanced version has new intakes and is larger overall

Notes: Some two-seat F/A-18Ds have been converted for use as forward air control aircraft. The F/A-18E/F can be recognised by its square cut intakes.

Vought F-8E(FN) Crusader

Type: carrier-borne fighter   **Accommodation:** one pilot

Dimensions:
Length: 54 ft 6 in (16.61 m)
Wingspan: 35 ft 8 in (10.87 m)
Height: 15 ft 9 in (4.8 m)

Weights:
Empty: 19 925 lb (9038 kg)
Max T/O: 34 000 lb (15 420 kg)

Performance:
Max Speed: Mach 2
Range: 1042 nm (1930 km)
Powerplant: one Pratt & Whitney J57-P-20A turbojet
Thrust: 18 000 lb (80.07 kn)

Armament:
four 20 mm Colt cannon; Matra 550 Magic, AIM-9 Sidewinder AAMs

Variants:
none still flying

Notes: The entire wing section can be angled up from the fuselage on take-off to provide high angle-of-attack.

Index

A–1E, 82
A–1H Skyraider, 75
A–4, 91, 95, 102, 126, 130, 144, 149
A–6, 84
A–6E, 164
A–50 Mainstay, 129
AA–2 Atoll missile, 67, 111
AA–8 Aphid missile, 111
AAA (anti-aircraft artillery), 80
AAM (air-to-air missile), 66–7, 68, 77, 126, 127, 154, 170
Abd al Hakim 'Amr, Marshal, 96, 97
AD–4 Skyraider, 29
Afghanistan War, 114, 150
AH–1W SuperCobra, 41
AIM–120 AMRAAM, 126, 127
Air Defense Command (ADC), 57
Air Tasking Orders (ATOs), 158–9, 164
AIR–2A Genie, 55, 65, 66
Alelyukhin, Colonel A V, 28
Amen, Lieutenant Commander William Thomas, 29
An–2 biplane, 41
Arab-Israeli conflicts, 94–113
Arado Ar 234 Blitz bomber, 18
ARM (anti-radiation missile), 84
Auld, Commander Andy, 142
AV–8, 131, 150
AWACS aircraft, 131, 132, 159, 167

B–26 Invader, 23, 25
B–29, 25, 26, 27, 28, 29, 31, 32, 34, 35, 36, 37, 38, 39, 42, 53, 82
B–36, 53
B–52, 55, 82, 92–3, 164, 165
B–57, 80
B–58, 68
Bagley, Major Bobby, 82
Bär, Oberstleutnant Heinz, 20, 23
Beaudralt, Captain 'Val', 8

'Bedcheck Charlie', 38, 40–1
Bf 109 fighter, 20
Bf 109G, 23
Bloodhound SAM, 68, 122
Blue Flag exercises, 136
Boeing 707, 105, 111
Boeing 727, 169
Bolo, Operation, 86, 88
BOMARC, 55, 68, 122
Bordelon, Lieutenant Guy P 'Lucky Pierre', 38, 41
Bosnia, 147, 168–9
Brown, Lieutenant Russell, 26, 28
Buccaneer, 131, 134
Bullpup air-to-surface missile, 77

C–130, 105, 149
Canberra, 97, 134, 146
cannon, 64, 77
CF–100, 57
Chatto Tzidon, Major Yehoash, 96–7
Clausewitz, Carl von, 140
Clostermann, Flight Lieutenant Pierre, 10
Cold War, 32, 44–69, 90, 94, 114–36, 146, 156, 162
'Colonel Tomb', 79, 83, 92
Combat Tree, 91
communications, 62–3
Cricket missile, 110
cruise missile, 122
Cuban Missile Crisis (1962), 44, 54–5
Cummings, Captain John D, 72–3
Cunningham, Lieutenant Randy 'Duke', 79, 83, 92

datalinks, 62–3
'decapitation' attacks, 96–7
de la Billiere, General Sir Peter, 166
Desert Storm, Operation, 117, 123, 159, 164–7
DEW (Distant Early Warning), 54

Ding Dong see AIR–2A Genie
dissimilar air combat training (DACT), 79
Driscoll, Lieutenant William 'Willie', 79, 83, 92
Dunn, Lieutenant J P, 75

E–2 Hawkeye, 159, 169
E–2A, 82, 84
E–2B, 129
E–2C, 105, 129, 164
E–3 AWACS, 129, 131, 159, 164, 169
EA–3, 84
EA–6A, 84
EA–6B, 164
EB–66, 82, 84, 86
EC–121 AWACS aircraft, 84, 91, 129
EC–130, 159, 164, 165
EF–111, 164, 165
ejection seats, 21
Exocet ASM, 144, 146, 149

F2H, 26
F3D Skynight, 38, 39, 67
F3H, 67
F–4 Phantom II, 67, 76, 78–9, 80, 93, 95, 102, 105, 118, 119, 134, 151
F–4B, 70, 75, 90
F–4C Phantom II, 75, 86, 92, 93
F–4D, 78, 82, 88
F–4E, 77, 82, 90, 91, 92, 93, 108
F–4G Wild Weasel, 165
F–4J Phantom II, 72–3, 90
F4U, 26
F4U–5N Corsair, 38, 41
F–5 Lightning, 16
F–5E, 126
F–7, 160, 165
F7F Tigercat, 38, 39, 40
F–8, 78
F–8E, 82

F9F Panther, 26, 29, 35
F–14, 10, 97, 118, 126, 128, 134, 160
F–14A, 150
F–15, 10, 104, 105, 110, 111, 118–19, 126, 141, 169
F–15A, 108–9
F–15C, 41, 63, 112, 159, 164, 165
F–15E, 97, 118, 165
F–16, 10, 63, 104, 105, 110, 111, 118–19, 124, 141, 146
F–22, 127, 141
F–51, 25, 26
F–51D, 25, 28
F–80, 29, 46, 57
F–80C, 25, 26, 28, 29
F–82, 25
F–84 Thunderjet, 26, 35, 39, 43, 46
F–84D, 32, 59
F–84E, 32, 59
F–86 Sabre, 28, 30–7, 40, 43, 46, 58, 60, 64, 140
F–86A, 42, 57
F–86D, 57, 65
F–86E, 37, 42
F–86F, 42
F–89, 57, 65
F–94 Starfire, 38, 39, 40–1, 57, 96
F–100, 46, 47, 60, 80, 91
F–100F Wild Weasel, 84
F–101, 57
F–102, 57, 76–7
F–102A, 82
F–104, 47, 57, 91, 146
F–104C, 75
F–105, 60, 70, 76, 78, 86, 90
F–105D, 82
F–105F, 84
F–106, 57, 60
F–111, 93, 105, 131, 164, 165
F–117, 131, 160, 164, 165
F/A–18, 10, 112, 118, 134, 165
Fagan, Ensign Ronald J, 75
Falklands War (1982), 126, 130,

138–55
Fernandez, Captain Manuel, 31
Fesenko, General M I, 72
FH–1, 46
Fighter Weapons School, 79
Firefly V, 25
FJ–1, 46
Fw 190, 20, 23

Galland, Generalleutant Adolf, 10, 14–15, 16, 17, 21, 22, 23, 25
Gannet radar aircraft, 131
Gloster Meteor I, 18, 23
Gloster Meteor III, 18
Göring, Herman, 23
Grachev, Captain M F, 29
Green Flag exercises, 136
Gulf War (1991), 126, 127, 136, 147, 156–67

Harpoon missile, 131
Harrier GR.1, 150
Harrier GR.3, 142, 149
Hawk trainer, 79
Hawker Hunter, 53, 64, 104
Heinkel He 162, 10
Heinkel He 280, 14, 21
Hercules, 105
Hermes, HMS, 142
Hewitt, Group Captain Ludlow, 124
HH–53 Jolly Green Giant helicopter, 82
Hitler, Adolf, 15
Holmes, Major 'Mike', 162
Howard, Sir Michael, 162
Hughes Falcon, 66
Hussein, Saddam, 97

Ilyushin Il–28, 42–3, 50, 54, 72, 96, 98, 100
Ilyushin Il–76, 129, 160
Immelmann, Max, 17
Invincible, HMS, 142

J–5, 72, 75
J–6, 72
Jabara, Captain James, 31, 35
Jaguar, 119
Javelin, 53
jet aces, 31
Johnson, James K, 32
JTIDS (Joint Tactical Information Distribution System), 63
Junkers Jumo 004 turbojet, 12, 16, 18
Junkers Jumo 004B turbojet, 22

K–13 AAM, 66–7
KA–3B tankers, 75
Ka–50 'Hokum', 41
Karelin, Major, 31
KC–707 tanker, 104
Khar'kovskiy, Major, 29
Khruschev, Nikita, 60
Klimov VK–1 engine, 37
Korean War (1950–3), 24–43, 74, 123
Kozhedub, Ivan, 32

La–11, 39
LABS (Low Altitude Bombing System), 59
Lance missile, 110
Lasseter, Major Lee T, 72–3
Lauder, Oberfeldwebel 'Ronny', 8–9, 16
Lavene, Staff Sergeant Harry J, 29
Lebanon War (1982), 94, 110–11, 126
LGB (laser–guided bomb), 91
Lightning interceptor, 53, 134, 150
Linebacker I, Operation, 71, 89, 90, 92
Linebacker II, Operation, 71, 72, 90, 91, 93
Link 16, 63
'Lufbery Circle', 78

M—4 'Bison', 55
McConnell, Captain Joseph, 31, 43
Messerschmidt Me 163 Komet, 13, 61
Messerschmidt Me 262, 8–9, 10, 12, 14–23, 47, 63, 64, 65, 66, 74, 80, 91
Meteor, 10, 26, 35, 46, 53, 96
Meteor NF.13, 96–7
Mi–6 helicopters, 91
Mikoyan MiG–9, 46
Mikoyan MiG–15, 26–43, 46, 72, 96, 143
Mikoyan MiG–17, 44, 70, 72, 75, 77, 78–9, 80–1, 82, 83, 86, 88, 91, 92, 93, 96, 97, 104, 106, 151
Mikoyan MiG–19, 46, 47, 72, 92
Mikoyan MiG–21, 20, 44, 47, 72, 79, 80, 82, 83, 86, 88, 91, 92–3, 98, 100, 107, 110, 111, 120
Mikoyan MiG–21J, 103
Mikoyan MiG–23, 110, 111, 112, 120, 160
Mikoyan MiG–25 Foxbat, 108–9, 116, 117, 128, 160, 165
Mikoyan MiG–27 Flogger, 120, 135
Mikoyan MiG–29, 91, 118, 120, 126, 129, 151, 160, 166
Mikoyan MiG–31 'Foxhound', 116, 117
Milton, General T R, 141
Mirage, 154
Mirage III, 100, 102, 119, 144
Mirage IIIC, 98
Mirage 2000, 118, 119, 160
Mirage F1, 118, 119, 160, 165
Mirage F1EQ, 159
Moab missile, 112
Mosquito, 16, 22
Murphy, Lieutenant Terence M, 75
Mystere IVA, 96

Nasser, Gamal Abdel, 94, 98
Nesher, 144

Nguyen Van Coc, 83
night operations, 38–9
Nike–Ajax, 68
Nike–Hercules, 55, 68
Nimrod, 131
Nowotny, Major Walter, 16–17

October War (1973), 94, 95, 106–9, 112, 116
Olds, Colonel Robin, 72, 86, 92
Ouragan, 96

P–38, 96
P–47 Thunderbolt, 8, 9, 17, 29
P–51, 8, 58, 60
P–80, 25
P–80A Shooting Star, 23
Patriot missile, 127
Pepelyaev, Colonel Yevgeni, 31
Peters, Lieutenant 'Pete', 8
Pham Tuan, 93
Phantom 2000, 104
Phoenix AAM, 126
Pocket Money, Operation, 92
Podkryshkin, A I, 32
Polikarpov Po–2 biplane, 38, 39, 40–1
Powers, Francis Gary, 68
Pucara turboprop aircraft, 148, 149

RA–5, 82
RA–5C, 93
RC–121, 82
RC–135 Rivet Joint, 165
Red Flag exercises, 136, 141, 146, 158
Redeye SAM, 68
RESCAP, 132
RF–4, 82
RF–101, 82
rockets, 65
Rolling Thunder, Operation, 70, 72, 75, 79, 88, 90, 92, 93, 159
Rolls–Royce RD–45F turbojet

engine, 27
Rolls–Royce W2B Welland turbojet engine, 18

SA–1, 68
SA–2 SAM, 68, 72, 80, 86, 92, 93, 100, 102, 116
SA–3 SAM, 102, 112
SA–5 SAM, 116
SA–6 SAM, 110, 112, 165
SA–7 SAM, 68, 127
SA–8 SAM, 110
SA–10 SAM, 127
SA–12 SAM, 127
SA–16 SAM, 127
SAGE (Semi–Automatic Ground Environment), 65, 68
SAM (surface–to–air missile), 55, 65, 68–9, 107, 110–11, 112, 122, 127, 170
Sandys, Duncan, 68
Schenk, Flägkapitan Otto, 21
Schwarzkopf, General Norman, 166
Scud missile, 160
Sea Eagle missile, 131
Sea Fury, 25
Sea Harrier, 130, 138, 140–1, 142–4, 146, 148–9, 150–1, 152, 153, 154
Sea King helicopter, 152
SEAD, 132
Second World War, 8–23, 58
Shabanov, Senior Lieutenant Fedor, 35
Shackleton AEW, 131
Shafrir missile, 111
Shchegolev, Lieutenant, 28
Shchukin, L K, 31
Sidewinder missile, 66–7, 79, 91, 93, 111, 126, 151, 153
situational awareness, 40–1, 128–9, 152
Six Day War (1967), 94, 100–1

Skyflash missile, 119, 126
Sparrow AAM, 67, 77, 78, 91, 93,
    108, 111, 126, 164
Späte, Major Wolfgang, 13
Spitfire, 12, 53
Spitfire Mk XIV, 12
SR–71, 116–17
SR 177, 60
SS–20 missile, 114
Stalin, Joseph, 50, 53, 60
Steinhoff, Oberst Johannes 'Macki',
    23
Stinger missile, 127
Sukhoi Su–7, 106, 120
Sukhoi Su–15, 120
Sukhoi Su–17, 120
Sukhoi Su–22 'Fitter–G', 111, 120
Sukhoi Su–24 Fencer, 120, 135,
    160
Sukhoi Su–25, 160
Sukhoi Su–27, 91, 118, 120, 126,
    128, 129, 151
Suez War (1956), 94, 96–7, 104
Super Etendard, 144, 146, 149
Suyagin, N V, 31

T–33, 57
T–38, 79, 91
tanker aircraft, 84
Tempest, 17, 53
Thyng, Colonel Harrison, 32
Tornado, 118, 119, 126, 164, 165,
    166–7
Tornado F.3, 79, 119, 131, 134,
    160, 166
Tornado GR.1, 134, 166
Tornado GR.1B, 131
Trenchard, Major–General 'Boom',
    20
Tupolev Tu–4, 50, 66
Tupolev Tu–16 'Badger', 55, 96, 98,
    100
Tupolev Tu–22, 68
Tupolev Tu–95 'Bear–As', 55
Tupolev Tu–126 Moss, 129
Tupolev Tu–128, 120

U–2 spyplanes, 68
Udet, Generaloberst Ernst, 14

V/STOL aircraft, 131, 150–1

Valiant, 97
Vampire, 10, 46, 53
Vatour fighter, 104
Vectoring in Forward Flight
    ('VIFFing'), 150–1
Vietnam War, 70–93, 123
Vulcan bomber, 148

War of Attrition (1969–70), 94,
    102–3, 106, 112
Ward, Commander 'Sharkey', 142
Wild Weasel, 84, 164, 165, 167
Woodward, Admiral Sir John, 140
World War II, 74

XF–108, 60
XP–89, 57

Yak–11, 40
Yak–15, 46
Yak–18 trainer, 38, 40
Yak–38 'Forger', 150
Yamamoto, Admiral, 96
Yom Kippur War (1973) see
    October War

Picture Credits

8: David Isby/Philip Jarrett. 9: David Isby/Jerry Scutts. 10:Bruce Robertson. 11: David Isby/Bruce Robertson/Bruce Robertson. 12: Bruce Robertson/Bruce Robertson. 13: Jerry Scott/Bruce Robertson. 4: David Isby/Bruce Robertson. 15: Philip Jarrett. 16: David Isby. 17: Philip Jarrett. 18: Bruce Robertson. 8/19: Bruce Robertson. 19: Bruce Robertson/Bruce Robertson. 20: Bruce Robertson/Bruce Robertson. 21: David Isby. 24: Bruce Robertson. 25: Jerry Scutts. 26: Bruce Robertson. 27: Aerospace Publishing/Bruce Robertson/T. Holmes.28: Jerry Scutts. 29: Aerospace Publishing. 30: Philip Jarrett/Bruce Robertson. 32: Aerospace Publishing/Jerry Scutts. 34: Bruce Robertson/Philip Jarrett. 35: Aerospace Publishing. 36: USAF/T. Holmes. 37: Bruce Robertson. 38: Philip Jarrett 39: Philip Jarrett. 42: Philip Jarrett. 43: Bruce Robertson. 44: Bruce Robertson. 45: Flight International. 46: Bruce Robertson/Bruce Robertson. 47: Bruce Robertson/T. Holmes. 48: Bruce Robertson/Philip Jarrett. 49: Bruce Robertson/Bruce Robertson. 50: T. Holmes/Bruce Robertson. 51: Philip Jarrett. 52: Bruce Robertson. 53: Bruce Robertson. 54/55: Bruce Robertson. 55: David Isby. 56: Philip Jarrett/Bruce Robertson. 57: T. Holmes/Bruce Robertson. 58: Bruce Robertson/Bruce Robertson. 59: Bruce Robertson. 60: Philip Jarrett. 61: Bruce Robertson/David Isby/Jerry Scutts.62: Jerry Scutts/Bruce Robertson. 63: Bruce Robertson. 64: David Isby. 65: Bruce Robertson/Bruce Robertson.

66: Bruce Robertson. 67: Bruce Robertson. 68/69: Philip Jarrett. 69: Philip Jarrett. 70: Bruce Robertson. 71: Bruce Robertson/Jerry Scutts. 72: David Isby. 73: Bruce Robertson/Aerospace Publishing/T. Holmes. 74: Bruce Robertson. 75: Aerospace Publishing. 76: Bruce Robertson/Philip Jarrett. 77: Bruce Robertson. 78: Bruce Robertson/Bruce Robertson. 79: M.J. Hooks/Bruce Robertson. 80/81: Aerospace Publishing. 80: Aerospace Publishing. 82/83: Bruce Robertson. 83: David Isby. 84: David Isby. 85: USAF/David Isby. 87: David Isby. 88/89: Jerry Scutts. 88: Bruce Robinson. 90: USNavy. 92: USNavy. 93: USNavy. 94: Aerospace Publishing/Philip Jarrett. 95: T. Holmes/David Isby. 97: Aerospace Publishing. 98: Bruce Robertson. 99: Bruce Robertson/Philip Jarrett. 100: Aerospace Publishing/Philip Jarrett. 101: Bruce Robertson. 103: David Isby. 104: David Isby. 105: David Isby. 106: Aerospace Publishing/Bruce Robertson. 107: Aerospace Publishing/Aerospace Publishing. 108: Aerospace Publishing. 109: Aerospace Publishing. 110: Bruce Robertson. 113: David Isby/David Isby. 114: Jerry Scutts.115: David Isby/Bruce Robertson. 116: Bob Munro 117: David Isby. 118: David Isby.119: Jerry Scutts/T. Holmes. 120: Jerry Scutts. 120/121: Aerospace Publishing. 121: David Isby. 122: Bruce Robertson. 123: Jerry Scutts. 124: Bruce Robertson. 125: David Isby. 126/127: T. Holmes. 127: David Isby. 128: David Isby. 129: T. Holmes. 130: David Isby. 131:

Jerry Scutts. 132: David Isby/David Isby. 133: Aerospace Publishing. 134: Jerry Scutts. 135: Aerospace Publishing/Aerospace Publishing. 136: T. Holmes. 137: David Isby/David Isby. 138: David Isby. 139. T. Holmes. 140: T. Holmes. 141: BAC. 142: Aerospace Publishing. 143: Jerry Scutts. 144: Aerospace Publishing. 145: Aerospace Publishing/Aerospace Publishing. 146: BAe. 147: BAe 148: Aerospace Publishing. 149: Aerospace Publishing. 150: BAe. 151: Jerry Scutts. 152: Aerospace Publishing/Bunbury.153: David Isby/Topham. 154/155: David Isby. 154: Aerospace Publishing. 155: Jerry Scutts. 156: T. Holmes. 157: Aviation Photos International. 161: Aerospace Publishing/McDonell Douglas.162: Lockheed/BAe. 163: General Dynamics 164: David Isby. 165: Lockheed.167: T. Holmes. 168: T. Holmes. 169: Aerospace Publishing 170: Saab 171: Dassault/Aerospace. 173: Dassault. 174: Dassault. 175: Dassault. 176: Eurofighter/Paul Jackson. 177: Jane's Information Group. 178: Peter J Cooper/Peter Steineman. 179: Jane's Information Group. 180: Peter Steineman/Piotr Bukowski. 181: Jane's Information Group. 182: Saab/Saab. 183: Saab/BAe. 184: Grumman/General Dynamics. 185: Paul Tomkins/Jane's Information Group. 186: McDonnell Douglas. 187: US Navy/Peter J Cooper.